Life of Dreams

MERCER
UNIVERSITY PRESS

Endowed by
Tom Watson Brown
and
The Watson-Brown Foundation, Inc.

Life of Dreams

The Good Times of Sportswriter Fred Russell

Andrew Derr

Mercer University Press

Macon, Georgia

MUP/H841

Books published by Mercer University Press are printed on acid-free
paper that meets the requirements of American National Standard for
Information Sciences—Permanence of Paper for Printed Library
Materials.

Mercer University Press is a member of Green Press Initiative
(greenpressinitiative.org), a nonprofit organization working to help
publishers and printers increase their use of recycled paper and
decrease their use of fiber derived from endangered forests. This book
is printed on recycled paper.

 Library of Congress Cataloging-in-Publication Data

Derr, Andrew.
 Life of dreams : the good times of sportswriter Fred Russell /
Andrew Derr. -- 1st ed.
    p. cm.
 Includes bibliographical references and index.
 ISBN-13: 978-0-88146-278-4 (hardback : alk. paper)
 ISBN-10: 0-88146-278-0 (hardback : alk. paper)
 1. Russell, Fred, 1906-2003. 2. Sportswriters--United States--
Biography. I. Title.
 GV742.42.R88D47 2012
 070.4'49796--dc23
   [B]   2011050962

To my grandfathers, Llewellyn and Melvin

Contents

Preface

In retrospect, my interactions with Fred Russell paled in comparison to the thousands who knew him before me. I was just eighteen when I first met him, and he was in his mid-eighties. We were two generations apart, and after that first meeting, how I wish I could have known him more. Little did I know that almost twenty years after that first meeting, I would have the honor to tell his story with this book.

In 1992 I attended Vanderbilt University on a full-tuition, once-in-a-lifetime scholarship. It was for sports journalism, and it was named after two Southern sportswriters who had both attended Vanderbilt years before: Fred Russell and one of his boyhood idols, Grantland Rice. Rice had died in 1954, but Russell was still alive in the early 1990s...and *still writing* for his hometown paper, the *Nashville Banner*. I would see Mr. Russell at least once a semester, when he came on campus to visit the four current Russell-Rice scholars. We would dine at the University Club for lunch, Mr. Russell would ask us how things were going with school, and then we would ask him about the times he interviewed some of the greatest sports icons in American history. His answers were far more interesting than ours.

Six years after graduating, our paths crossed again, when I worked at Vanderbilt University. On the side, I was doing freelance writing for a sports magazine published by the Vanderbilt athletic department, and I was hoping to interview Mr. Russell for an article. The former scholarship recipients who had become successful professional sportswriters comprised an impressive list, and I wanted to see if Mr. Russell could comment on his "living legacy" of former Commodore writers. As it turned out, by that point in his life, Russell was in declining health. I wasn't able to get a quote that autumn day in 2002, but his daughter Carolyn told me later that Mr. Russell was smiling when he heard me on the phone describing the article I was writing.

When I hung up the phone, I remember wondering how much time Mr. Russell still had to live. It couldn't be long. As it turned out, it was just a few months later, in January 2003, when I received a call one afternoon from Carolyn, and she told me that her father had passed. He was ninety-six.

When plans were coming together for the funeral in the days that followed, I wanted to see if there was anything the former scholarship recipients could do. I spoke with Carolyn and asked politely if it would be possible for me to speak on behalf of the young men and women her father had so profoundly influenced. Carolyn said the family would be honored. I felt the same way. It was a privilege to eulogize a man who had touched so many, and that January 2003 day remains one of the more humble moments of my life.

It was almost two years to the day after the funeral that the idea of the Fred Russell biography occurred to me. Russell had written his own autobiography earlier in life, when he was in his fifties, but that book had been published in 1957. What about the final four-plus decades of Russell's life? Since no subsequent biographies had been written since 1957, I realized the complete story of Fred Russell had not been told.

With permission from the Russell family in spring 2005, I started down the long road of researching his sixty-nine-year career at the *Nashville Banner*, an astounding number any way you look at it. Because of such longevity, I knew it would be next to impossible to document every year of Russell's life. But what I wanted to do, and what I have tried to do, is capture the highlights of his career, the sports figures he treasured the most, his colleagues in the business, and the friends and family members with whom he shared his life for almost a century. I wanted a book that could be read in a long weekend, something that sportswriters and fans, young and old, could sit back and enjoy without having to set aside weeks on end to make it through seven decades of success. In my research and in my writing, I have placed a premium on the stories and the memories of those who knew Russell, worked with him, learned from him, or simply enjoyed life with him. This biography is not an exhaustive, analytical piece of literature, but rather a more personal and light-hearted piece. One thing I learned along the way, and something that I believe will turn the pages a little easier, is that Fred Russell was the ultimate prankster and storyteller. It is these humorous anecdotes sprinkled throughout his life that people remember the most, and after interviewing more than 100 coaches, athletes, writers, and friends, I wanted these stories to come to life again, in their own words as much as possible. Little did I realize that there was so much material from this part of Russell's life that I would be able to dedicate an entire chapter to his sense of humor.

Beyond his humor and beyond the astounding list of sports figures and other journalists who were in Russell's life, there was a more significant, farther-reaching purpose to why I felt compelled to write this book. Russell represented a bygone era, when our heroes of sport were recognized simply for their achievements on the field, or in the ring, or on the court. Russell celebrated the spirit of sport and sportsmanship for the better part of the twentieth century, and such devotion is a rarity today. Without hesitation, he celebrated the inspirational moments of sports, and he wanted his readers to share in that inspiration. In an era before reporters deemed it acceptable to search for and report on every aspect of an athlete's life, Russell lived by that age-old advice passed down from one generation to the next: if you don't have anything nice to say, don't say anything at all. And for the better part of seventy years, Russell was successful with that approach.

In telling the story of Fred Russell, then, my aim is simple: honor the man and honor the path he walked for as long as he did. As talented as he was as a writer, Russell was equally as demanding as a sports editor and equally as skilled at scouting and developing sportswriting talent. Through his many years as a sports editor, and with the aforementioned Russell-Rice scholarship now more than fifty years old, Fred Russell's influence continues to have an impact on sportswriters to this day. He has a living legacy, and those who had the privilege to work for him, or attend Vanderbilt University because of the scholarship, remember the role he played in their lives. They now carry the Russell torch, and they carry it proudly. Telling the Fred Russell story and sharing this legacy has been my honor.

Acknowledgments

If I tried to thank the countless people who made this biography possible, I dare say that you might need a break before even starting chapter one. Ironically, this is Fred Russell's own fault. He lived so long and he impacted the lives of so many in such a profoundly positive way that my initial estimate of a few months of research turned into a year's worth of interviews. After completing that phase of the project, I remember thinking this book would just write itself once I put the stories in some sort of logical order. Of course, the book did not write itself, despite my repeated requests for it to do so, so it now becomes appropriate that I make the humble attempt to thank those who made this book a reality.

First and foremost, my thanks to the Russell family, who gave so willingly and freely of their time during the past seven years. In particular, to Fred's daughter Carolyn, I can say without hesitation that this book would not have been possible were it not for your patience, time, and willingness to put me in touch with the right people and to assist me in gathering the information I needed to tell this story correctly.

While there are hundreds, if not thousands, of people who consider themselves a "friend" of Fred Russell's, there were two close friends who I leaned on heavily to research this man's life thoroughly. To Joe Biddle and Dick Philpot, I thank you for the many phone calls we shared and the emails we exchanged. Your assistance and encouragement never went unnoticed.

As a first-time author, I am compelled to thank two other biographers—David Maraniss and William Harper—who not only offered me advice during that first year on how to approach this biography, but who were experienced enough to tell me to never give up, knowing there would be times when I would hit a wall, which I did.

While it would take too long to thank all of those I interviewed for this book, there were several notable interviews that warrant an appreciative nod. My thanks to Roy Kramer, Buster Olney, John Seigenthaler, and Edwin Pope, for taking as much time as you did to share your memories; to some of the twentieth century's most iconic sports figures, such as Lou Holtz, Bobby Knight, and Archie Manning; and to those who have sadly passed away since we spoke: Ernie Harwell, Eddie Jones, George Steinbrenner, and Sparky Anderson—may you rest in peace.

To the patient editors and staff at Mercer University Press, I offer a profound thank you. Specifically, to its director, Dr. Marc Jolley, for taking a chance on this book, and to Marsha Luttrell for answering all my "rookie" questions. Thank you for seeing what I saw in the Fred Russell story and agreeing that it needed to be shared.

Importantly, this book did not become a viable endeavor without financial assistance that I must acknowledge. Most notably, to Charles Cella, who has given so much to promote and fund the Russell-Rice sportswriting scholarship at Vanderbilt University, thank you for your remarkably generous donation to fund the book's publishing. Additionally, the donations from Dr. Thomas Frist, Brownlee Curry, and Lee Barfield were significant, as was the assistance from Vanderbilt University's athletic department. A final thank you for individual financial assistance goes to Aubrey Harwell, Wilson Sims, David Wiley, Bill Brittain, John Cain, Matt Dobson, Roy Elam, Edward Graham, Beverly Landstreet, Richard Norvell, Dick Philpot, Henry Jamison, and Homer Gibbs. This publishing would not have occurred with your donations.

Lastly, my sincerest of thanks to my family. To my wife, Molly, who sacrificed more than she may realize in order for me to make it across the finish line; to my siblings, parents, in-laws, and extended family, all of whom have been so selfless in their support, genuine interest, and even editing of the manuscript; and, finally, to my four beautiful children, who I believe set a record for the number of times that it can be asked, "Daddy, are you done with your book yet?"

1

Vanderbilt Roots

"He was Fred Russell of the *Nashville Banner* but he was 'Mr. Russell' of Vanderbilt. He made no bones about his love for Vanderbilt, and he tied Vanderbilt to key people throughout the sporting world in a real way."[1] —C. M. Newton, Vanderbilt University basketball coach

In May 1994, at the age of eighty-seven, Fred Russell walked slowly but confidently to the podium, ready to address the crowd, just as he had countless times before over his long and storied career as celebrated sportswriter, banquet speaker, and master of ceremonies. This evening, however, the attendees were more reserved than usual. It was the induction ceremony for new members of Vanderbilt's Quinq Club, and there were quite a few Commodore alumni present. The previous December, Vanderbilt's football team had completed its eleventh straight losing season, and the seventeenth in its last eighteen seasons. The crowd was anxious to hear what one of Vanderbilt's most famous sportswriters might say.

Russell opened his speech with the following remarks:

"I'm not dealing with any current affairs, except for one thing. Yesterday, a member of the Vanderbilt football coaching staff was praising you for your support, your tolerance, your patience. Indeed, he gave me a little note that he had just received the day before from a very loyal alumnus. He even gave me a copy of it, and I read it now.

> Dear Coach,
> Do not feel bad about last year's record. Winning isn't everything. As for the 1994 season, it really makes no difference to us alumni whether your record is 11–0, or 0–11. Just as long as your young lads have fun and wholesome recreation on game day.
> The reason I am writing this in crayon is because they won't let me have anything sharp here.[2]"
> —Fred Russell

For almost seven decades, his column was a daily slice of sports Americana. It was a Sunday drive on the sun-drenched Natchez Trace Parkway with the top down and the soft summer air blowing through your hair. From the 1930s until the 1990s, it gave you a glimpse into the biggest names in sports, and along the way, it made you laugh, it kept you informed of sport's biggest stories, and it made you laugh some more. It was informed, it was accurate, and it was honest. It didn't hide its love for hometown Tennessee heroes and minor league characters, and when you were thirsty for something more, it gave you a drink of major league water from the big cities across the country. It was written more than 12,000 times, and its author would bleed each and every time. Within its paper, it was an institution unto itself, and when that rolled-up paper landed on Tennessee doorsteps, he was there waiting for you. The title of the column was "Sidelines," and its author was a dyed-in-the-wool Southerner who left his mark on a grateful nation.

His name: Fred Russell.

From the late 1920s to February 1998, throughout his long and celebrated career as a sportswriter, Russell wrote for one newspaper and one newspaper only: the *Nashville Banner*. Russell's career at the *Banner* began in 1929, and within a decade, he was an established sports editor with opportunities to jump to the bright lights and big cities away from Middle Tennessee. Each time a new opportunity came, though, Russell stayed. Not because he feared the competition, but because Nashville was home, and he was a man of character and conviction, a man who valued hometown roots and camaraderie more than the financial allure of a place devoid of the Southern charm and loyalty to which he was accustomed.

In 1953, at a celebration of his twenty-fifth year with the *Banner*, the paper hosted a banquet in his honor that attracted over 600 people, many of whom were some of the nation's biggest sports names and most celebrated writers. The following day, another sportswriter from a different city, Tom Siler, wrote in his column just how far Russell had come.

"Time was when a newspaperman had to comb the straw out of his hair and hit the road to New York or Chicago—that is, if he ever expected to 'make good' Grantland Rice was a virtual unknown until he left the

South and went to New York. Bill Corum is an old Missouri boy and Red Smith hit Broadway by way of Green Bay, St. Louis, and Philadelphia.

"Fred Russell is now the exception. He is a living illustration of how things have changed. You don't have to leave home to make a newspaper 'name' anymore. Russell is renowned from coast to coast as a distinguished sports editor, as a thorough reporter, as an entertaining columnist, as a clear thinker and a sound sportsman.[3]"

That was 1953. Four years later, Russell wrote his autobiography, *Bury Me in an Old Press Box: Good Times and Life of a Sportswriter.* From the time that book was published in 1957, Russell would continue to write for four more decades, emerging as one of the century's most celebrated journalists. From his small Nashville office at 1100 Broadway, the small-town sportswriter attracted big-league audiences and held them captive. Whether it was through his daily column being picked up by other papers or his annual college football preview, which he penned for the *Saturday Evening Post*, Russell's words resonated with his readers, his peers, and his subjects. Along the way, he developed a sports department whose charge was simple: beat their rival, the *Tennessean,* and beat them mercilessly. The *Banner* sports department was an underdog for much of the twentieth century, but Russell and his team fought the noble fight until the bitter end. As a result of his mentoring, when Russell's own career was winding down, he looked in the rear-view mirror of his life and saw a countless supply of journalists filing their own columns in newspapers and magazines across the nation.

Put simply, by the time he stepped away from his old, worn-out Remington typewriter in 1998, at the age of ninety-one, Fred Russell was a sportswriting superstar. He had become the most successful and most well-known Nashville sportswriter in the city's history, and the awards and acclaim bestowed upon him put Russell in the company of sportswriting greats such as Grantland Rice, Red Smith, Jim Murray, and Shirley Povich.

Russell's path to national stature and success was neither overnight nor easy. He earned it on his own steam, one column at a time, and it started in his hometown of Nashville, Tennessee, and at his alma mater, Vanderbilt University. Russell lived and died with the Commodores. He was a loyal alumnus, and there's no better place to begin the Fred Russell story than with the tree-lined campus off West End Avenue.

A Commodore from Day One

To say that Vanderbilt University was a part of Fred Russell's life would be like saying that the Commodores' beating state rival Tennessee in football was only somewhat important. Vanderbilt was an integral part of Russell from his birth in the twentieth century's first decade until his final days in the first decade of *this* century. And in between those years (1906 to 2003), Russell lived two lifetimes of Vanderbilt memories. From working extra shifts after prep school to earn enough money to attend the university, to falling asleep in law class once he made it there, to ultimately pulling some of the most outlandish pranks on chancellors and coaches one could imagine, Russell's association with Vanderbilt was a strong one, one that he cherished until the day he died.

Vanderbilt benefited from its relationship with Russell as well. As the university gained prominence and recognition over the years and across the country, the name Fred Russell became synonymous with two entities: the *Nashville Banner* and Vanderbilt University. From his days as a student, through the 1930s when he became the *Banner's* sports editor, and certainly through his glory years with the *Banner* from the 1940s through 1970s, one could not think of Vanderbilt sports without thinking of Fred Russell. Remarkably, for a period of time in the middle of the century, Russell was considered by many to be Vanderbilt's de facto athletic director. Hardly any important decisions or announcements came out of the athletic department without having first crossed the sports desk of one of its most famous alumni.

And in the closing years of Russell's life, even when he had retired to Richland Place, the old scribe still found a way to get Vanderbilt information that no one else seemed to have. While he grew up merely wishing to attend the university, Russell eventually became one of its most noteworthy champions. He left an indelible mark on the university, and in doing so, one of Vanderbilt's native sons died a Vanderbilt man.

Before he was even born, Russell had a destiny to be associated with the Commodores. In 1897, Vanderbilt celebrated the unveiling of a statue of Commodore Cornelius Vanderbilt, and part of the pomp and circumstance that day was the playing of "The Vanderbilt University Waltz," a song written by Russell's mother, Mabel Lee McFerrin. Nine years later, Russell was born in August 1906 and spent his boyhood years growing up in Wartrace, Tennessee, just fifty miles southeast of

Nashville. Years later, in his 1957 autobiography, Russell could only make it to page two before making his first reference to Vanderbilt. Russell wrote of his family's move to Wartrace in fall 1906 and the fact that it coincided with a Vanderbilt football game. He commented that "it was a dirty trick not letting me see that game."[4] Russell was just three months old.

As a boy, Russell made it to Nashville on a fairly regular basis, as he would join his father for trips by train from Wartrace. Wartrace was a main-line town back then, on the way from Nashville to Chattanooga, and the fifty-mile trip took about an hour and a half along the rails. Russell became infatuated with Nashville, longing for his return trips to the train station.

"There was just something fascinating about Union Station," Russell said in a 1986 interview looking back on his youth. "It was so big, and you would come up the steps and I would never forget the aroma, the smell of freshly ground coffee. These were the early days of Nashville, 1912 or so."[5] Compared to the quiet railroad town of Wartrace, Nashville was a bustling center of growth and activity. Russell enjoyed twenty-five-cent meals on Union Street at Mrs. Fitzhugh's Dining Room, clothing shops to get outfitted for the fall and spring each year, and even mid-town arcades that would capture the attention of just about any boy Russell's age.

When Russell's father changed jobs several years later, the family moved permanently to Nashville. Russell was thirteen at the time of the move, and in 1920 his parents enrolled him at Duncan College Preparatory School. Duncan School was located at 401 25th Avenue in Nashville. Today, Vanderbilt's Memorial Gym occupies the land in the 400 block of 25th Avenue, but in the first part of the twentieth century, it was home to a two-story brick schoolhouse whose owner, Mr. Marvin Duncan, catered to the education of approximately 100 students each year.

Russell entered Duncan School intimidated and not sure what to expect. He was small for his age, and because he had skipped a grade early in his grammar school days (from first to third), he was particularly self-conscious about his stature in the new school. However, something as simple as alphabetical seating "saved his life."[6]

In what became the first meeting of a lifelong friendship, Russell found himself seated next to a young boy named Henry Sanders. "Red," as he was known, was a popular student and a talented baseball and football player. Much to Russell's delight, Sanders shared his dry sense of humor and they hit it off from the start. Sanders introduced Russell around the school, and for the thirteen-year-old Russell, that made a world of difference.[7] Ultimately, Russell and Sanders attended Vanderbilt together, the latter one day becoming one of the Commodore's most successful football coaches, further cementing their friendship through the years.

Russell excelled at Duncan School and graduated at the age of fifteen. Among other things, Russell learned consistency, structure, and integrity during his prep school years, traits that he would fine-tune into daily values throughout his life and his career. Russell's success at Duncan proved that he possessed the academic ability to succeed at Vanderbilt. However, his financial resources—or lack thereof—prevented Russell from enrolling in 1922. Russell needed additional money, so he went searching for a job to help pay for college. Ever since his youngest days, he had loved the sports pages, so Russell considered being an "office boy" at one of the local papers in Nashville. But that paid $3 per week, and Russell found he could make $15 per week as a "soda jerk" working at a local store's soda fountain. He worked long hours, upwards of seventy hours per week at a time, working at the store for a year before saving enough money to enter Vanderbilt University in fall 1923.

At Vanderbilt, Russell studied law, joined the Kappa Sigma fraternity, and played baseball for the Commodores. He and Sanders were good friends through their years at Vanderbilt, and if their time together as Commodores accomplished only one thing, it paved the road for a life spent pulling practical jokes and making one another laugh, oftentimes at the other's expense.

One such instance, which was destined to be told and retold by Russell and others through the years, occurred when Russell was a freshman.

"This was the most embarrassing experience that ever happened to me at Vanderbilt," Russell began. "It was in the spring of 1924, in a law school class, taught by a very stern, no-nonsense man named Fitzgerald Hall. And I couldn't have possibly dozed off for more than four or five seconds, when the student next to me nudged me and I heard the whisper from him, 'Called on you!'

"And in a very loud voice, I said, 'I'm not prepared on that case, Mr. Hall!' Well, he had not called on me," Russell continued. "I had interrupted his lecture. The close, close friend who did that to me was Red Sanders."[8]

Russell and Sanders played pranks on each other back and forth during their undergraduate days. Not all of Russell's gags involved Sanders, of course, but most either involved Vanderbilt people or occurred on Vanderbilt's campus. One such case was Russell's "Vanderbilt manure" prank, a story that Russell's youngest daughter, Carolyn, said she heard multiple times over the years.

As the story went, there was a certain professor at Vanderbilt who was unpopular with a large number of students. The prank was to not just have a truckload of manure delivered to this man's home, but to do so in such a way that it wouldn't get turned away. The pranksters employed the innocent support from the delivery man, but with specific instructions in case the tenant became upset.

"The truckload of manure was delivered and dumped on the front yard, and they instructed the driver to continue unloading even when the owner protested," Carolyn Russell recalled. "Their instructions were that he was getting older and losing his mind. In fact, the homeowner was so crazy, old, and forgetful that he would say he did not even order the load! So please ignore him…and don't make him mad!

"And, as the teacher screamed at him, the delivery man just smiled and waved and kept on shoveling."[9]

Russell didn't limit his collegiate pranks to off-campus acts. During his Kappa Sigma fraternity days he certainly found his way into trouble as well. The end result of one of his pranks was Russell sprinting across campus in an effort to out-run Vanderbilt's All-American football player, Lynn Bomar, in the early morning hours before class. What had led to this scene? As a freshman pledging the Kappa Sigma fraternity, of which Bomar was a member, Russell had been given the task of making sure Bomar was awake in time for his classes each day. When the school year was almost over, Russell concluded that lighting the biggest firecracker he could find underneath Bomar's bed was a fitting tribute for the last day of his fraternal responsibility. Thus, the aforementioned scene occurred, which included Bomar being angry enough to conduct his part of the chase wearing only his underwear.[10]

Despite the countless gags he either orchestrated or participated in during his Commodore days, Russell nonetheless remained focused on his education at Vanderbilt through the mid-1920s. He was a member of the Vanderbilt baseball team, studied at the university's law school, and ultimately became a member of the Kappa Sigma fraternity. Interestingly enough, Russell never graduated, despite passing the state bar exam and being a member of the Class of 1927.

Joining the *Banner*

Once Russell's student days were behind him, his first career choice was in the mortgage business. However, it was not more than a few years before Vanderbilt became part of Russell's work life as well. In June 1929, Russell joined the *Nashville Banner* staff as a cub reporter making $6 per week. Only a few weeks after being assigned the police beat, Russell learned of his new assignment: Vanderbilt football. The young reporter was now a sportswriter. Russell was just twenty-two, and, unbeknownst to him, he began the first of sixty-nine consecutive years with the paper. Beginning with Herbert Hoover, who had given his inaugural address as United States president in March 1929, Russell's watch over the Nashville sports scene covered a dozen presidents, from Franklin Roosevelt to Dwight Eisenhower, from Jimmy Carter to Bill Clinton, who was president in 1998 when the *Banner* abruptly folded.

The first half of the twentieth century was an era when sportswriters were much closer with their subjects than writers are today. While the nation had a healthy and growing appetite for sports information, it paled in comparison to the twenty-first century sports audience of today, a culture of information-starved sports junkies who crave and consume 24/7 sports coverage via cable TV, talk radio, the Internet, and a number of social computing networks.

But before sports blogs and Twitter, it was the newspaper medium that delivered sports information to the American public. Long before ESPN anchors, such as Stuart Scott, Dan Patrick, Chris Berman, became names known across the country, America's cities and towns relied on their well-known newspapermen to inform them of what was going on throughout the sports world. In New York, there was Red Smith; in Los

Angeles, Jim Murray. Washington, D.C., had Shirley Povich, and in Baltimore, there was John Steadman.

In Nashville, there was Fred Russell. And for the better part of the twentieth century, Vanderbilt athletics was at the top of the Nashville sports scene, so what Fred Russell had to say meant a great deal to a significant number of people in Middle Tennessee. Russell leveraged that position throughout his career at the *Banner*, and from fall 1930 to the final decades of the twentieth century, if you lived in Tennessee, you could not think of Vanderbilt athletics without thinking of Fred Russell.

"Whether it was Coach [Paul 'Bear'] Bryant or Coach [Ray] Graves from Florida, whoever it was throughout this league, they associated him with Vanderbilt," former Commodore basketball coach C. M. Newton (1982 to 1989) commented once, when speaking about Russell's place within the Southeastern Conference. "And it added an element of class to Vanderbilt."[11]

As an alumnus and a fan, Russell bled black-and-gold. His passion for the Commodores made Russell a fierce competitor as a newspaperman. The *Banner* was Nashville's afternoon paper, and one of its primary advantages was its ability to have breaking news from the morning hit the newsstands in the afternoon. Russell did everything he could to exploit that advantage, especially when it came to using his connections within the athletic department.

The *Banner's* archrival was the *Tennessean*, and Jimmy Davy was a member of that morning paper's staff from the 1960s until 1984. Davy covered Vanderbilt, and he battled Russell every day for over twenty years.

"We were just terrific rivals, especially Vanderbilt sports," Davy recalled, wincing at the memory of how Russell's connections at Vanderbilt made his life that much more difficult. "He had been a student there, and he had a virtual lock on VU news."

The athletic department "would just wait and make sure that every announcement that had to do with athletics would be in the morning, which of course killed us," Davy laughed.[12]

Davy was not the only one to voice that opinion during the Russell years. John Seigenthaler was one of the central figures and voices of the *Tennessean* in the second half of the twentieth century, as he became editor in 1962, publisher in 1973, and chairman in 1982. He retired in 1991 as chairman emeritus, and for the majority of his years at the helm, Seigenthaler's answer to Fred Russell was Raymond Johnson. But Seigenthaler knew that when it came to sports editors, he could only do so much to counter Russell, especially when it came to Vanderbilt.

"Freddie had absolute dominance over Raymond in terms of breaking news at Vanderbilt," Seigenthaler said. "The *Tennessean*, despite being the larger paper, found itself often beaten on important stories."[13]

Toward the latter stages of his career, Russell's years of dominating Vanderbilt news in Nashville's papers ensured a legacy of sorts at the *Banner*: the sought-after Commodore beat. Even when Russell was no longer the day-to-day sports editor (in 1981, he became vice president emeritus), he presided over the *Banner* sports desk in an intimidating but dignified way, demanding respect from his staff and his peers without ever having to ask for it.

During the emeritus years, Russell's influence over the Vanderbilt beat remained strong. Mark McGee, who covered sports at the *Banner* from 1981 to 1994, was one of the first to cover the Commodores during that era.

"That's what everybody worked for, but it also had the most scrutiny because of Mr. Russell," McGee said of the Vanderbilt beat. "Mr. Russell had such a love for the school, and such a connection. You knew how much he knew, and you never knew if you might step on somebody's toes who he had a loyalty to."[14]

In recognition of the years he covered Vanderbilt sports, the university honored Russell by naming not only the football press box after him in 1982, but also the baseball press box in 2001. A notable member of Nashville's current sports media is George Plaster, a popular afternoon talk-show host who grew up in Middle Tennessee reading Russell. Plaster attended Vanderbilt as well, and during his early years as a Commodore reporter, he came to realize just how much Nashville and its sports media members thought of Russell.

"I was either a freshman or sophomore in college, and Vanderbilt was playing Auburn. It was in that old rickety press box at Dudley Field," Plaster recalled. "When Mr. Russell walked in, it was like the president of the United States walked in there. It was as if somebody had blown a trumpet and said, 'Ladies and Gentlemen...' Everybody stopped what they were doing, and it was as if royalty had walked in there."[15]

The *Tennessean's* John Seigenthaler also remembered the Vanderbilt press box scene, but from a slightly different perspective.

"If you went into the press box before a Vanderbilt game, you'd see two things: you'd see Freddie surrounded by sportswriters, and you'd see Raymond (Johnson) sulking somewhere else in the press box, sometimes at the other end of the press box talking on the telephone to stay busy," Seigenthaler recalled with a laugh.[16]

Football and Influence

Within the Vanderbilt sport scene itself, no sport carried more weight during Russell's time than college football. It is only natural that this sport serves as the common denominator for Russell, when one thinks about the success the Commodores had during the first half of the twentieth century, his influence at the school during the second fifty years, and the good times and laughs that occurred throughout.

While difficult to imagine today due to its lack of recent success, when Russell first covered the team in the 1930s, Vanderbilt football was one of the institutions of college football. Legendary coach Dan McGugin was in his final years of leading Vanderbilt (1904 to 1934, 197–55–19), and the Commodores posted winning records almost every year.

Russell's style was founded on relationship-building. From his earliest days covering the Commodores, he forged lasting friendships with countless Vanderbilt football players over the decades. Because of his unassuming style and natural charm, players from the 1940s and 1950s, such as Dick Philpot, Art Demmas, and Jimmy Webb, became lifelong friends of Russell's.

Webb was a Commodore in the early 1940s, and in this case, Russell made a friend for life with one simple article.

"I was a freshman at Vanderbilt in 1940, and everybody read Freddie's column," Webb recalled. "In the spring game ending my freshman year, he wrote a column and said a nice thing about me.

"Of course, I admired him a lot before that, but that really endeared me to him," Webb added with a laugh. "Through the years, we remained friends, as a young man would be to an older person."[17]

Relationships with coaches in those days were easier as well. Not only was access to the coaches less of the hurdle that it is today, but sportswriters had more time to invest with the coaches of the schools they covered. Russell's disarming personality was a perfect fit for his time, and he maintained strong relationships with the coaches.

Beyond the coaches, though, Russell stayed involved with the administration too. As the years went by and his reputation and success as a journalist grew, so too did his power base at Vanderbilt. And in the middle of the twentieth century, as foreign a concept as it seems today, it was not uncommon for a university to seek the counsel of a respected sportswriter when important athletic matters were at hand. Vanderbilt chancellors and administration officials did this repeatedly with Russell, and while it was never formally acknowledged, of course, Russell essentially functioned as athletic director for the Commodores at times.

Speaking from experience, Roy Kramer is one to know. Kramer came to Vanderbilt as its athletic director in the mid-1970s, and he became one of Russell's close friends until Russell died.

"Fred did have a tremendous amount of influence," Kramer said when asked about Russell's involvement with athletics decisions at Vanderbilt. "Fred loved Vanderbilt, he had a great respect for it, and he had a phenomenal feel for the tradition of McGugin. Because of his knowledge, and his so many contacts in the sporting world, the administration at the university relied on Fred."[18]

John Beasley is another Commodore voice who recalled Russell's close ties to the athletic department. Beasley arrived in 1948 as a Vanderbilt undergraduate, and for more than half a century, he served the university in a variety of capacities. He retired as vice chancellor for alumni and development in 1999, but retains the title vice chancellor emeritus today.

"When Rob Roy Purdy was senior vice chancellor here and athletics came under him, he and Harvie Branscomb and (Alexander) Heard would frequently turn to Russell for information and advice," Beasley commented of the time when Branscomb was chancellor from 1946 to 1963. "If we had to hire a coach, Russell would know things such as who we ought to look at. He was great friends with many coaches, and his view was always sought on athletics."[19]

Beasley recalled specific instances of Russell's name coming up behind closed doors.

"I was certainly in meetings where somebody would say, 'See what Fred Russell thinks about this.' It was just a different time," Beasley added. "There were other sportswriters back then, but people turned to Russell. One, he was a Vanderbilt man. And two, he would never betray a confidence and I don't think he ever misused a source."[20]

The rarity of this type of relationship, even in the days of easier access and less volatility between sportswriter and athletic department, is not lost on members of the media today.

Plaster, the afternoon talk-show host who grew up reading Russell and also attended Vanderbilt, shakes his head when thinking about the role a member of his industry played just fifty years ago.

"He was a real power-broker, and his influence helped determine key hires," Plaster commented. "Today, if anybody is going to sway a chancellor or an athletic director, that person is called the 'key donor,' it's the person who gives the most money. Back then, before they would make a hire, they would at least seek his counsel."[21]

Trademark Sense of Humor

While there is no disputing the weight and influence that Russell wielded within the athletic department, by no means should history reflect that Russell's time spent with Vanderbilt coaches and athletic officials was always serious. On the contrary. Russell eventually injected his natural sense of humor into his friendships with many of the coaches he covered in the paper.

Being a Vanderbilt man, and then having the Commodore sports beat in his early years, it was almost too much to pass up for Russell. His gags were always good-natured and he considered no one off limits over at West End Avenue. One of the first times this happened was in 1944, when Chancellor Harold Carmichael was unwittingly associated with one of Russell's gags, as was a poor interim coach named Doby Bartling. Earlier that year, Coach Red Sanders had joined the Navy to serve his commitment, and Vanderbilt had a war-time team that played a limited schedule of games. In an interim role, Bartling led the Commodore teams of 1944 and 1945, and in the final game of the 1944 season, Russell got involved.

"In late November, they were playing the final game of the season on a real, real muddy field," Russell remembered. "Chancellor Carmichael was staying until the very end, in his box, which was not far from the Vanderbilt bench. And all but one player on that bench had a muddy jersey, and you could not even read the numbers."

"From the press box, I sent a note by *Banner* office boy to Coach Bartling," Russell continued. "He gave him this note, saying it was from Chancellor Carmichael. Doby opened it right away. It said, 'Dear Coach, Vanderbilt player number 28 is the nephew of one Vanderbilt University's most generous donors. I would consider it a personal favor if you could get him in the game.' He was in the game within a second and a half."

In familiar Russell style, he laid low afterwards. "No harm was done and as far as I know the chancellor never knew about it. And Bartling never knew until years later," Russell admitted.[22]

As good-natured as most of them were, a few of Russell's jokes did manage to push the envelope a bit. They were funny nonetheless, and as it turned out, coach Art Guepe just happened to be the recipient of a couple of classics.

Longtime friend Dick Philpot laughs every time he is asked to tell the "Liberace" story. It occurred during Guepe's years of coaching the Commodores (1953 to 1962), when the famed pianist was coming to Nashville on a personal appearance.

"Sometimes Fred imitated a woman's voice," Philpot recalled, "and before Liberace arrived in town, Art Guepe received a phone call.

'Mr. Guepe, this is Mrs. T. Graham Hall. Our latest group is having a meeting this week, and we noticed that Mr. Liberace is coming to town. Since you and he are from the same town, we thought it would be appropriate for you to introduce him.'

'Well, uh, that would be a high honor, but I'm afraid my schedule is too full to do this.'

'Well, Mr Guepe, our entire ladies' group would be very disappointed if you turned us down. We're sure that you all being from the same spot would mean a lot to us.'

'Listen, I can't do it. I'm just too busy.'

"And then Mrs. T Graham Hall says, 'Well, they told me you'd be an uncooperative son of a bitch.'"[23]

Also in classic Russell style, the jokester couldn't leave the gag at just the one phone call. As Philpot explained, Russell picked things up later that afternoon at spring practice.

"So Fred goes out there, and at one point, Guepe turns the practice over to his brother," Philpot said. "Art sits down next to Fred on a bench and lights a cigarette. They talk for a minute, and finally Art says, 'Fred, do you know a Mrs. T Graham Bell?' Fred says, 'Well, I don't know her, but I know *of* her.'

"Art says, 'Well you can't imagine the conversation we had today.' And he proceeds to tell Freddie the whole conversation, including the last line, to which Freddie says, 'No, she did not.' Guepe says, 'Oh yes she did. That's exactly what she said.' And Freddie Russell never let him off the hook. Ever."[24]

Closing Thoughts

While there were plenty of humorous Vanderbilt-related moments for Russell and his friends over the years, Russell's legacy at his alma mater is clearly his sportswriting. He remains one of the university's most accomplished and famous alumni. Within his trade, Russell was one of the top ten sportswriters of the twentieth century, and some would put him behind only his idol, Grantland Rice, and his New York pal, Red Smith. He parlayed that success into a household name, and that bode well for his relationship at Vanderbilt as well. Russell's national reputation, connections, and knowledge opened numerous Vanderbilt doors for the sportswriter and afforded him significant power within the university's athletic department, particularly in the middle years of the century.

Beyond his behind-the-scenes influence, two additional themes come to mind when summarizing Russell's connection to Vanderbilt. The first is how sportswriters across the country would strike up conversations with members of the Nashville media once Russell stopped covering Commodore events. Whether it was a writer for the *Nashville Banner* or the rival *Tennessean*, he or she would invariably be approached by writers from other towns with the simple question, "How's Freddie doing?" His reputation had grown from local to regional to national stature, and Vanderbilt's reputation benefitted from Russell's success.

Secondly, when thinking of Fred Russell and Vanderbilt, one must acknowledge his *living* legacy of sportswriters, the Vanderbilt-educated journalists who became Commodores thanks to the Fred Russell-Grantland Rice TRA (Thoroughbred Racing Association) Sportswriting

Scholarship. The scholarship was established in 1954, when Russell petitioned the university to honor Rice, Vanderbilt's most well-known sportswriter at the time. In 1986, Russell's name was added to the scholarship, and in the fifty-plus years of its existence, the number of talented and well-known sportswriters in the business today who have this scholarship on their resumes is impressive. From Roy Blount (1959 recipient) to Skip Bayless (1970) and from Dave Sheinin (1987) to Tyler Kepner (1993), there is an impressive number of sportswriters writing today who have a direct link back to Russell.

Bayless attended Vanderbilt in the early 1970s and has enjoyed success both as a columnist (in Miami, Dallas, and San Jose) and a television commentator (currently with ESPN). Before that success, however, he was a Commodore, a scholarship recipient, and a loyal reader of Russell's.

"The highlight of my days was hearing that paper land outside my door in the afternoons, because I knew I could read Fred Russell," Bayless said, when describing his days as a student. "For me, Vanderbilt was hard, but the most peaceful moment of every weekday was reading Fred Russell in the *Banner*."[25]

In the years since college, Bayless has been in the business long enough to realize just how fortunate he was to not only read Russell the writer, but to appreciate the writer as a person as well.

"Class, gentility, and that decency that a good human being has: like [Grantland] Rice and [Red] Smith," Bayless commented, when asked to describe what set Russell apart from his peers. "You don't see that anymore, that dignity, that class, that caring for sportswriting brethren up and down the totem pole. That era is dead."[26]

2

The *Banner* Part 1: Beginnings

"Fred was an innovator from the start. He popularized his newspaper by originating the Banquet of Champions for the high school teams of Tennessee. In the first year of the Southeastern Conference, 1933, he began presenting a new *Nashville Banner* trophy to the league's most outstanding football player. Two years later, he arranged a similar award for the SEC's 'Coach of the Year'. Red Sanders won it in 1941. Red's former assistant at Vanderbilt, Bear Bryant, won it eight times."[1] —Dan Miller, at the 1986 Fred Russell-Grantland Rice scholarship banquet

From 1930 to 1972, Jimmy Stahlman was publisher of the *Nashville Banner*, and in those forty-two years, he was Russell's boss. Russell kept Stahlman on his toes, however. In the first half of the twentieth century, telephone technology was still developing, and as described by a longtime *Banner* colleague below, this presented an opportunity for the young Russell.

"One time Russell called the city editor from outside the office and said he was representing the Bell Telephone Company. Freddie convinced him that they were going to put a heavy charge on the lines to dislodge carbon out of the telephone lines and that everybody ought to cover up their telephones between 9 and 10 o'clock. So Jack Drury, the city editor, got everybody to turn their wastebaskets upside down on their desks over top their telephones.

"Well, Stahlman comes walking through, and there's his whole newsroom just sitting around, not doing anything but looking at these wastebaskets on the desks waiting for the big blow to blow the carbon out of the telephone line.

"He walks up to Drury and says, 'What in the hell is going on here?'

"Jack says, 'Well, Mr. Stahlman, they're cleaning the telephone lines because—'

"'Cleaning the telephone lines, my ass. It's Russell. Get those baskets off the desk and put this staff back to work.'"[2] —Eddie Jones, *Banner* editor

***

After his Vanderbilt years in the mid-1920s, Russell did not immediately arrive in the field of sports journalism. He leveraged his legal acumen and attention to detail for a position with a real estate title company in Nashville.

"When I got out of Vanderbilt law school, the first person I went to work for was Manning Kirby [who had been a teacher in Wartrace before WWI]," Russell recalled during a television interview in fall 1986. "He was in Nashville then, and the head of a new title company. He gave me a job there, and I was with his firm as a lawyer before I went to the *Banner*."[3]

Russell held this position with the title company for eighteen months, joining in June 1927. As he came to learn, the business of titles and liens was just that: business. For Russell, it was not intriguing work, and even after passing the State Bar in January 1928, he began to consider other options for a career.

"It was not the most exciting kind of work," Russell admitted years later. "You were dealing all the time with deeds, and mortgages, and taxes. You found out pretty quick that it probably wasn't something you were going to spend your whole life doing. And Manning Kirby knew that, too. He knew that I wanted to get on the newspaper."[4]

Kirby contacted his friend Jimmy Stahlman at the *Banner* and arranged for Russell to meet him. "He gave me a choice: an opening on the classified ad desk at $25 a week or a cub reporter at $6 a week. I jumped at the reporting job."[5]

It was summer 1929, and as the *Banner* adjusted to sports editor Ralph McGill leaving for the *Atlanta Constitution*, a political writer managed the sports desk on an interim basis. Like many first-year reporters, Russell's first assignment was a somewhat morbid one.

"When I first got to the *Banner*, they put me on obituaries. You had to do about eight to ten of those a day," Russell recalled years later.[6] It wasn't long before he was assigned the police beat, and then within a few weeks, Russell began covering Vanderbilt football. "I got the luckiest break in the world in June of '29," Russell said in summer 1986. "In weeks, I knew that I didn't ever want to do anything else."[7]

Long Hours and a "Kidnapping" Break

During his initial years as the *Banner* sports editor, Russell and the rest of the country battled through the Great Depression, with its effects trickling down to almost every facet of one's life and business. It was no different for Russell's sports department, as the tough times forced him to make due with a staff of only three or four people.

Working with a skeleton crew meant long hours for the staff. At that time, though, work was work, and employees were grateful.

"Nobody minded work. There were 70-hour weeks, more often 80," Russell wrote of the Depression years in his autobiography. "I can remember driving to Knoxville to cover a University of Tennessee football game, filing a brief bulletin lead for the bulldog edition, then racing back to Nashville to write the story, thus saving the telegraph toll."[8]

Long hours were just one part of the sportswriting culture during those years. It was a tough business to be in, it did not pay well, and it attracted a tough crowd. A common stereotype of a sportswriter in the 1930s/1940s was that he was prone to heavy drinking, late-night carousing when traveling on the road, and generally possessing character flaws that made him a less-than-upstanding member of the community.

"It was a real grind for them, and there weren't a whole lot of Southern gentlemen in sportswriting back then. It was a pretty rough-and-tumble business," Edwin Pope of the *Miami Herald* noted. "Some of the real hard-up ones were hard-drinking people. They would just drink during the games, and they would even have fights in the press boxes. There was a certain air of desperation in that business, because it truly was a job from payday to payday." [9]

The athletes these reporters covered often did things far worse themselves, almost all of which stayed off the sports pages. What made it into the daily papers in the 1930s was what happened on the field, not anywhere else. A famous story, probably somewhat exaggerated over the years because of its context, involved Babe Ruth, who was known for his hard-charging lifestyle off the baseball field. As the story goes, several writers were covering the Yankees and they were on a train from one town to the next. It was late and they were playing cards, and all of a sudden, Babe Ruth ran through the car naked, with a naked woman chasing after him, armed only with a knife. They continued on through the car, leaving one writer to say, "You know—if she stabs him, we're going to have to write about it."[10]

For Russell, his interests in sports and his ambitions (for himself and for the *Banner*) kept him focused on his duties at the paper. His goal was simple: build the *Banner* sports department into the best-led, best-staffed sports team not only in the city, but throughout the South.

1930s Nashville was similar to other Southern cities: college football and minor league baseball received the most attention from fans and the media, with other sports such as boxing, horse racing, and golf next in line. With a small staff, in addition to the long hours, Russell had to be creative. One such instance occurred in the early 1930s when golfers from Vanderbilt and other Southern schools competed in an annual collegiate golf tournament. This was before the Southeastern Conference formed in 1932, and Russell recalled how the *Tennessean* was promoting this tournament for a full week ahead of time, whereas at the *Banner*, "We didn't know what to do, we didn't have money enough to cover it ourselves."[11]

In a pinch, Russell fell back on his personal connection to Vanderbilt, and took a creative chance. He called up Vanderbilt's best golfer—a young man named Huck Wheeler—and "hired" him to cover the event himself.

"I told him, 'I'll be down here each night. You just call me—that's all you have to do,'" Russell recalled telling the young Wheeler. "What happened? Huck Wheeler *won* the tournament, covering it for us. He called Saturday, and he told us every stroke, every play. He got the byline, and that was probably the luckiest experience of that time in my life."[12]

Ever the humble Southerner, Russell often attributed this element of "luck" and good fortune to his beginnings at the *Banner*. In truth, it was Russell's instincts as a reporter that put him in the right place at the right time. In no instance was this more evident than in 1934 when Tom Robinson, a former classmate of Russell's at law school, reentered the sports editor's life, albeit in a rather sensational fashion. It began 10 October 1934, when Robinson kidnapped a young woman from

Louisville, Kentucky, named Alice Speed Stoll and held her for ransom. He received $50,000 in ransom money and spent nineteen months crisscrossing the country before his capture 11 May 1936, in California. Authorities in California sent Robinson back to Louisville for trial, and Russell entered the picture, along with interested press from all over the country.

Russell told *Banner* publisher Jimmy Stahlman that he had known Robinson in college and suggested that this relationship could be their entrée with Robinson to understand where and how he had spent that time on the run. Russell drove to Louisville with Robinson's father under the pretense that he (Russell) was one of Robinson's attorneys. It backfired—Russell couldn't even get in to the court clerk's office, let alone stand up as one of Robinson's attorneys. Robinson's trial was set for 5:00 P.M. that afternoon, so Russell had to stand in court like everybody else.

"He pleaded guilty and was sentenced so quickly—all within less than two minutes—that everybody was taken by surprise and the whole place was in confusion," Russell wrote. "As Robinson was led back to jail, I fell in with his mother, father, and other relatives, just to see how far I might get without being stopped. I got all the way, right into his cell."[13]

Russell did not know it then, but his quick thinking in that Louisville courthouse and jail set off a series of events that had as much to do with his launching his career as a journalist as any other story he covered, sports or otherwise.

Several days after sneaking into Robinson's cell, his "Freddie Russell" byline appeared on the Sunday morning front page of the 17 May 1936 *Banner*, under the giant headline of "Kidnapper Tells of Gay $45,000 Spree in Which He Crisscrossed Continent Three Times Spending Stoll Ransom."

Russell's hunch that his friendship with Robinson from ten years before would pay off was correct. In the opening paragraphs of his 17 May exclusive, Russell commented that "Hundreds of times I asked myself the question of Tom Robinson's whereabouts and howabouts during those nineteen months. At last, I have the answer and the only authentic answer. It is from the mouth of Thomas H. Robinson, Jr., himself."[14]

It is not clear exactly how long Russell had with Robinson in that jail cell, but given the level of detail Russell shared just days later in the *Banner*, perhaps it was close to an hour before authorities realized he wasn't part of the family. After hardly saying a word for nineteen months to anyone about who he was, Robinson came clean. Russell must have known that his jailhouse interview could end at any moment, and as he wrote years later, "Tom told me the highlights of his hiding-out as Public Enemy No. 1, his narrow escapes, and what led up to his capture."[15]

Russell's time with Robinson came to an abrupt end, although not without a touch of ironic humor. The FBI eventually discovered that Russell was not supposed to be in the cell. Up to that point, however, they had believed Russell was an attorney, not a reporter. When they learned of his intention to use the interview information publicly, the FBI threatened action against Russell.

"I was hustled out promptly and not tenderly," Russell recalled. "The FBI man said I positively could not make use of any information I had obtained from Robinson.

"'What if I should?' I asked.

"'You would be barred forever from practicing law in Kentucky!' he said.

"A deplorable fate, thought I, but the story had to be used."[16]

Not surprisingly, having been the sports editor at the *Banner* for six years already, Russell took the "heartbreaking" news in stride.

Remarkably, the law-educated sports editor turned interim criminal reporter had scored the interview of a lifetime. And on the front page of the *Banner* that following Sunday, Russell shed light on how the interview came to be and how he was able to gather so much information from a national fugitive.

"It was natural that this boy, who had so closely guarded every word for almost two years and now was headed for the silence of an Atlanta cell, should smile and talk to the only friend he had seen since that autumn afternoon in 1934."[17]

Part of the national interest came from the sensational kidnapping itself and the amount of money involved. Robinson spent more than $45,000, and not a single dollar of it was ever traced. Russell wrote in all capitals on the front page, "THE MONEY COULDN'T BE TRACED,

AND FOR THE FIRST TIME EVER PUBLISHED, I'LL TELL YOU WHY."[18]

A bit sensational? Perhaps, but journalistic standards and styles in the first half of the twentieth century favored such an approach. Directly beneath his byline that day, before the article itself, an italicized text box read:

> Because of the nation-wide interest in the facts revealed in this exclusive interview by Freddie Russell with the kidnaper of Mrs. Alice Speed Stoll, the Banner is sharing it with a large number of the country's leading newspapers. It is being prominently displayed today in approximately forty metropolitan papers from coast to coast.[19]

Up to this point, Fred Russell was an unknown name outside of Middle Tennessee. However, for his personal jailhouse interviews of Robinson and subsequent writings, Russell earned the prestigious National Headliner's Award in 1936. The award offered the first glimpse into his eventual status as a preeminent journalist on the national stage.

Lifelong Foundations

Beyond the Stoll-Robinson kidnapping experience, the 1930s was a foundational decade for Russell on numerous levels, with residual effects that were evident until his final years with the *Banner* and up to his death in 2003. Professionally, despite his brush with success as an investigative reporter with the Robinson case, Russell returned to his first love of writing: sports. He settled into his role as sports editor for the *Banner* and helped established the paper as the clear competitor to the *Tennessean*. Competition between these two papers would become legendary in the later decades of the twentieth century, and Russell's sports desk battles with the *Tennessean*'s Raymond Johnson and later with John Bibb were as well known as they were heated.

Personally, Russell found love as well.

He was re-acquainted in 1931 with a young woman he had known in his youth, Katherine Early. As adults, the connection was immediate, and it wasn't long before Russell and Early were engaged. They married 2 November 1933, and at the ceremony, Manning Kirby—the man who gave Russell his first job out of college and then connected Russell to

Jimmy Stahlman at the *Banner*—stood as Best Man. Appropriately, Russell's great boyhood friend Red Sanders was one of the groomsmen as well.

Despite Russell's long hours and ever-changing schedule as a newspaperman, his lifestyle was a good fit for his new bride. Years later, Russell commented on his Kay's affinity for his industry.

"She loved being near sports, and near the newspaper business," Russell said. "Thank goodness she thrived on going everywhere. You couldn't imagine anyone more wonderful for a sportswriter."[20]

Shortly after getting married, the Russells started their own family. In October 1934, Fred and Kay welcomed the first of their four daughters, Katherine Early Russell. Daughters Ellen, Lee, and Carolyn were born in 1937, 1942, and 1946, respectively. On having four girls, Russell would later say, "That's the luckiest thing that ever happened."[21]

As Russell balanced his new roles as husband and father in the 1930s, he established himself as one of the *Banner*'s rising stars as well. Russell wanted his paper to be a *regional* leader in the sports business, and in 1933 the *Nashville Banner* initiated its annual Southeastern Conference Player of the Year award in football. The SEC Football Coach of the Year award followed in 1934, and for the next ten years, Russell used the *Banner* to announce these SEC awards as well as Nashville high school awards in football, baseball, basketball, golf, and tennis.

In 1943, Russell formalized the process, and the "Banquet of Champions" was born. The event brought the South's most celebrated collegiate players and coaches to Nashville for an annual December dinner and awards ceremony. The tenure of this event was a testament to its popularity and success, as it was held for the next fifty-five years (1943 to 1997) until the *Banner* ceased publications in February 1998.

Through the years, Russell handed out trophies to collegiate stars, such as Georgia's Charley Trippi in the 1940s, to modern-era recipients, such as Florida's Emmitt Smith (1989) and Tennessee's Peyton Manning (1997). The Coach of the Year award highlighted names just as prestigious, with Southern icons such as Bobby Dodd (Georgia Tech), Robert Neyland (Tennessee), and Bear Bryant (Alabama) winning the award.

Two athletes—Tennessee's Johnny Majors and Florida's Steve Spurrier—each won the SEC Player of the Year during their playing days and then received the SEC Coach of the Year award later during their clipboard-toting days on the sidelines. Majors won the player award in 1955 and 1956, and then won the coach award thirty years later in 1985. Similarly, Spurrier won the coach award three times (1994 to 1996) after being the SEC Player of the Year in 1966.

During that late 1960s period, Georgia's Vince Dooley twice received the SEC Coach of the Year award. Dooley would later become one of Russell's dear friends over the years.

"It was a very prestigious SEC Coach of the Year award," Dooley recalled of the annual *Nashville Banner* award. "They would ask the coaches to vote on the Coach of the Year, and it was a nice plaque that you received. It was a prestigious banquet, and it always brought me into contact with Freddie."[22]

Eventually, the awards would be expanded to include other leading sports, such as basketball, and Vanderbilt's C. M. Newton reflected on Russell's role with the banquet, its popularity, and the award he won in the 1980s.

"I got the Coach of the Year one time, and it was the Southern version of the Downtown Athletic Club. The *Banner* and Fred really took the lead in doing something like that," Newton commented, comparing the regional Nashville event to the national Heisman Trophy award presentation held each year in New York. "He was very instrumental in all of that."[23]

In terms of its impact within Nashville, by mixing the collegiate awards with the local area high school awards, Russell and the *Banner* popularized their paper. Russell had a penchant for celebrating local athletes at the high school level, and he used both his role at the paper and the Banquet of Champions event to promote Nashville's most successful young athletes.

Early Competition with the *Tennessean*

As the *Banner*'s sports pages increased in popularity, the competition with its city-rival, the *Tennessean*, heated up as well. By the 1930s, the two papers had been competing long enough to establish a genuine dislike for one another, as opposing political views sharpened and fueled the growing rivalry. Historically speaking, the *Banner*'s first date of publication was 10 April 1876, and in 1893, a local railroad executive, Major Edward Bushrod Stahlman, purchased full ownership of the paper. Representing the railroad industry, the business-savvy Stahlman carried a Republican stance during his tenure with the paper. After Stahlman's death in 1930, his grandson James G. Stahlman became president and publisher of the *Banner*. Subsequently, the *Banner* continued to reflect a conservative viewpoint through the Stahlman years.

As for the *Tennessean*, its roots go back to the early 1800s with the *Nashville Whig*. After a series of mergers throughout the nineteenth century, the first issue of the *Nashville Tennessean* was printed 12 May 1907. It was established by Colonel Luke Lea, a political activist who butted heads with the elder Stahlman when he and his political associates conspired unsuccessfully to have the German-born Major Stahlman declared an "alien enemy" after World War I began.[24] Such events helped to shape the competitive spirit between the papers, and during these early years of the twentieth century, each paper operated with daily morning and evening editions.

The Depression of the 1930s had a sobering effect on the financial viability of both papers, however. For a short period of time, it appeared that the *Tennessean* would not survive, as compromising legal situations developed with its ownership. In March 1933, the newspaper was placed under federal receivership, and for the next several years, federally appointed directors ran the *Tennessean* until it was ultimately placed on the auction block. In 1937, Silliman Evans, a former reporter for the *Fort Worth Star-Telegram*, purchased the paper for $850,000. Shortly after that purchase, despite the financial and personal competition that existed between the two papers, Evans and Stahlman came together in an effort to strengthen each paper for the long term.

In an unprecedented move, the two papers established a Joint Operating Agreement in 1937, the nation's first "JOA." Under this agreement, the *Tennessean* ceased publication of its evening editions and the *Banner* ceased publication of its Sunday edition, in part to save operational costs, in part to provide each paper a specific market advantage. The *Tennessean* would have Sundays to itself, while the *Banner* would become the city's only afternoon/evening paper.

The papers maintained their editorial and political independence. The operational and business goodwill that brought Stahlman and Evans together to form the JOA didn't necessarily filter down to the respective staffs of either paper.

"The competition between the *Banner* and the *Tennessean* was intense," retired *Tennessean* editor John Seigenthaler recalled. "It was two separate news and editorial groups, with a joint operation among everything else. One paper was very conservative, and the other was very Roosevelt/New-Deal liberal."[25]

The most remarkable aspect of this agreement was that these two rivals essentially moved in with each other. The JOA created the Newspaper Printing Corporation as a business agent for both papers, and together, the two newspapers built a new facility in 1938, located at 1100 Broadway in downtown Nashville. For sixty years, the two papers shared services, such as printing and classified advertising as well as meeting rooms, office space, and even parking lots, where rival staff members would pass each other coming and going from work.

"This was a strange relationship between the *Banner* and the *Tennessean*," Seigenthaler commented in 2005, when looking back at how the respective staffs arranged the shared space. "After you got in the front door, there was a customer service counter in the center of the entrance hall. Quite naturally, if you turned to the right, you went to the *Banner*, and if you turned to the left, you went to the *Tennessean*. And that was more than a physical arrangement."[26]

Even the most private of rooms, the bathroom, was a place where one writer never knew for sure just who might be in the stall next door.

"The bathroom was in the rear of both city rooms, and there reporters would occasionally meet," Seigenthaler recalled. "There were occasional barbs exchanged back and forth, of course, but if you were at a urinal talking to one of your colleagues about a story, you always checked to make certain that nobody was in the stalls and might overhear what you said."[27]

It was within this unique, shared-space environment at 1100 Broadway that Russell honed his sportswriting craft and skills as an editor. Working for Stahlman, Russell was loyal to his boss, but it was a harsh business and Stahlman was as demanding as he was tough.

Edwin Pope, a sportswriter for decades with the *Miami Herald*, recalled a distinct conversation he had with Russell some years later, when the two of them were covering a sporting event together. Pope had heard flattering things about Stahlman, and mentioned this to his friend.

"He looked at me, and fixed me with a very level look, and said, 'Edwin, the nicest publisher that ever lived is a sonofabitch,'" Pope recalled. "I've told about six publishers at the *Miami Herald* that line over the years, and they thought it was pretty funny, because there's so much truth in it. They had to be that way. It's part of what got them there."[28]

Stahlman's toughness was critical to his success, and coupled with ambitious editors and writers like Russell, it served both men and the *Banner* well. Each knew their respective roles and how the newspaper game needed to be played in order to be successful. Over the years, Stahlman's paper and personal reputation benefited from having the region's most successful sportswriter, while Russell leveraged Stahlman's power position within the community and at Vanderbilt to get his name in the right public circles of influence. Russell navigated the competitive waters with his exemplary people skills, not only within the papers, but within the community as well.

"The power-brokers knew that if you needed to get to Jimmy Stahlman, you went through Freddie Russell," Eddie Jones said. "And if you wanted to get the *Banner* lined up to support something for the Metro government or something for the community, you'd line up a secret meeting with Russell and sell him first. If you sold it to Freddie, you had a pretty good chance of him bringing the paper along to support what you wanted."[29]

Eventually, the working relationship between Stahlman and Russell became one of friendship.

"Oh, people said he was a tyrant. Everybody can tell you that. But Daddy admired and respected him," daughter Carolyn said, when asked of her father's relationship to Stahlman.[30]

Russell's growing reputation on the national scene in the 1930s and 1940s only contributed to the competitive nature between the two Nashville papers as well. As a nod to Russell's relationship skills, though, the *Tennessean's* John Seigenthaler recalled how Russell was perceived during those early years after the Joint Operating Agreement of 1937 was in place. His uncle, Walter Seigenthaler, was circulation direction for both papers, had known Russell well from the early days, and witnessed how competitive the sports departments were.

"He [Walter] was friendly with both sides, and he made it clear to me that there were some people at the *Banner* that would be hostile to the *Tennessean* folks no matter what happened," Seigenthaler said of his uncle. "Walter also said that Freddie Russell effectively had no enemies."[31]

Leading the *Banner* Forward

With that kind of reputation surrounding him even from his competition, Russell had the advantage over one of his earliest rivals at the *Tennessean*: Raymond Johnson. Johnson was an established and respected writer, but even Johnson's own boss, John Seigenthaler, acknowledged the disparity in talent: "Freddie simply could write rings around Raymond."[32]

Further fanning the competitive flames between the sports departments was the fact that Russell had the influential Stahlman in his court. During these times, Vanderbilt sports highlighted the city beats, and with Stahlman's position with the university's board of trustees, not to mention Russell being a Vanderbilt man, Johnson faced a constant uphill battle.

"Particularly with stories coming out of Vanderbilt, Stahlman opened for Freddie all the doors that anybody could ever open for another person, where Raymond Johnson, it seemed, couldn't get people to return his calls," Jones recalled with a laugh. "In the early days, I really can't think of many big stories breaking in the *Tennessean* before Freddie had it in the *Banner*."[33]

Of course, no matter how much one paper or one reporter dominated, there were always moments when the underdog won. Not surprisingly, Russell never liked getting beat once.

"He had a very bad temper when things didn't go right at the paper," daughter Carolyn recalled. "I can remember as a child that breakfast could be a pretty tense time. He would be reading the morning paper, and if Raymond Johnson had something that beat the *Banner*, he would just blow up."[34]

More often than not, though, Russell had stories in the *Banner* first. And if he was scooped on a story, or if a story appeared in both papers on the same day, readers gravitated towards the *Banner* sports section to read Russell. This tendency underscored the readers' appreciation for Russell the writer, as opposed to Russell the competitor.

"I think it was his personality and his people skills, his ability to communicate with people," former *Banner* sports editor and current *Tennessean* columnist Joe Biddle reflected. "Mr. Russell could get better quotes. With the ethics and integrity that he had, the wit that he had, and then the feel that he had for sports and for people. Those are the things that made him special, made people want to read his columns." [35]

Russell's readers were not just the casual public, either. Even in those days, the athletes that Russell covered would glance at the sports pages themselves.

"I was a freshman at Vanderbilt in 1940, and everybody read Freddie's column," former Commodore Jimmy Webb recalled with a laugh. "In the spring game ending my freshman year, he wrote a column and said a nice thing about me. I admired him a lot before that, but that really endeared me to him."[36]

Webb stayed in Nashville after his Vanderbilt years, and he and Russell eventually forged a friendship that lasted until the latter passed away in 2003. Before Webb passed away in January 2009, he commented on his friendship with Russell, and how he remembered him from his time playing football at Vanderbilt.

"He had something that gave everyone a warm, happy feeling. When he would meet a Jack Dempsey or a Gene Tunney, he would always follow up with them," Webb said. "Russell would stay in touch, send a Christmas card, and so they always knew about Fred Russell, they would always remember him, and then they would gradually become friends. He just had that way about him," Webb said.[37]

One of Russell's additional skills, often reflected in his daily column, was his sense of timing, knowing when to step away from the sports world when "real life" warranted attention. An example of this from his early days at the *Banner* occurred during World War II, when many coaches, players, and journalists themselves were called up for duty.

One of Russell's good friends at the time was Tom Siler, a fellow sportswriter from the *Knoxville News-Sentinel*. Siler was in the Army, stationed in Paris with the press corps, and one of his jobs was to take newspaper men to the front lines for stories. Toward the end of the war, shortly after Berlin fell, Siler and a small group of men had access to

Hitler's office building. As they rummaged through items, Siler found a pile of papers and letters from a prisoner of war camp based in Crossville, Tennessee.

As it turned out, the Crossville POW camp housed well over a 1,000 German and Italian prisoners. In their spare time, many of the Germans wrote to Hitler, and it was these cards that Siler stumbled upon in Hitler's office building.

As Siler's wife Nancy retold the story, her husband gathered up what he could and thought it might make for an interesting read back in Nashville.

"Tom sent these postcards to Fred Russell, and Russell put them in the Nashville paper," Nancy Siler said. "They said things like, 'Happy birthday, my Fuhrer' and 'Can't wait to get home and fight for you again; we love you.' All the cards were dated March 1943, and Freddie's story ran in September 1945."

Over the years, Russell kept his column alive by departing from the normal day-to-day sports world every once in a while, and this World War II example underscores his ability to connect his readers to the important events of their time, events that had little to do with sports.

In that general sense, Russell's early columns in the *Banner* from the '30s and '40s were no different than those he wrote during the second half of the century. He remained sensitive to his reader's interests, and the foundations Russell established early on—relationships, writing style, and family—were pivotal ones that yielded a lifetime of success.

3

Rites of Spring

"People will come, Ray. The one constant through all the years has been *baseball*. America has rolled by like an army of steamrollers. It's been erased like a blackboard, rebuilt, and erased again. But baseball has marked the time. This field, this game—it's a part of our past, Ray. It reminds us of all that once was good and it could be again. Oh, people will come, Ray. People will most definitely come."[1] —James Earl Jones as Terrence Mann in *Field of Dreams*

Horse racing certainly has its share of hard-luck stories where its fans just can't seem to cash in at the track. For Fred Russell, a man who loved horse racing, one man's misery could be another man's punch line. The story below, as told by one of his Nashville golfing acquaintances, would appear in his column every once in a while, and it never failed to illicit a laugh from the reader.

There's this compulsive gambler who bet on horse races, and he had a bad run of luck and just couldn't pick a winner. One night, he had a vision, and it said, "Bet the hat." So he gets up the next morning, calls his bookie right away, tells him about the vision, and that he wants to "bet the hat." He asks him about what's running at the local track, wants to know if there's anything running with a hat in the name. And the guy says, "Well, let's see. Hey, in the first race, the clear favorite is 'Top Hat.' How about that?" The guy goes, "That's unreal. Let's go with that. What about in the second race?"

"Well, 'Bluebonnet' is there, but he hasn't been running real well."

"That's okay. Let's go with it. How about the third?"

"Oh, 'Save the Straw' is the favorite there."

"Great. And the fourth?"

"Well, 'Green Beret' is running here. It's a new horse, but looks like he's going to be all right. And, hey, 'Son of Stetson' is running in the fifth. Does that work?"

"Oh yeah. What about the sixth?"

"Whoa, wow. 'Brown Derby' is running there. What do you think?"

"Absolutely, and in the seventh?"

"Hmm, no, no, no—wait a minute...the favorite is 'Check-Room.' That's where you put all your hats, isn't it?"

"Yeah, I think so. Let's do it. $10 on the nose for every horse, and let's double-up each time and see what happens."

So he called his bookie later that afternoon to see what happened.

"Well, how'd we do?"

"You're not going to believe this," the bookie says, all excited. "They're running the last race now, and Top Hat, Bluebonnet, Green Beret, Brown Derby, they've *all* won, all six of your horses. I can't believe this. And right now, Check-Room is leading, he's *comfortably* ahead, coming around the last turn right now. This is great!"

"Now hang on, just hang on. You just tell me what happens."

"I'm telling you, Check-Room is looking *great*. Running strong. I just want to know how you're going to spend all this—oh no. Check-Room just...he just stumbled at the end. He lost by a nose."

"You're kidding! Oh my gosh. You mean I've lost everything?"

"Well, yeah, looks like it, because I doubled up every time, like you said."

"I can't believe it, I just can't believe it. You have to tell me: who beat Check-Room?"

"Well, let's see here. Hang on, they're posting it right now. There it is. Looks like...some Mexican horse named 'Sombrero.'"[2]

* * *

As Fred Russell settled into his routine at the *Nashville Banner* during the 1930s and 1940s, he gravitated toward his natural sports passions. Baseball and college football were clearly his top two, with horse racing and golf rounding out his top four. With the spring season came the annual awakening of three of these Russell favorites: spring training, the Masters Tournament, and the Kentucky Derby.

Whether it was caravanning with legendary writers Grantland Rice and Red Smith to Florida each March to cover baseball, befriending Bobby Jones at Augusta, or making his annual pilgrimage to Churchill Downs for the Kentucky Derby, Russell regularly witnessed sport's most celebrated events and their heroes. Russell once described the start of the Kentucky Derby as "the most electric instant in sports,"[3] and he would know: Russell attended more than fifty consecutive Derbies.

Each year, however, before the big race in Louisville, and before walking beside the lush green fairways at the Masters, there was baseball. This was Russell's first love, and he was a faithful follower his entire life.

Baseball

When Russell was eighty-two in 1989, the movie *Field of Dreams* was in theatres, and it quickly became one of Russell's all-time favorite films. With its connections to Shoeless Joe Jackson and other stars from Russell's youth, the movie's focus on baseball and its depiction of simpler times in the first half of the twentieth century resonated with Russell. The movie was a nostalgic event for Russell, since it was during that part of his youth when baseball captured his attention. In the opening pages of his 1957 autobiography, Russell wrote about going to the drugstore to get a new baseball. "How beautiful the new ball, stitched in red and blue and so slick that it almost squirted out of the tissue paper," Russell wrote. "The smell of a new baseball, the feel of a glove when you ran your fingers way up in it and pounded the pocket where a drop or two of machine oil had been rubbed—those things never leave you."[4]

As a boy and a young man, baseball became Russell's sport of choice, and he was good at it. He played well enough to earn a spot on the Vanderbilt baseball team as a pitcher, and during his Commodore years, he was classmate and teammate of Red Sanders. Sanders, of course, played football as well and eventually went on to garner his own fame in coaching as the head man at Vanderbilt and UCLA in the 1940s and 1950s. Their playing days together on the Commodore baseball team were some of Russell's finest memories as a young man.

While Russell's skills on the diamond prevented him from playing beyond the collegiate level, his passion for the sport never waned. It was inevitable that baseball would rise to the surface of Russell's sportswriting preferences. Major League Baseball's "spring training" proved to be a perfect mix of the things Russell appreciated most in the business: camaraderie with friends, closeness with the players and coaches, and a relaxed atmosphere. The advent of March led to annual trips to Florida with Rice and Smith, two of his closest friends in the business, and these were treasured sojourns for the Nashville writer. As Russell commented in his autobiography, "Baseball, with its sun and fun (ever hear of anyone getting tired of batting practice?) had been my favorite game, and from the first days on a newspaper it was the sport I liked best to cover."[5]

Russell enjoyed the pace of it all, adding that "One reason I'm so fond of spring baseball is that on gloomy days columns can be written two or three days in advance, with little chance of spoiling."[6]

Minor League Town, Major League Connections

Russell's time spent in Florida each spring allowed him to connect with players and coaches from all over the country; and as his stature grew, he developed friendships and relationships of respect with some of the sport's biggest names. The New York Yankees were as big during Russell's time as they are today, and with Yankee pitching coach Jim Turner being a Nashville native and a Russell friend, the *Banner* sports editor spent a majority of his time covering the Yankees. Russell particularly enjoyed his time covering the Yankees in the 1950s.

"Casey Stengel was better than any show anywhere," Russell said of Stengel's managing stint with the Yankees from 1940 to 1960. "Training in St. Petersburg, around hotel lobbies at night, after the exhibitions—the greatest days I've known."[7]

As far as relationships went, Russell and baseball in the spring were a perfect fit. Years later, *Banner* staff members would bump into ex-players who remembered Russell well. One example included a run-in with Yankee great Joe DiMaggio.

"In his time, everybody knew him, no matter how famous they were," former *Banner* sports staffer Mark McGee said. "I would cover Major League All-Star games, and one time Joe DiMaggio saw my '*Nashville Banner*' credential. He said to me, 'How's Freddie doing?' They were always shocked that he was still writing, and they all knew him as 'Freddie.'"[8]

Part of the allure of spring training for Russell (and for so many writers in the era before television and night games) was the relaxed access to players and coaches, coupled with the camaraderie with colleagues. In his early days, Russell made the trip with Rice and Smith; later he would meet up with more contemporary writers such as Edwin Pope and Tom McEwen. It was during these times that he would gather his best material, things you wouldn't get once the season started. Russell typically made the Tampa/St Petersburg area his home for a couple of weeks each year.

"It has always been the center for spring training, because about ten teams are all within driving distance," McEwen said of his hometown Tampa, where he still writes today. "Russell would come down to Tampa all these years for spring training, write a few stories, let people know that he was still covering baseball."[9]

"Spring training was one of the places the old writers most enjoyed. They would sit around the hotels in Tampa and St. Petersburg and tell old stories," Pope recalled. "That was back when they really used those lobbies. Coaches and managers and some players would sit around the lobbies in these big, stuffed chairs when they weren't in the bar and would just tell stories all night long. And Russell loved to collect these stories. It was paradise for him."[10]

Russell made his own impression on countless baseball men, from players to managers to all those in between. Former Los Angeles Dodger skipper Tommy Lasorda was one of them.

"I saw him on many occasions, and he was always so polite, so cordial," Lasorda said of his encounters with Russell. "He was so well thought of, and everybody thought the world of him. You know, usually writers can't get 100 percent devotion or support, but this guy did."[11]

Ernie Harwell, longtime radio voice of the Detroit Tigers (1960 to 2002), remembered Russell from his own early trips to Florida, when Harwell was doing play-by-play for the New York Giants (1950 to 1953). Harwell recalled the different pace of baseball life during the middle part of the twentieth century as well.

"It was a different time back then," Harwell recalled. "Remember, there was no night baseball. The players and writers would drink together and party together.[12]

"I remember 1951, in particular. I was with the New York Giants at the time. In St. Pete, Russell had a place, and we stayed there together with our families," Harwell continued. "The Giants players and families would join us on the beach and at the cottages. We played charades and played on the beach with our families."[13]

Russell's daughters remember vividly their times spent not only in St. Petersburg with their father for spring training, but also their time out of school in order to do so. Lee (Russell) Brown remembers one year in particular.

"One time I met Lefty Gomez," Brown recalled, thinking back to one of the years her parents took the whole family on the road. "We went to St. Petersburg with Mother and Daddy for about a month. Mother needed to light this gas stove in this funky little house we used to stay in, and I went up and asked this man for a match. Turns out it was Lefty Gomez, and we ended up playing with his two daughters the rest of the time."[14]

Having the entire family on the spring-training trips was a rarity, however, and there were many times when he was away more than he was home. Over time, the investment paid off. Not only did Russell establish himself as a spring-training regular, but because he was a member of the *Nashville Banner* staff, he paved the way for other *Banner* sportswriters in the years that followed.

Mark McGee, who wrote for the *Banner* from 1981 to 1994, remembered the time he struggled to get an interview with one of baseball's legendary managers. As persistent as he was, McGee couldn't find a way in, until he dropped Russell's name.

"The *Banner* wanted me to do a big story on Sparky Anderson," McGee said, recalling a story from his 1984 spring-training trip. "Sparky's a nice guy, but he tried the patience of the writers. He wanted to test you, see how much of the game you knew."

Towards the end of camp, growing more worried each day, McGee finally caught up with Anderson on the practice field to request an interview. He received the rather brief reply, "Yeah, we'll get to that."

"Well, not sure why I even thought about it," McGee continued, "but I said, 'Well, Fred Russell told me you'd help me out.'

"And he just stopped and sat down right where he was standing and said, 'What do you need to know?' It was like the floodgates just opened up. It was remarkable that his name could get that kind of response."[15]

It is worth noting that Russell developed his baseball acumen and astounding network of contacts without having a major league team in his hometown to cover. The Nashville Vols were a minor league team with its own rich history, but Southern League baseball was a far cry from the big leagues. And yet Russell was known throughout the majors, a frequent and recognizable face in press boxes, especially around the World Series.

Russell focused on covering the regional teams of interest. The *Nashville Banner* paid closer attention to the teams from St. Louis, Chicago, Atlanta, and Cincinnati, respectively. During spring training at first, and then throughout the season when possible, Russell established and cultivated relationships with other writers from those towns, guys like Si Burick, who covered the Reds for the *Dayton Daily News*, and Bob Broeg, who covered the Cardinals for the *St. Louis Post-Dispatch*.

These friendships provided Russell a means of establishing relationships with players and coaches from other teams, and Russell was an opportunistic newspaperman. He knew the business reality that sometimes your next story was only as good as your network of contacts, the players you could call if you had to have a fact confirmed (or denied), or the coaches who would return your call, even if it wasn't a convenient time to do so. Over the years, Russell built up a network of friends in the business that was second to none.

As an example, McEwen was Russell's connection point to legendary Yankee owner George Steinbrenner, someone in the late twentieth and early twenty-first centuries who was known for being combative with the media at worst, distant and apathetic at best. When asked to comment on Russell, Steinbrenner's mood was so relaxed, it was as if he had gone back in time for an interview in the 1950s, when members of the media weren't so critical.

"[Fred] was a class act, he never tried to hurt people, and if he didn't have anything to write positive, he didn't write," Steinbrenner said. "Fred wrote about the game they played, and he'd report the facts, not so much his opinion."[16]

For all the contacts Russell made, it was never about name-dropping for him. Just the opposite, in fact. As shown in the story below, Russell's interest in building friendships was as evident at the top of the organization with owners as it was with those collecting tickets.

"Mr. Russell wore his dignity so well, with everybody," former *Nashville Banner* reporter Tom Robinson noted, reminded of a time when Russell called to let him know that he was returning home early from the World Series. It was 1976, the Yankees and the Reds were playing, and Russell had a sideline pass if Robinson was interested.

"Mr. Russell tells me to go to Gate 12, not 'will call' or a press tent or anything, and ask for this older gentleman," Robinson recalled. "Well, this older gentleman was the gatekeeper, sitting in his folding chair, waiting for the stadium to open. I see Gate 12, and I walk up to him.

"'Hey, I'm Tom Robinson.'

"'Yeah, you got Freddie's pass for tonight, right? Yeah, I've known Freddie a long time. He's been coming up here for years seeing these Reds games.'"[17]

One year the Reds were in Nashville to play an exhibition game against Nashville's minor league team. It was years after Russell was needed for day-to-day sportswriting, so he was there in the stands with his wife to enjoy the game. Roy Kramer, former Vanderbilt athletic director, SEC commissioner, and close friend of Russell's, recalled the evening that night

"About a half hour before the game, we were sitting up there with Fred and Kay. All of a sudden, here comes Sparky Anderson climbing over the railing coming up to sit with Fred and tell stories," Kramer recalled. "I'll never forget Sparky saying, 'I really hate having to go back to the dugout, Fred. I'd rather sit up here and tell stories and watch the game with you.' That just gave you a feel for the kind of respect he carried with him."[18]

Early Baseball in Nashville: Sulphur Dell and the Vols

Without a major league team, Nashville's baseball traditions of the twentieth century were that of the Southern League variety, with the Nashville Vols playing in downtown Nashville. The Vols played in Nashville from 1901 to 1963 and represented one of the more significant sporting attractions in Tennessee's growing capital city.

The talent equivalent of today's Double-A or Triple-A minor league teams, the Southern League had notable teams in Nashville, Atlanta (the Crackers), New Orleans (the Pelicans), and Birmingham (the Barons), to name a few. The Vols played at Sulphur Dell, the name of their field in downtown Nashville, and it was the main event in town. It was synonymous with Nashville baseball, and up until 1963 when the franchise left Nashville, Russell often pointed out that "Organized baseball had been played on that spot longer than at any place in the United States."[19] As a fan first, long before his duties at the *Banner*,

Russell attended games as often as he could. He carried that passion to his own family, when Russell took his wife and the girls to games.

"I remember that place really well," Russell's oldest daughter, Kay Beasley, recalled. "Sometimes the whole neighborhood would go down there on Sunday nights and we would watch from the top row, up near the office."[20]

"It was unbelievable. You should have seen the doubleheaders we had out there on Sundays," former *Banner* staffer and copyeditor Bill Roberts said, when asked about the popularity of Southern League games in Nashville. "These were the days before television, and there was nothing to do on those Sundays. You couldn't get a car out of the parking lot."[21]

"When I grew up in the 1940s, they were *the* story," Larry Schmittou, founder and still owner of the Nashville Sounds, recalled. "They were on WSM radio, Larry Munson was the announcer, Mr. Russell and George Leonard covered them, and the Vols were the front-page story."[22]

For Russell, these players were some of his first subjects to garner attention in the *Banner*. True to his style, Russell never just reported the game; he knew that readers needed more to keep their interest throughout the long season and the proverbial dog days of summer. One of his favorites was tough guy Buster Brown, a Nashville first-baseman and pitcher from the 1920s.

Before games, Brown would stick his head into opposing dugouts, all but challenging his opponents to a fight if they tried to pull anything rough or out of line once the game started. As Russell described in his autobiography, Brown was ready in case anything broke out.

"He carried a spring-lock knife with a blade about five inches long—actually kept it in his uniform—a fact well known to visiting players," Russell wrote.[23]

No matter how serious Brown might have been, Russell appreciated more than most the indirect humor and irony associated with a player actually being armed during a game. Things one might never see at the major league level were rarely considered out of the realm of possibility in the minor leagues.

"It was easier to write, too, especially on the lighter side," Russell said of the 1930 season, his first covering baseball. "One of the greatest thrills of my life, Clarence 'Pants' Roland managed Nashville, and the Nashville team went to Anniston, Alabama, to play Toledo, managed by Casey Stengel. I thought it was the greatest."[24]

Through his early years covering baseball in Nashville, one of Russell's all-time favorites was Larry Gilbert, who managed the Nashville Vols for ten years from 1939 to 1948. All told, Gilbert spent thirty-nine years within the Southern League, first as a player, then later as a manager with both New Orleans and Nashville. Russell's fondness for the manager was apparent, as he dedicated an entire chapter of his autobiography to Gilbert. About the time Gilbert finished his managerial career with the Vols in 1948, the clock started ticking on the Vols, unfortunately. The advent of television and a loss of financial viability started to wear on the teams of the Southern League, and the uniqueness of Sulphur Dell became more of a liability.

"As attendance dwindled and ballparks decayed, the minor league teams could not make any money," Schmittou recalled of the Southern League's troubles. "That's what made the Nashville Vols go broke. When TV came in, towards the end of their reign, they were dead before they died."[25]

Similar to Russell, Schmittou loved baseball and he loved Nashville. When Sulphur Dell was torn down in 1969, marking the end of professional baseball in Nashville, it was Schmittou who played the key role in bringing baseball back to his city. Russell lent his support in the late 1970s, and wrote encouraging things about Schmittou in his column at the *Banner*.

"With Mr. Russell, an age-old fan of baseball, I remember him telling me, 'If there's anyone who can do it, it's you Larry.' That meant something," Schmittou noted.[26]

In 1978, Schmittou succeeded in his efforts when the Nashville Sounds played their first season in Greer Stadium, marking the return of baseball to a city that had not seen it for a decade and a half. For Fred Russell, as his column went from daily to weekly in the later stages of his career, the timing was perfect. Similar to his boyhood days when he visited Sulphur Dell, going to Greer Stadium became an opportunity to enjoy minor league baseball, be close to the players and coaches, and most importantly, simply be a fan again.

From Spring Training to Amen Corner

While the month of March was a favorite of Russell's, there was not much time between the end of spring training and the beginning of the golf season. The Masters—still one of the four major golf tournaments for professional golfers—kicked off the heart of the annual golf season. There were tournaments played in warmer climates during the early months of the year, but it wasn't really until the golfing world descended upon Augusta, Georgia, in early April that things heated up.

Augusta and the Masters were a favorite destination for Fred Russell. From his close friendship with golfing legend Bobby Jones to the venue's proximity to Nashville to the opportunity to spend time at the "Tennessee Cottage" each spring, Russell rarely missed his annual sojourn to Augusta.

"In the good times and life of a sportswriter, the Masters tournament gets a top spot," Russell said in his 1957 autobiography. "This is the most pleasant spectator event in sports, the best course in the world for seeing golf. It has become one of the game's shrines."[27]

The Masters ascended to that status in a remarkably short period of time. The tournament began informally in 1934, when organizer Bobby Jones wanted an opportunity to play against the top players in the world. For the first couple of years, the tournament was titled the Augusta National Invitational, and 1937 marked Russell's first year covering the event.

"At the early tournaments, Bobby attracted the biggest galleries the first two or three days," Russell wrote in 1995. "They thinned considerably by Sunday's final round if he wasn't in contention."[28]

In 1938, the tournament's name officially became the Masters. Over the years, there has been debate as to who came up with this name, since it was one that Jones eventually came around to accept but did not originally favor. Some argued that it was legendary golf writer O. B. Keeler from the *Atlanta Journal*, while others believed it was sportswriting icon Grantland Rice. To settle the debate, Russell recalled what his good friend Rice had told him years before.

"No, it was Cliff Roberts," Rice told Russell. Roberts was the cofounder of Augusta National Golf Club, along with Jones. "Cliff wanted the name from the beginning, but Bob thought it sounded too presumptuous."[29]

Ultimately, it was a fitting name for the tournament. With its picturesque location, the Southern charm of Augusta, and golf's greatest players wanting to take part in Jones's tournament, it was immensely popular. From Gene Sarazen to Sam Snead and Walter Hagen to Ben Hogan, Augusta National was an annual stop. This carried over to the next generation of golfers that Russell covered, men such as Arnold Palmer, Jack Nicklaus, Lee Trevino, and Johnny Miller. In the television era, the tournament blossomed, and it is today perhaps the most cherished victory in golf.

Palmer won the tournament four times (1958, 1960, 1962, and 1964), and the retired golfer retains vivid memories of his playing days.

"I pointed my entire season, especially the winter season, to the Masters. I played as hard as I could possibly play so that when I got to Augusta, I was ready," Palmer recalled in November 2005. "I looked forward to getting there, and you walked in with a great deal of pride. The way the tournament was conducted, the condition of the golf course, it was a place of inspiration for me."[30]

Augusta Charm: Bobby Jones, the Quonset Hut, and the Tennessee Cottage

What Palmer loved about the tournament and its location during his playing days is what Fred Russell had been appreciating for more than twenty years.

"He loved going down there," Jake Wallace, one of Nashville's current members at Augusta National Country Club, said. "But the thing about the Masters was that it wasn't just that he loved the place, it's that everybody down there that knew him loved him."[31]

Nowhere was this more evident than in his friendship with Jones. Russell and Jones met first in the late 1920s, and Jones impressed Russell more than any other athletic figure during the sportswriter's time.

"Without question, one of the greatest privileges of my life was to be a friend of Bobby Jones. Bob Jones, actually. He liked for you to call him Bob," Russell said in the late 1990s, acknowledging the personal friendship he had with Jones. "As far as my idols, I place Bob Jones and Grantland Rice in the company of Robert E. Lee."[32]

43

Russell did not meet Jones through golf. In his early days at the *Banner*, before he was a sportswriter, Russell met Jones through baseball. Jones was a part-owner of the Atlanta Crackers, a minor league baseball team in the same Southern League as the Nashville Vols. "Minor league baseball was the thing back then, and Nashville and Atlanta were great rivals through the years," Russell said. "A group of Atlanta people bought the Atlanta baseball club, and Jones was in there doing them a favor."[33]

Ultimately, it was Jones's golfing success and Russell's ascendancy at the *Banner* that put the two men on the same sports page. When Russell made his way to Augusta each year, visiting Jones was a priority and a highlight. While he often commented on Jones's kindness and friendly personality, Russell never forgot Jones's true talents on the golf course.

"He would be my top golfer of all time," Russell said years later when reflecting on the golfing greats of the twentieth century. "There's a lot of argument about [Jack] Nicklaus, and [Ben] Hogan, and Jones—but for Jones's time, and the equipment he played with, I would have to put Jones number one."[34]

One of the accomplishments that impressed Russell the most was Jones's "Grand Slam," when he won the open and amateur championships in both the U.S. and Britain in 1930. "When you go back and see how impossible that is to accomplish, winning those four big tournaments, I don't know how he did it," Russell marveled.[35]

Like Russell, Jones was a great storyteller, and this was one of the foundations of their lasting friendship. One of the stories that stuck with the sportswriter throughout his life was Jones's trip to Great Britain to play in the British Amateur one year. The tournament was held at St. Andrew's, and Jones was playing in a practice round several days before the main event. Jones was assigned a caddy as well as a playing partner for the day. Of his partner, Jones later told Russell that he was the "most unpleasant human being he had ever been around." As Russell recalled the story, Jones had more regard for the caddy that day than his partner.

"The guy was bogeying every hole, cursing to himself, and it was just a horrible experience," Russell remembered Jones telling him. "They were winding up, and he said it loud enough for everybody to hear, 'I do believe you are the *worst* caddy in the entire world.'

"And Jones never forgot how gentlemanly the caddy was. He said, 'Oh no, sir. Oh no, sir. That would be far, *far* too great a coincidence.'"[36]

Russell and Jones remained close long after Jones's playing days ended, and it was a friendship that lasted until Jones died 18 December 1971.

Years later, reflecting on his friend and the tournament he founded, Russell still carried strong feelings. "My fondest and most enduring memories of April in Augusta surround my visits to the Bob Jones Cabin on the course, facing the 10th tee," Russell wrote once. "The heart and soul of the tournament is the spirit of Bobby Jones."[37]

It wasn't just players who carried strong memories of their experiences in Augusta. For Russell and his colleagues in the sportswriting business, the Masters was also home to one of the most recognized names for press facilities: the Quonset Hut. From 1953 to 1989, the Quonset Hut was the media headquarters at Augusta National, and while media headquarters have since been updated to the more modern Press Building, the old headquarters had its share of quirky characteristics.

As John Boyette reported for the *Augusta Chronicle* in 2004, the hut could be considered cozy and intimate by some, noisy and cramped by others.[38] Longtime *Miami Herald* columnist Edwin Pope spent many years at the Quonset hut and could speak authoritatively to its nuances.

"The press tent was literally a tent, located over by the first fairway," said Pope. "It had planks on the floor and 12 or 13 typewriters. Each one had a big barrel of whiskey beside it, in various stages of emptiness. Mostly empty."[39]

"In those days, at the Quonset hut, you sat in a room at long tight tables, and if you had a big fat guy in front of you and he leaned back, you'd get knocked over," Tom McEwen of the *Tampa Tribune* added with a laugh. A longtime friend of Russell's, McEwen also remembered the technical limitations of that era, and the press accommodations at the Masters were not immune to trouble.

"Lightning hit one time, and we were all about halfway through our stories. Those were the very early days of computers, and you knew that you'd lose everything if anything happened," McEwen recalled. "It hit the lines of the Quonset hut, and you've never heard a moan like that in your life. Everyone had to start all over that year."[40]

Augusta and the Masters were a popular destination for Tennessee fans as well, in particular those from Nashville who could make the trip in a day's drive or a quick flight. In the mid-1950s, several Nashville businessmen who were members of Augusta National built a cottage on the course. It was a place to stay during their golfing trips to the country club and a popular place to be during that first week in April each spring.

The cottage was built by Sam Fleming, Elden Stevenson, and O. H. "Hank" Ingram, and it was appropriately dubbed the "Tennessee Cottage." The Masters tournament was a cherished trip, not only for those from Nashville who made their way down to Augusta, but for Russell as well, since he was able to spend some of his on-the-job time with friends from home. On several occasions, Russell flew down with Cohen Williams, whose family had founded Martha White Food. On the company plane, Russell would also spend time with renowned entertainer Ernie Ford, who was a spokesman for Martha White and had the nationally recognized nickname, "Tennessee Ernie."

Buzz Davis, one of Nashville's current members at Augusta National, said some of his fondest memories at the celebrated tournament were the ones that included Russell.

"Every Tuesday night of the Masters, Fred Russell, Judd Collins, who was a TV announcer in Nashville at Channel 4, and Ernie Ford, we would have dinner, usually downtown at the Pinnacle Club," Davis recalled. "Listening to these guys swap stories, I wished I had tape recorder. My guess is, they told the same stories, but they got funnier each and every year."[41]

One of the classic stories is one Russell himself recalled when he reminisced about the Masters and spending time at the Tennessee Cottage. It was a gag they pulled on Ford, who Russell said was "probably the most identifiable figure there, and, boy, did he love the Masters."[42]

It was the late 1970s, and Russell was flying to Augusta from Salisbury, North Carolina, home of the National Sportscasters and Sportswriters Association (NSSA), where "Tennessee Ernie" had been booked as an entertainer. It was a group of about eight or nine folks, including Ford, Cohen Williams, Russell, and fellow sportswriter Tom McEwen. They went to dinner that night, and someone suggested that they organize a pool on the Masters that week, and they would draw names from a hat.

"We had all the names of those who are playing, and we'd put in $10 a piece, and we'd have about $100, and we'd make it $70, and the runner-up would get $30," Russell recalled. "Ernie wasn't overeager to participate, but he did it anyway. The guy who had suggested it told me what he was up to, and he said you make out like you are drawing out of the hat, but use these other six slips."

As the gag played out, Ford's "luck" with the names he drew was downright terrible.

"The first one that Tennessee Ernie got was Ralph Guldahl. He had won it 1937; well this was maybe 1977 or later. Ernie was visibly disappointed," Russell continued. "Well, I got Gary Player first, and the second time around, I drew Jack Nicklaus. Ernie drew an amateur. The climax was about the fifth time around, and he still didn't have anybody, and Ernie drew Freddie McLeod, an honorary starter. He was close to ninety-two. Oh, Lord. That busted it up."[43]

Bob Hope and Billy Graham

Storytelling was a natural part of Russell's life, and when it came to golf—a sport in which Russell never professed to be very skilled—the sportswriter found himself in his share of humorous situations. On one occasion, comedian Bob Hope was in town for a performance at Vanderbilt's Memorial Gym, and Russell's golfing "skills" were on display earlier that day.

"We played golf that afternoon, and I was using left-hand woods and right-hand irons," Russell remembered during an interview in the mid-1990s. "It was about the third hole and he couldn't believe what he saw. He said, 'Did you hit the last one off the tee left-handed?' and I said, 'Yes.'

"That night, Hope referred to it at the concert," Russell concluded. "He said he had studied my swing, and it reminded him, more than anything, of Kate Smith trying to get rid of a boomerang."[44]

Many years after the Bob Hope visit, Russell was a guest speaker at a banquet in 1990. The master of ceremonies that night was Dick Horton, the president of Tennessee Golf Foundation in Nashville, and he introduced Russell.

"He mastered almost everything he ever attempted...except golf," Horton said of Russell. "When he retired from active play, which is the nicest way I can say it, he was pretty well messed up. He was hitting his woods right-handed, and his irons left-handed, and he never knew which side he'd go at it with his putter."[45]

Despite this unique style of play, Russell was no stranger to using the golf course to welcome guests or dignitaries to Nashville. In 1955 the Reverend Billy Graham was in town, and the two were part of a foursome one afternoon that attracted quite a few onlookers. As Russell recalled, the good reverend made quite a shot during that round.

"Billy swings cross-handed, but at the spot on the course where the biggest gallery had congregated, he holed out 110 yards off the green. Many of the witnesses attended his services that night," Russell recollected.[46]

From Augusta to Churchill Downs

Each year, after spending weeks in Florida chasing down baseball coaches and players, and after a long weekend in Georgia at the Masters, Russell capped off his spring sports season with a few "electric" moments in Kentucky. It was the first Saturday in May, and that could only mean one thing for Fred Russell: the Kentucky Derby.

Russell loved Churchill Downs. For more than half a century, he never missed the race. In 1983, the year he attended his fiftieth consecutive Derby, the National Turf Writer's Association (NTWA) presented Russell with one of its highest honors, the Walter Haight Award for excellence in writing.

In terms of favorite sports during his early years of writing, horse racing was behind only baseball and football for Russell. Before his streak of consecutive Derbies was too far along, he enjoyed what his city had to offer in the sport. The Iroquois Steeplechase, the oldest of its kind in North America, began in 1941 and has been running continuously at Percy Warner Park, with the exception of one year off during World War II. The annual event, held in early May, typically the week after the Kentucky Derby, was a Russell favorite and tapped into the sportswriter's love for horses and racing.

But prior to the steeplechase was the derby, and it was this event and all its trimmings that captured Russell's spirit. He once described the derby as "a one-day madhouse with more circus atmosphere and carnival spirit than any show in sports."[47] Just as it is a premier event in today's sports world, it was one of the biggest national attractions of the year during Russell's prime as well. In his autobiography, Russell did not hold back his thoughts on where it ranked within the sports world.

"I doubt if there is a more electric instant in sports than the start of a Kentucky Derby," Russell wrote back in 1957.[48] When covering the race, it was more than just a Saturday race. "Derby Week" would begin on Tuesday, and for five days, Russell and other writers worked whatever hours necessary to get the scoop on the big race that weekend.

"For one thing, it's the only time a sportswriter will get out of bed at five or six o'clock for three of four mornings and visit the barns, watch the workouts, and talk to the trainers," Russell commented.[49]

For Russell, putting in the extra hours to get to know those within the sport fit with his personality. It didn't matter whether he was tracking down one of the wealthy horse owners or the jockey or the trainer. It was about getting the story right, and as fellow sportswriter Tom McEwen remembers from his countless Kentucky trips with Russell, this was information they desperately needed.

"We didn't know that much, really, about race horses. We all had to learn," McEwen said, adding with a laugh that they turned to colleagues within their fraternity for assistance as well. "I don't know what he or I would have done if we hadn't had Joe Hirsch of the *Daily Racing Forum* to take us around the barns before and identify who the horses were and give us stories."[50]

When it came to covering the race itself, Russell's longevity at the derby earned him a spot in the front row of the press area, seat number 3. McEwen and others marveled at Russell's success at picking the race winner in the days leading up to the race. In particular, one of Russell's closest friends in the thoroughbred industry, Charles Cella, remembered Russell's prognostication skills well.

"For about twenty-five years, I would see him at Churchill. We were pretty devout about being there, and Freddie had an absolutely uncanny ability to pick Kentucky Derby winners," Cella recalled. "He couldn't dodge the bullet, because he would print it before the race. It was unbelievable how many times he picked the winner."[51]

49

Russell commented once that it was part preparation and part instinct, but really something you won't know unless you're there walking the stalls.

"Prior to the big race, I rely more on what I hear than on what I see. I try to find the winner by eliminating other horses from consideration," Russell wrote in his autobiography. "Sometimes this is possible when a jockey can't or won't conceal his low opinion of his horse. Other times a realistic owner will confide certain unfavorable circumstances."[52]

One particular derby memory from a colleague had nothing to do with the race itself; rather, it highlighted Fred Russell as the true friend he was to so many. In this case, it involved longtime *Baltimore Sun* writer John Steadman.

Tom Robinson began working for Russell at the *Banner* in 1976 and was there until 1981. Years after he had left the *Banner*, he was in Baltimore visiting a client at the *Sun*. Robinson had a chance to meet John Steadman, and with it came a touching memory about his former boss in Nashville.

"I told him I used to be a sportswriter in Nashville. He asked me where I worked, and I told him the *Banner*," Robinson recalled. "Steadman just stopped cold and said to me, 'If you need a phone call made in this state, you tell me. I don't care if it's the governor, the mayor of Baltimore, you let me know. You worked for Freddie, so anything you need, any call you need around Maryland, I'll do it.'"[53]

There was a reason Steadman felt so strongly about Russell, and it had very little to do with sports. Robinson remembered vividly the story Steadman told him that day in Baltimore.

"One year covering the Kentucky Derby, I was there at the derby and my mother passed away. Well, I can't get a flight out of Louisville on Derby Day, everything's booked going out. Saturday night, after the derby and after filing my story, I'm sitting in my hotel room. There's a knock on the door, and it's Freddie. He says to me, 'John, you've lost your Mom, and you don't need to be by yourself tonight. I'm staying with you.' And he stayed up with me all night."[54]

4

Hangin' with Granny

"Both of our Southern gentlemen of sport paid just as much attention to the intangibles—to the more abstract and ethical values of right conduct, friendship, loyalty, courage, and generosity—as they did the tangibles. This they did against the philosophical direction of this entire century."[1] —William Harper, Grantland Rice biographer

By the mid 1950s, when Russell was working on his autobiography, he had spent close to a quarter-century with his mentor and friend, Grantland Rice. There were numerous references to Rice in Russell's book, an entire chapter, in fact, and there was no denying Rice's penchant for enjoying the horse races during spring training with friends.

"His favorite spot each March was Sunshine Park, a cozy and not easily accessible track at Oldsmar, Florida, about twenty miles equidistant from Tampa, St. Petersburg, and Clearwater," Russell wrote in his autobiography. "Every spring we spent at least one afternoon there, usually with Granny's steadiest traveling companions, Red Smith of the *Herald Tribune* and Frank Graham of the *Journal-American*."[2]

Russell remembered Graham's humorous recollection of those episodes as well. When they would meet for lunch at the track, Rice's fellow New York writer would say, "Just follow the waiter who has a martini, tomato juice, a dill pickle, and Camembert cheese on his tray."[3]

* * *

In May 1954, Fred Russell traveled to New York City to speak at a Vanderbilt alumni meeting. As often was the case when he visited New York, Russell made it a point to visit Grantland Rice. On this particular trip, Russell and Rice gathered for lunch at Rice's favorite restaurant, Toots Shor's. They were joined by their good friend Bill Corum, who had been a successful writer with the *New York Journal-American* before being appointed track president at Churchill Downs in 1949. The three friends sat in Rice's regular corner table—an indication of how much Shor thought of Rice—and their lunch turned easily into a long afternoon of laughs and storytelling from their days of being on the road, churning out daily columns, and grinding away at the sportswriter life.

For Russell, it was one of his many memorable moments with Rice. Eventually, this particular memory would turn somber. In an interview more than thirty years later, Russell remembered that May afternoon in 1954 well, and for good reason: it was the last time he would see his friend alive. Rice died just two months later on 13 July, four months before his seventy-fourth birthday.

Not only did Rice's death represent the passing of the nation's founding father of sports journalism, it also signified the loss of Russell's boyhood idol. The following day, Russell's column in the *Nashville Banner* opened with the following:

"Along about sunset Tuesday, the most beloved, respected man in the history of his profession left this earth. Grantland Rice was all this, and more—a virile saint. His personality, his sense of honor and fairness, along with his gift of poetry and prose, contributed more to the wholesome development of sports in America than any one factor. He was the greatest gentleman ever to grace the business."[4]

When it came to sportswriting, no one had a greater impact on his trade than Grantland Rice during the first half of the twentieth century. Nor did a writer pen more recognizable phrases still quoted (and even misquoted) today than this 1901 graduate from Vanderbilt. Born in 1880, Rice was a natural poet and a lover of sports. Combining the two, he drafted one of the most famous lines in all of sports lore:

"For when the one Great Scorer comes to mark against your name,
He writes not that you won or lost—but how you played the Game."[5]

When Rice died, Russell was one of the many sportswriters across the country who put into words the heartfelt sadness of a nation. It was only natural for Rice's brethren to comment on how Rice himself had "played the game." Rice's time had been the Golden Age of sports, the era before television, and if a journalist wanted to be successful, the newspaper business was *the* business in which to do it. Rice's byline had been gracing newspapers for more than fifty years, and he was one of the most revered figures of the twentieth century at the time of his death thanks to his ability to celebrate the pureness of sport and the innate decency of not only the athletes he covered but his readers as well.

For these traits alone, Russell had reason to dedicate this column to Rice. However, it was for other aspects of his friendship with Rice that Fred Russell mourned the deepest. He mourned the things that come only with a shared history, shared experiences, and times spent together.

Russell mourned the loss of one of his strongest, most meaningful friendships, the loss of his fellow Commodore and his fellow Middle Tennessean, and his steadfast road-trip companion when they made their annual trek to Florida for spring training. There had been countless trips to the Sunshine Park race track in Florida with Rice as well as trips to the Bluegrass State for the Kentucky Derby. There were memories with Rice each April in Augusta for the Masters as well as the special dinners he and Rice had enjoyed with golfing great Bobby Jones.

In short, on that July day in 1954, Fred Russell lost a best friend.

"He was my hero as long as I can remember," Russell noted in an interview years later, thinking back to his earliest memories of Rice. "I devoured the sports pages, and I read everything I could."[6]

As history would show, Russell and Rice had much in common, certainly more than just their Tennessee roots. A significant foundation for their friendship was a shared set of values, and it is not hard to fathom that a friendship between the two was inevitable.

"Greater even than his talent was his heart, his natural courtesy, and his all-embracing kindness," Russell said of Rice years later.[7] Rice was also one to provide well-timed advice to his fellow Commodore, in particular about not being too eager when Russell was still finding his niche early in his career.

"I was twenty-seven or twenty-eight and thinking how wonderful it would be if I applied in New York or Philadelphia," Russell said, believing that a position covering a major league club in a big city would be the best assignment he could land. When he approached his good friend with these thoughts, the response Russell received was vintage Rice, who quoted the Romantic poet John Keats: "Time, that ancient nurse, Rock me to patience."[8]

Russell and Rice shared many of the same perspectives on sports. Rice's desire to celebrate the contest rather than the individuals resonated with Russell, and Rice's penchant for glorifying honor and integrity above all else struck a chord with the younger Russell as well.

"Rice was never satirical, rarely inclined to be over-critical. His approach was idealistic. He stressed the nobility of maximum effort and gracious losing," Russell said once during a speech at Vanderbilt that honored Rice. "It's my belief that Grantland Rice, through more than fifty years of daily writing, wielded the greatest influence for fair play and was the finest factor for good the sports world has ever known."[9]

Russell did more than just admire the way in which Rice approached his trade—he learned from it, and realized the value in building relationships and celebrating the effort, not always the result.

"Most of all, Fred loved to write about people. He loved to get to know them, have anecdotes about them, to visit with them," former Vanderbilt athletic director and SEC commissioner Roy Kramer said, when asked to comment on similarities between the two Vanderbilt alumni sportswriters. "He had a way of opening a conversation without having to talk about how a guy had struck out three times that day. He had an uncanny ability to bridge life with sports, and that gave him access, a bridge into people's lives the way few people are able to do it."[10]

Similar Paths

While their friendship did not develop until later in Russell's adult life, the similarities in the paths each man took during his early years are striking, and this common path laid the foundation for a lifelong friendship.

In the late 1800s, Rice enrolled in Vanderbilt University, and he graduated in 1901. Rice tried his hand at a number of sports while in college, and baseball was the one which he played exceptionally well. In his senior campaign, Rice was elected captain and led the Commodores to the Southern Conference championship.[11] As Rice did before him, Russell played for the Commodore baseball team as well. Russell was a pitcher and an infielder, and, like Rice, he was talented enough to play during his entire tenure in college, but not enough to make it a career. Each man found journalism not long after leaving their collegiate years behind. For Rice, it was briefly with the *Nashville Daily News*, and in 1902, he moved to Atlanta where he assumed the sports editor position of the *Atlanta Journal*. He spent three years in Atlanta covering sports, and as biographer Charles Fountain noted, Rice "came of age as a journalist."[12]

Unlike Russell, who ultimately chose Nashville as his permanent home after leaving Vanderbilt, Rice fine-tuned his talents in a number of cities. He spent four years in Atlanta, and after a short stint in Cleveland in 1906, he returned to Nashville in 1907 and wrote for the *Nashville Tennessean*, a new paper that set out to compete with the *Nashville Banner*. After four successful years, Rice had an opportunity to take his talents to the grandest of stages: New York. He seized that opportunity, and it was the last of his career moves to a different city. He wrote initially for the *New York Evening Mail* (1911 to 1915), and from 1915 to 1930, Rice's byline graced the pages of the city's most respected paper, the *New York Tribune*. At that time, other notable writers of the day in New York included Frank Graham, Bill Corum, and Jimmy Cannon, to name just a few. Over time, Rice's popularity eclipsed them all. In January 1930, Rice left the Tribune Syndicate for the *New York Sun*, and his column became syndicated nationally. It was picked up by more than eighty newspapers across the country, and Grantland Rice became a nationally recognized name. By the end of the first half of the twentieth century, as Rice was entering the twilight of his career, he had established himself as the "Dean of America's Sportswriters."

Toward the end of Rice's career, several other up-and-coming writers in New York were gaining prominence. One such writer was Red Smith, who began his own syndicated column in 1945 with the *New York Herald Tribune*, after working on newspapers in St. Louis and Philadelphia. Smith eventually joined the *New York Times* in 1972, and just as Fred Russell was the leading sportswriter of the South, Red Smith assumed that position in the North.

In 1960, Smith was the first recipient of the National Sportswriter of the Year award, an award given by the newly formed National Sportscasters and Sportswriters Association (NSSA). In 1962, when the NSSA created a Hall of Fame to celebrate the giants of the industry, Rice was selected as its first member. Fittingly, Red Smith was asked to deliver the induction speech.

"Who knows what will become of this Hall of Fame? It might never be heard from again," Smith said. "No matter. It cannot be improved, for it is perfect tonight with only Granny enshrined."[13]

Smith and Russell became friends through the business as well, and several years after Smith died (in 1982), Russell was interviewed by a Grantland Rice biographer. He commented on the respect others had for Rice, in particular Smith.

"I think what's pertinent is what Smith had to say at Rice's death, about his great respect for him, and the warm personal friendship they shared," Russell noted. "Some of the younger sportswriters would refer to Rice as sort of a 'gee whiz' writer. But he thought Rice was the greatest, personally. And this is from Smith, anything but a rah-rah writer."[14]

Passing the Torch: From Granny to Red and Freddie

Sadly, Grantland Rice did not have the opportunity to retire his daily column on his own terms. By 1950, the *Sun* could not compete within the increasingly competitive New York newspaper market. In a somber end to one of New York's most celebrated and traditional daily papers, the *Sun*—along with Grantland Rice's column—was consumed by the *World-Telegram*. The *Telegram* carried his column for one final year, but Rice's contract was not renewed past 1951.

By this time, larger markets across the country were producing more and more sportswriters, and in the latter stages of Rice's career, as his readership declined, there was an opportunity for other writers to emerge. For several reasons, it was two of his closest friends—Fred Russell and Red Smith—who rose to the top of that group.

Russell was Rice's constant connection to the South and to his Middle Tennessee and Vanderbilt roots. Shared passions for baseball, golf, and horse racing cemented their lifelong friendship, even though it was a long-distance one between writers a generation apart. In the North, Smith began to make his own mark in an area where Rice's popularity was highest, and he proceeded to dominate the New York sportswriting scene from the 1950s through the 1970s in the same way that Rice was the leading byline during the 1930s and 1940s.

It wasn't just readers and other writers who recognized the talent of these three leading journalists. Many times, the subjects of their columns did as well.

Legendary college football coach Lou Holtz remembered the impressions these writers made back in the middle part of the twentieth century, specifically the way in which Russell followed the success of his mentor.

"When you talk about Red Smith and Grantland Rice, you put Fred Russell in that class," Holtz said. "But it was a different era, just like with coaching. You had Bear Bryant and Darrell Royal, and then you had Joe Paterno, Ara Parseghian, and Bobby Bowden."[15]

While Smith emerged in New York as the most-read columnist, it was Russell who slowly emerged on the national scene. By the 1940s, he was one of the leading sports editors in the South, and his popularity was extending beyond Middle Tennessee. A catalyst for this development was Russell's opportunity to write for a national magazine. Similar to how Rice had written for *Collier's*, Russell began writing for the *Saturday Evening Post*, a freelance position which resulted in Russell establishing a national presence of his own. Beginning in the late 1930s, he wrote occasional articles for the *Post*, and from 1949 to 1962, Russell authored his "Pigskin Preview," an annual summer feature in advance of the upcoming college football season. These writings became immensely popular as the *Post* spread across the country, and Russell landed on the national stage much like his predecessor had with *Collier's* two decades before him.

By 1962, in the year that Smith gave his introduction speech for Rice's induction at the NSSA Hall of Fame, these three giants of the business had dominated sportswriting for over three decades. Smith and Russell would continue their daily columns for two and three more decades, respectively, with Russell writing into the late 1990s.

Rice's "Natural Heir"

Due to that longevity, it was Russell who served as the bridge between the Rice-era and today's modern sportswriters. With his years of writing, coupled with his more natural ties to Rice, there are those who believe it was Russell who ultimately filled the shoes of Grantland Rice. Some folks even made the argument that Russell more than filled those shoes, with one such example coming from within the college football arena.

"I've met all the big names in sportswriting. I knew Grantland Rice, but Fred was my gospel," legend Red Grange once said. "He didn't butcher you up. He reasoned things out. He understood sports as well as anyone today, and whether he liked you or not, it didn't show in his writing."[16]

John Seigenthaler was the longtime editor of the rival *Tennessean* in Nashville, and he too elevated Russell to the status of elite sportswriter.

"He was Grantland Rice's natural heir, I think," Seigenthaler said. "Some people would say Red Smith, but Freddie wrote with grace and insight and humor that set him apart."[17]

As he entered the same profession as Rice, Russell discovered that the two had very similar interests within the world of sports. In line with Russell's primary sports interests of the day, Rice's footprint was evident in college football, golf, and horse racing as well. Specific to the gridiron, Rice's early twentieth century writings were, in effect, game stories providing readers a unique insight and perspective on the football games that had occurred the previous Saturday. They were poetic, flowery and, by today's standards, would elicit more laughter than praise due to Rice's style. But in his time, Rice was the acknowledged authority on the biggest games each weekend.

In the golf world, Rice was a close friend of Bobby Jones even before Russell shared that friendship. When Jones started his invitation-only tournament in Augusta, Georgia, in the 1930s, Rice was an annual guest of Jones at the Masters. When another of golf's four majors, the PGA Championship, came to Shoal Creek in Birmingham, Alabama, in 1984, Russell wrote a feature article on Rice for the tournament program. Rice had been dead for thirty years at this point, and Russell reflected on Rice's love for the game.

"He seemed to personify the game of golf and all of its virtues. One reason might have been that this patron saint of sportswriters didn't look funny wearing knickers," Russell wrote.[18]

Rice also dearly loved horse racing, as did Russell. A sport that was more popular in the first half of the twentieth century than the latter half, horse racing attracted Rice with its relaxed style and the touch of class it brought to the sports world. More than any other event, the Kentucky

Derby was the quintessential race within the industry. For both Rice and Russell, the annual trip to Churchill Downs that first Saturday in May was a special one, not only for the race itself, but for their friendship as well. Once Rice had made New York his hometown, the Kentucky Derby became one of the few times the two men would see each other in person.

While golf, football, and horse racing each appealed to these two great writers, no sport connected Russell and Rice more than baseball. Both had played the sport competitively as young men, and once they embarked on their writing careers, covering baseball was as much a pastime for Russell and Rice as it was a sport played by the men they covered. Major leagues, minor leagues, amateur level—it didn't matter. Russell and Rice just loved the game, and whether they were covering league games in the Southern Association or the World Series, come October, they embraced each game as if it were one in which they were back playing.

In Nashville and throughout Middle Tennessee, baseball in the first half of the century started and stopped with the Nashville Vols, a minor league team that competed in the Southern League. Minor league ball in Middle Tennessee dated back to the Reconstruction Era, but it did not finally become permanent until the Vols began play in 1901 at a field called Athletic Park. The park's most striking feature was in right field, where the fence was not only close (less than 300 feet, compared to left field at 365 and deep center at 400-plus), but there existed a steep embankment that right fielders had to navigate if they wished to avoid errors and gaffes. As noted by minor league baseball historians Bill Weiss and Marshall Wright, the area had been a sulphur springs and picnic spot in the pioneer days. As Rice covered the team in its early years, he penned the name "Sulphur Dell Park," and it took.[19] Up until the Vols' demise in 1963, the term Sulphur Dell was as much a part of Nashville's dialogue as "Music Row" is today. Nashville owes that piece of its historical lexicon to Grantland Rice.

When thinking of baseball and these two celebrated writers, spring training is not only part of the discussion, it is required reading. Russell and Rice used their annual baseball pilgrimage to Florida as an excuse to spend time together and often made the trip together. Since he still had family members in or around Nashville, Rice would travel from New York to Nashville, and the two men would drive together down to the

Sunshine State. There were times when Rice was joined by fellow New York writers Red Smith and Frank Graham, but many times, it was Russell and Rice, along with their wives, who made the trip to Florida.

Once they arrived in Florida, the demands of covering baseball were not nearly as involved or as competitive as they are today. A typical spring training sidebar involved a trip to the horse track, something for which Rice was well known, in particular. As Russell and others came to know over the years, Rice rarely saw a Daily Double he didn't like.

"By the time I came around, in the late 1930s, the racetrack had the greatest hold on him. He'd rather be at the track than anywhere," Russell told the late Jerome Holtzman, who wrote the popular *No Cheering in the Press Box* in the early 1970s. "He was a good bettor, the kind of guy who had twenty or thirty doubles going."[20]

Horse racing also allowed Rice and others to relax, enjoy an afternoon at the track, and, of course, the occasional opportunity to gamble. As is usually the case, it didn't always work out the way the gambler intended. In later years, one of Russell's good friends in the business was *Tampa Tribune* columnist Tom McEwen. From the area and knowing its history, McEwen knew Sunshine Park well.

"That was Grantland Rice's favorite track, and out at Sunshine Park, anything could happen," McEwen recalled with a laugh. "There are all kinds of stories from that place, like when the starting gun went off sometimes, everyone stood up in their gates except for one, because this was his race, his turn to win."[21]

Death of the Dean

In reality, such a "fix" would have mostly evoked disdain from Rice. Rice celebrated the contest and the spirit of the game more than any other writer of his generation, and that approach had a profound impact on Russell.

"He had more influence on fair play than any one person of his time, just through his writings," Russell said in a television interview years after his mentor had died. "He was the absolute North Star that many sportswriters tried to follow."[22]

Russell treasured his time with Rice, especially in the latter's later years, when he was stepping into the shadows as readers, editors, and writers turned away from the classical, poetic style that Rice favored. The

May 1954 lunch Russell shared with Rice and Bill Corum in New York was one of his favorite memories. One story turned into 100, and lunch became an all-day affair at Toots Shor's restaurant.

"It was about 5 P.M. that afternoon, we were still there from lunch," Russell remembered with a laugh. "Shor would join us every few minutes, and repeatedly, he would slap Rice on the shoulder, and say, 'I tell you, when you're seventy-five years old, I'm going to give you the greatest birthday party that's ever been given. I'm closing the joint.'"[23]

As it turned out, though, there would be no seventy-fifth birthday party for Rice, as he died a few months shy of his seventy-fourth. However, that did not stop Shor from hosting a commemorative birthday party for Rice on Halloween night in 1954. Russell attended the black-tie affair, as did close to 250 others—all there by invitation only—and they spent the evening celebrating Rice. Russell's opinion was that there had never before been such a collection of celebrities in one room.[24] To note just a few who were present that night: Gene Sarazen, Jack Dempsey, Ed Sullivan, Jackie Gleason, Yogi Berra, Eddie Arcaro, Walter Hagen, and Gene Tunney. From the writing profession, the list was long and distinguished as well. Russell shared the evening with Red Smith, Bill Corum, John Kieran, and Frank Graham—again, just to name a few.[25]

With Rice as the figurative president of these writers and others within the sportswriting fraternity, his career had positive ramifications throughout the industry and for those trying to make a career out of sports journalism. Blackie Sherrod, one of Texas's most respected and well-known sports journalists, acknowledged as much when he recalled his friendship with Russell, and how Russell spoke so highly of Rice. "He talked at length about Grantland Rice and the love and respect he had for the man," Sherrod said, adding that Rice brought respect to the press box. "I remember Freddie saying, 'Granny put a necktie on all of us.'"[26]

Years after his friend had passed, Russell still carried with him strong memories from that time, and he recalled the feelings of his peers as well.

"On the day Granny died, Red Smith—in my opinion, the most gifted sports columnist of the '50s and '60s and '70s—said, 'The most treasured privilege I have had in this world was knowing Grantland Rice and going about with him as his friend,'" Russell said years later. "Rice's fellowship was a truly wonderful thing. His presence had the warmth and glow of an open fire on a winter's night."[27]

The Grantland Rice Memorial Award and the TRA Scholarship

A final connection between Rice and Russell stems from two awards that came about in the late 1950s: the Grantland Rice Memorial Award and the Thoroughbred Racing Association (TRA) Grantland Rice Scholarship for Sports Journalism.

When Rice died in 1954, it did not take long for the sports community to realize the importance of honoring one of its leading champions during the twentieth century. Fred Russell was directly involved in both. Within a year of Rice's passing, the New York Sportsman's Brotherhood Association created the Grantland Rice Memorial Award, and Russell himself was the award's initial recipient in 1955. As he shared in an interview, "Nothing could have brought me more joy."[28]

During this same period, Russell was looking for a way to honor his fellow Commodore, and it seemed natural to consider a scholarship of some kind, one that was specific to Vanderbilt (Rice's alma mater) and one that celebrated academics and journalism. Russell worked with former sports columnist and good friend Bill Corum to establish a partnership with the Thoroughbred Racing Association and endow a scholarship that would bring students interested in journalism to Vanderbilt University.

The TRA scholarship has been in existence since 1956, and for over fifty years, the recipient has received financial support to attend Rice's alma mater. Up until the mid-1990s, the scholarship provided full-ride assistance, and it attracted some of the nation's most promising prospective journalists. From Roy Blount (1959 recipient) to Skip Bayless (1970), from Dave Sheinin (1987) to Tyler Kepner (1993) and Lee Jenkins (1995), aspiring writers descended upon Nashville each fall to walk the same campus that was home to both Rice and Russell in the early part of the twentieth century.

The scholarship was so important to Russell that he chaired the selection committee well into the 1990s. He stayed involved and in touch with the recipients during their years at Vanderbilt as well as after they graduated, many of whom found success in the industry. During Bayless's Vanderbilt years in the early 1970s, Russell was still a force in the business, carving out his column for the *Nashville Banner* each day. Through his relationship with Russell when he was a scholarship recipient, Bayless came to appreciate not only the connection between Russell and Rice, but the sportswriting style they represented.

"Russell was an era unto himself. Class, gentility, that decency that a good human being has—like [Grantland] Rice and [Red] Smith," Bayless commented. "You don't see that anymore, that dignity, that class, that caring for sportswriting brethren up and down the totem pole. That era is dead. The old style, sometimes it was melodramatic, sure. But 'The Four Horsemen'—it was great stuff."[29]

College Football: A Lifetime of Service

"There are two types of people: those who walk into a room and say, 'Here I am'...and then there are those who walk into a room and say, 'There you are.' When Fred Russell walked into a room, he always said, 'There you are,' regardless of what he had accomplished or where he had been."[1] —Lou Holtz, college football coach and current TV analyst

"I don't think there's been a finer gentleman representing the sports world in writing and in college football than Fred Russell. The guy was just as wonderful a human being as you could ever find."[2] —Lee Corso, college football coach and current TV analyst

In the middle of the twentieth century, sportswriters from all over the South would take part in the "Skywriters Tour" each summer, piling into an old plane and traveling from one SEC school to the next to preview that school's football team for the upcoming season. Sports columnists would have two weeks away from their home base of operations, and lifelong friendships were often formed through the course of the trip. In the years that followed once the Skywriters trips ran their course, the annual National Sportscasters and Sportswriters Association (NSSA) awards banquet became a natural gathering place to rekindle friendships. Based in Salisbury, North Carolina, the NSSA was formed in 1959 and today consists of roughly 700 leading sportscasters and sportswriters from around the country. Since 1962, more than eighty sports media legends have been inducted into the organization's Hall of Fame, and its annual program each year remains an opportunity for folks within the business to gather. Tom McEwen (*Tampa Tribune*) has been a member for decades, and he recalled one of the annual award shows from a year he was not able to make it.

I got a call from Salisbury, and it was Freddie and Jim Murray. It came in after midnight, and I was already in bed. Jim's first wife played the piano, and she would always play so people could sing. Blackie Sherrod was a great friend of his, and he'd take his guitar out, and all of them would stand around the piano and sing. Well, they call me, and it's safe to say, the bar was still open. I talk with Jim, and then Freddie grabs the phone, and he kind of slurs out, 'Whaddya wanna hear?' I said, 'What?' Freddie goes, 'Whaddya wanna hear?' I figured out what he was asking, and the only thing that came to mind was this old Irish song called 'Danny Boy.' Well, they sang it, and I'm just standing there on the phone in my pajamas. When they were done, he came back on and said, 'What else you wanna hear?' I told him to sing 'Danny Boy' again, and with that, I put the phone down and went back to bed. I left it off the hook and there's no telling how many times they sang that song with no one listening on the phone. Of course, it wouldn't have bothered them a bit."[3]

Baseball was Fred Russell's favorite sport to play as a young boy, and it was admittedly his favorite sport to cover as a journalist in his adult years. But neither his love for baseball nor his reporting of the sport translated to the mainstream popularity and success that Russell achieved. Rather, in order to transcend decades and regions, Russell needed college football to gain a national reputation. As his career unfolded and as his contributions to the sport continued up to the turn of the century, history has revealed that college football needed Fred Russell as well.

Perhaps in no other sport did Russell have so many contacts. If it seemed that he knew people everywhere, it's because he did. Not just football figures specific to Vanderbilt or Tennessee, and not just players within the Southeastern Conference. Across the nation, Russell's reach was impressive, and his name became synonymous with college football. He started with his regional connections, such as his relationship with Paul Bryant in the mid 1930s, well before Bryant put Alabama football on the map. That friendship lasted until "the Bear" passed away in early 1983. Russell covered Archie Manning and Johnny Majors in the 1960s as players in the SEC, and then stayed connected to them long after their playing days had ended. He had a relationship with Manning which extended down to his son, Peyton, who played at Tennessee during Russell's final years with the *Banner*. Russell also got to know coaches in their early days—men such as Lee Corso and Lou Holtz, coaches who are still connected to college football today.

Russell's big break within college football (and by extension, the sportswriting business) came via the *Saturday Evening Post*. At the time that his daily "Sidelines" column was gaining popularity beyond Tennessee, Russell had an opportunity to write a feature for the popular national magazine. That successful story in 1939 marked the beginning of a twenty-three-year relationship with the *Post*, as Russell ultimately parlayed that opportunity into a more significant role with the magazine on an annual basis. When the Nashville writer authored his first "Pigskin Preview" feature in 1949, Russell had hit on a successful formula that catapulted him into the national spotlight.

While the "Pigskin Preview" resulted in national attention for Russell, he always stayed true to his Southern roots of Vanderbilt and the Southeastern Conference. Living and covering the Vanderbilt-Tennessee rivalry was an annual affair for Russell, and his writings on this subject alone reflected his passion for college football. In the second half of the century, when the SEC Skywriters Tour was established, Russell continued to build relationships with players and coaches, further cementing his reputation as a leading authority within the sport. Ultimately, from his Southern allegiances and writings to his national "Pigskin Preview," which ran annually until 1962, to his subsequent thirty-plus years with the Honors Court of the National Football Foundation Hall of Fame, Russell left an impressive and lasting footprint on the college football world.

Russell's Big Break with the *Saturday Evening Post*

By the late 1930s, Fred Russell was nearing the end of a decade at the helm of the *Nashville Banner* sports department. His popularity was strengthening beyond Nashville and into the South in general. His 1936 Headliners Award for his coverage of the Alice Speed Stoll kidnapping case put Russell's name on the national stage, and while this award was not tied to his sportswriting, it nonetheless highlighted him as a promising, intelligent, and ambitious journalist. Once the attention from the Stoll case died down, Russell refocused his full efforts on covering sports in Nashville, the state of Tennessee, and throughout the South. His presence as a sportswriter continued to grow across the region, and in 1939, an opportunity developed that Russell could not turn down.

Just as Russell had matured as a sportswriter during the 1930s in Nashville, something similar was happening 180 miles to the East at the University of Tennessee. The Volunteer football program had been suffering through a number of rough seasons, and in late 1925, the university hired a man named Robert Neyland to turn the program around. Neyland's first assignment: beat Vanderbilt and then get Tennessee back to being respectable on the football field. While he lost his opening game to the Commodores in 1926, Neyland ultimately achieved long-lasting success in this rivarly. In the 1930s alone, Tennessee posted a 7–2–1 record against Vanderbilt.

In fall 1939, Neyland compiled arguably one of college football's greatest teams ever. From a statistical perspective, the numbers were staggering: the Volunteers were *undefeated*, *untied*, and *un-scored upon* in the regular season. The only blemish against the team would be its final game, a 14–0 shutout at the hands of the USC Trojans in the Rose Bowl on 1 January 1940.

As Tennessee's remarkable 1939 season unfolded, interest from around the country intensified. In the fall, the *Saturday Evening Post*—one of the nation's most popular weekly magazines—wanted to run a story on Neyland. As was its practice at the time, in order to have a national presence, the *Post* occasionally offered freelance opportunities to local or regional writers. For the Neyland article, the *Post* needed a sportswriter from the South, preferably from the state of Tennessee. Someone who covered football, was familiar with the Volunteer program, and, of course, was a strong writer.

The *Post* found their man in Nashville's Fred Russell.

In December 1939, on the eve of Tennessee's Rose Bowl appearance against USC, Fred Russell made his debut in the *Saturday Evening Post*. The article was titled "Touchdown Engineer," and in it, Russell highlighted the successful early career the Volunteer coach had put together in his ten-plus years at the helm. The piece ran in the 30 December issue of the magazine, and for the first time in his burgeoning career, Russell appeared on the national stage as a sportswriter.

Genesis of the "Pigskin Preview": Making the Most of an Opportunity

Ultimately, the 1939 *Post* article was a watershed moment for the *Banner* sports editor, not only with regard to national recognition, but from a financial perspective as well. Russell would later comment that one the most exciting days of his life came that year when he opened his mailbox and in it found a check from the *Post* for $400. At a time when America was turning a corner and putting the Great Depression in its rear-view mirror, this was real money. To put this figure in perspective, $400 in 1939 equated to roughly $6,500 in 2012.

Russell's contributions to the *Post* did not end with his article on Neyland. In May 1942, Russell wrote a baseball piece entitled "They're Simply Wild about Larry" as he celebrated the success of Southern baseball coaching icon, Larry Gilbert.

Then came a second opportunity to cover college football for the *Post*. Charley Trippi was a two-time All-American at the University of Georgia in the 1940s. His playing days came both prior to and after fighting in World War II, and in fall 1946, the *Post* enlisted Russell to draft an article on one of college football's finest players.

Russell's article, "Big Bad Bulldog from Dixie," was a resounding success, particularly in the South, and he made quite a few friends at the University of Georgia with his coverage of its star player. Russell saved a series of Western Union telegrams that Jimmy Jones, the publicity director of the University of Georgia Athletic Department, sent to Russell and to the *Post* in late 1946. Take, for instance, this first one from Jones to Russell dated 31 October 1946: "All Georgia and particularly Athens raving about your swell story on Trippi in Saturday Evening Post, assure you that you will be a most welcome visitor Saturday."[4]

As Georgia prepared for its Sugar Bowl trip to New Orleans, Jones wired Russell again, this time with an invitation, dated 15 December 1946: "Coach Wallace Butts and the University of Georgia football team cordially invite you to be our guest on trip to Sugar Bowl and return with all expenses paid by University."[5]

The offer to pay for Russell's trip was not an uncommon practice at the time. What is noteworthy, though, is that Russell was starting to make an impact across the sportswriting spectrum. More importantly, to borrow from one of the more celebrated authors of that time, Russell was slowly "winning friends and influencing people."[6]

This leads to the third telegram from Jones, this one directly to Robert Fuoss, managing editor of the *Post*. Jones had wired Fuoss 30 October 1946, the day before he sent Russell his first note, and Fuoss shared Jones's message with Russell in a letter he sent out later that afternoon: "Trippi's story out today and all Georgia thrills to expert and sympathetic treatment given by Post. Just goes to show that old Nathan B Forrest was wrong. It's not a case of get there fust with the mostest but fust with the bestest and the Post and Fred Russell have rung the bell. Don't want to be quoted publicly for obvious reasons but this is by far the best piece yet done on a Southern football player."[7]

The importance of messages like this to the *Post's* editorial staff cannot be overstated. Keep in mind that even though Russell had been writing for over fifteen years at the *Banner* by this time, his article on Trippi was just his third for the *Post*. Both then and now, editors are more likely to receive negative feedback and complaints on articles than praise and compliments. So when Russell's writing started to generate acclaim from the readers of the *Post*, even the expected subjective opinions from someone like Jones, the magazine's editors took notice.

Ultimately, the *Post* took action as well. It was clear to the editorial staff that Russell was a popular writer, and the magazine wanted to introduce a late summer special that not only catered to its football-reading public, but served as a segue from the summer to the fall. When the *Post* married these together, they hit on the idea for an annual football preview. When Fred Russell was asked if he was interested in the topic, the "Pigskin Preview" came to life.

The first edition of the annual "Pigskin Preview" appeared in the 17 September 1949 edition of the *Post*. The feature was an instant success. From 1949 to 1962, Russell authored this annual feature, and his popularity soared. Russell included previews of each conference, as he projected the top teams for each and highlighted notable coaches and players. On the opening pages of the preview, Russell predicted his "Top Twenty Teams" for the upcoming season as well as his projections for individual All-Americans. In the early years of the feature, Russell correctly predicted the eventual national champion on several occasions, and with his bold picks, he earned the fun nickname of "Fearless Fred."

Across the country and certainly in his home state, Russell's feature was a popular one. The popularity of the feature transcended college rivalries as well as professional rivalries. The *Tennessean's* John Seigenthaler began his journalism career the same year the preview debuted in 1949, and he eventually became editor of the *Tennessean*.

"The 'Pigskin Preview' was something that everybody interested in college sports across the country read and relied on," Seigenthaler noted.

"Even members of the *Tennessean* sports department, they absolutely enjoyed the preview."[8]

And despite being penned by a "Vanderbilt man," Russell's regular summer feature was a big hit for folks in Knoxville at the University of Tennessee as well. Gus Manning was a former UT sports information director who was hired by Neyland in the early 1950s.

"It was *the* big authority," Manning said of Russell's annual report in the *Post*. "It was before *Sports Illustrated*, and that 'Pigskin Preview' was one of the biggest things in the nation."[9]

The payout to Russell was lucrative as well. The Curtis Publishing Company sent Russell a $2,500.00 check on 19 July 1949 for that first summer feature.[10] Even by modern standards, that's a hefty payday for an article of this magnitude; it would be the equivalent of nearly $24,000 today, in 2012.

Before the Preview, It Was "Vanderbilt-Tennessee" ...and It Was Personal

Well before the "Pigskin Preview," however, in his early years of covering college football, it was the fierce Vanderbilt-Tennessee rivalry that was at the heart of Russell's college football reporting. During his lifetime, from being a Vanderbilt student first to covering the Commodores as his profession to remaining a diehard fan through it all, this rivalry tugged at Russell's heart. He saw all sides of the rivalry and experienced the ups and downs as the Commodores went from dominating their cross-state foe in the early part of Russell's life to being dominated in his latter years. In the second half of the twentieth century, and up to the final years of Russell's life, the rivalry was marked by Tennessee victories, many of them lopsided. In the mid-1950s, Johnny Majors was the All-American leader for the Volunteers, and his teams posted victories over the Commodores in both 1955 and 1956. In addition to personal success on the field, Majors made a name for himself in the coaching ranks, leading Tennessee from 1977 to 1992. Suffice it to say, he was around for his share of Vanderbilt-Tennessee battles, and he came to know Russell very well.

"We all knew he was a Vanderbilt guy, and there's no question that he would have liked to have seen Vanderbilt win those games," Majors admitted. "But I never thought there were any prejudicial feelings that were shown outwardly or written.

"He was particularly objective when writing about the Tennessee-Vanderbilt rivalry," the All-American and head coach added. "His heart wanted Vanderbilt, but he never let that interfere with his writing."[11]

While Russell was the consummate objective reporter in his coverage of the Vanderbilt-Tennessee rivalry, the years of tough losses took their toll on the prideful Commodore. Every once in a while, even if it was only to family, Russell the Commodore fan made comments that Russell the journalist would never write for the public. His youngest daughter, Carolyn, remembered a particular game at Dudley Field. Like many games in the latter part of Russell's life, things had not started out well for the 'Dores. During halftime, the Tennessee marching band had taken the field, prompting Russell to share a couple of thoughts with his daughter. Or perhaps he just needed to vent.

"He leaned up to me," Russell's daughter recalled her father saying, "and he mumbled, 'They get all this money from the *state*, and orange is the *worst color.*'"[12]

The Rivalry's Early Years

When Russell was growing up a Commodore fan, his opinion of Vanderbilt started and stopped with his high praise for Dan McGugin, the legendary coach who began coaching the Commodores before Russell was even born in 1906. At that time, McGugin was about to start his third season as Vanderbilt's head coach. McGugin had started his Vanderbilt coaching career in exceptional fashion, going 16–1 over his first two seasons, and an impressive 72–13–5 over this first ten years coaching. The Commodore squads from a century ago dominated the way Ohio State and Southern California have succeeded in the modern era. Behind that domination was McGugin, and before Russell was a student at Vanderbilt, let alone a reporter covering the Commodores, he was a fan. He grew to respect the Vanderbilt head coach the way opposing squads feared McGugin's teams.

Sixty years after the coaching legend retired, Russell had a chance to share one of his favorite stories about McGugin. Russell was being inducted into the Vanderbilt Quinqs Club in 1994, and he reminded the audience of one of McGugin's greatest coaching accomplishments: a 0–0 tie with the mighty Wolverines of Michigan in 1922.

"He was the most inspirational coach I've ever been around, and he blended a sly humor with his inspiring," Russell told the crowd, recalling the story he had heard years before. "All McGugin said to them was, 'Never forget this. You boys are going against Yankees. Many of those boys, their grandfathers tried to kill your grandfathers in the Civil War.'"[13]

Russell's admiration for McGugin went beyond appreciating the coach's sense of humor or his coaching ability. He respected McGugin for his integrity off the field and his sense of fairness, and in the days following McGugin's death in late January 1936, Russell paid a glowing tribute to the coach.

"For Vanderbilt athletics, he rendered as great a service as Chancellor Kirkland has to the university," Russell eulogized. "He loved life, and friendships he treasured most of all."[14]

While most of McGugin's coaching days occurred during Russell's youth, the last few years took place as Russell assumed his sports editor role at the *Banner* in the early 1930s. And during those formative decades of Russell's tenure at the *Banner*, nowhere was there a more bitter and fierce rival than 180 miles to the east in Knoxville, Tennessee. From 1926 to 1952, the aforementioned Coach Neyland led the powerful Volunteers, and many of these Vanderbilt-Tennessee games were brutal contests more about state pride than the final score.

The rivalry between the two teams began with their head coaches. Neyland started his tenure in Knoxville in 1926, and up until that point, it was the Commodores who enjoyed regular success against the Volunteers. McGugin compiled a 12–2–1 career record against the Volunteers before Neyland assumed control at Tennessee.

"It was a very hard-fought series all through the years," former Tennessee Sports Information director Haywood Harris noted. "When Neyland took over in 1926, his instructions to the athletic faculty chairman were to do something about the Vanderbilt series to make it more competitive on *our part.*"[15]

Tennessee responded to its new coach, to say the least. In Neyland's first year, McGugin got the best of him in a 20–3 Commodore victory, but it would be McGugin's only victory over Neyland. Six losses and two ties later, McGugin retired from coaching in 1934, and Russell acknowledged the success of the new coach in Knoxville.

"He really respected General Neyland," noted longtime UT sports historian Gus Manning, hired by Neyland in the early 1950s. "Russell was a huge follower of Vanderbilt's, but he was fair to Tennessee."[16]

After McGugin's retirement, as well as Ray Morrison's brief five-year stint (1935 to 1939) running the Commodores, Vanderbilt's next coach was Henry "Red" Sanders, the same Sanders who had been Russell's childhood friend from high school at Duncan preparatory to college years at Vanderbilt in the mid-1920s. Sanders coached at Vanderbilt from 1940 to 1948, and to see his old friend return to coach his alma mater fifteen years later was a joyous time for Russell. Naturally, he wanted nothing more than to see Sanders do well, especially against their in-state rival in Knoxville.

That meant beating General Neyland, of course. It took Sanders six tries, but in 1948, in what would be his final season coaching Vanderbilt, Sanders posted his only victory against Tennessee, a 28–6 triumph at home. The following Monday, Russell praised the performance and relished in his alma mater's triumph, led by his friend and Vanderbilt coach.

"Today they pass each other and still grin, these Vanderbilt people, and nobody asks why. Everybody knows why," Russell wrote in his 29 November 1948 column. "There is no one exact word. What I am trying to say is that in beating Tennessee soundly, Vanderbilt also popped them in that capitalizing-on-the-situation, quick-reacting manner which the Neylandmen have flashed so often through the past twenty-two years of this long and raging rivalry. Red Sanders's Commodores, acting just as hungry as their followers who had been waiting eleven years, crackled with a smart, impromptu winning touch."[17]

Continuing the Rivalry: From Competitive to Lopsided

The celebration of 1948's triumph was short-lived. After the season, UCLA recruited Sanders away from Nashville, and new expectations faced Vanderbilt almost before its stellar 8–2–1 season had ended. No one faced this scrutiny more than incoming head coach Bill Edwards, who arrived in 1949 knowing that Vanderbilt needed to build on the 1948 victory over its rival. It didn't happen during the first two seasons, as Tennessee won 26–20 and 43–0 in 1949 and 1950, respectively. With consecutive losses to the state rival, Edwards faced the additional pressure of an athletic community that had grown tired of average play, made worse by notably poor play against its archrival to the east.

In the papers, Russell was not an overtly passionate fan of Edwards. He did not give the same benefit of the doubt to Edwards as he did to his predecessor (and longtime friend) Red Sanders. In fact, in his Monday, 4 December 1950, column that followed the 43–0 pasting, Russell declined to comment on Edwards, not even mentioning his name once. He pointed out defensive inadequacies and alluded to an inconsistent performance throughout the season, but in summarizing his opinion of the blow-out loss, all Russell could muster was, "Vanderbilt gave its best against Tennessee, which was good enough to make a sock-for-sock ball game of it the first half."[18]

Coming off the embarrassing home shutout loss by 43 points to close out the 1950 season, the pressure was on for Edwards and his staff. This backdrop of poor performance and the public's questioning of the coach (even if Russell had hesitated to do so at this point) led to the 1951 contest in Knoxville, arguably one of the greatest clashes of the twentieth century between the two schools.

Neyland and Tennessee were coming off their 1950 National Championship season and had started the 1951 campaign at 9–0. In December, Edwards took his 6–4 team into Knoxville as a heavy underdog against the Volunteers. It was the final game of the season for Vanderbilt, while Tennessee had its sights set on a second straight national title and would play Maryland in the Sugar Bowl the next month. The Volunteers exploded out to a 21–0 lead, only to see the Commodores storm back and make it 21–20. In the game's final dramatic minutes, Tennessee scored a late touchdown to win 35–27 and preserve its number-one ranking.

It was a heart-breaking defeat for Edwards and Vanderbilt, and a colossal sigh of relief for Neyland and Tennessee. Russell was there, of course, covering the game. So was Gus Manning, a member of Tennessee's sports information department. Manning recalled that game well, in particular a brief discussion he had with Russell regarding Edwards.

"After the game was over, Coach Edwards went running out on the field towards the officials, to complain about something, and his hat fell off," Manning recalled of the 1951 classic. "Freddie Russell saw it, and I overheard him say, 'That's the last game Bill Edwards will ever coach for Vanderbilt.' Well, it almost was. He only coached one more year."[19]

The following season, Edwards started the 1952 campaign with two losses and two ties through the first four games, and went into the final game of the season against Tennessee with a rather mediocre 3–4–2 record. Whether or not a home victory over the Volunteers would have saved Edwards's job, it mattered not in the end. Tennessee crushed the Commodores 46–0 in Nashville, in the process cementing Edwards's fate. It would be his last game as the Vanderbilt head coach. Russell was only one year removed from being correct after his 1951 prediction.

As for the Vanderbilt-Tennessee rivalry, it has been several generations (yes, that long) since it was competitive. Over fifty years removed from that game in 1952, the Commodore-Volunteer tilt has been woefully (or blissfully, depending on which side of the fence you sit) one-sided. Art Guepe, Jack Green, and Bill Pace followed Bill Edwards, but they fared no better against Tennessee. Over a twenty-year span, they collectively went 3–17. It only got worse. As the coaching carousel for the Commodores continued, the losses to Tennessee piled up. Steve Sloan, Fred Pancoast, George MacIntyre, and Watson Brown were a combined 2–14–1 from 1973 to 1990; from 1991 through 2008, a fresh set of coaches led Vanderbilt to a dismal 1–17 record against the Volunteers. All told, since the 46–0 debacle in 1952, eleven Vanderbilt coaches have totaled just six wins and one tie against the Big Orange Nation.

The Skywriters Tour and Football in the South

While Vanderbilt's football program took a turn for the worse in the 1950s and 1960s, fan interest in and media coverage of SEC football picked up dramatically. As fans around the South developed a thirst for additional information on teams throughout the conference, newspapers and the SEC itself realized there was a larger demand for regional coverage of the teams, coaches, and players. Feature articles, such as Russell's "Pigskin Preview," provided high-level coverage at the national level, but these articles stopped short of detailed team-by-team previews of the teams within each conference. Across the conference, universities and town/city newspapers that covered the teams looked for ways to effectively and affordably market and preview the fall football season for fans.

Interestingly enough, even though it wasn't Fred Russell, it *was* a Vanderbilt man who was part of a conference-wide solution to provide reporters with greater access to the teams and, ultimately, more information for the fans. Elmore "Scoop" Hudgens was Vanderbilt's first Sports Information director from 1949 to 1964, until he took the same position for the Southeastern Conference itself. One of Hudgens's initial programs was the SEC Skywriters Tour, a preseason tour of the conference's football schools for media members. In summer 1965, Hudgens and the SEC inaugurated the tour, and the concept was a relatively simple one: during football training days in August, load up a plane with sportswriters from around the South and fly them from school to school to interview coaches and players. Instead of coaches and players having to fit in interviews from newspapers at various times during training camp, the Skywriters Tour brought reporters to each school all at once, where combined press conferences were held and practices were open for the group of writers.

From the start, the Skywriters Tour was popular across the board. For starters, football fans were able to learn more about the upcoming season, the projected competitive balance within the conference, and players and coaches they normally would not read about unless their team was playing them during the season.

For the coaches and writers, Skywriters was a success as well. Longtime Georgia coach Vince Dooley (1964 to 1988) remembers the tour well, specifically the opportunity it afforded coaches and writers to get to know one another.

"They would spend the day with you, come watch practice, and each day they would write their columns," Dooley recalled of the reporters during the Skywriters Tour days. "It was a good relationship. You'd go out to dinner with them, and you got to know the writers that way pretty well."[20]

For Fred Russell, this format fit perfectly with his personality and style: cover the team on the field, and get to know the coaches off of it. In this setting, he either established or continued relationships with coaches across the conference. Dooley was certainly one example during the Skywriter Tour days. He entered the conference in 1964 and spent the next twenty-five years coaching the Bulldogs, plenty of time for annual visits with Russell. Other relationships included those with Coach Ray Graves (Florida), Russell's longtime friend Paul "Bear" Bryant (Alabama), Paul Dietzel (first LSU, then South Carolina), and even Johnny Majors (Tennessee) in the 1970s, when the former Heisman-trophy winner returned to coach his alma mater.

Russell had a leg up on his competition when the Skywriters Tour began in the mid-1960s. To say nothing of his reporting and writing talents, Russell had just spent the better part of two decades becoming one of the leading voices in college football. His cross-country treks each summer preparing for the annual "Pigskin Preview" served him well, and his competitors and friends within the sportswriting fraternity knew that.

"His connections from working with the *Saturday Evening Post* for all those years on the football preview were great," recalled former *Atlanta Constitution* sportswriter Jesse Outlar, who was in the business himself for forty-plus years. "He was very close to all these head coaches, and I never met a coach who didn't like Russell. That's almost impossible to imagine."[21]

Another contributing factor to the Skywriters Tour being a good match for Russell was the era in which it was set. Through the 1960s and even a good bit through the 1970s, there was general trust and discretion between coaches and reporters. Not everything needed to be prefaced with "on the record" or "off the record," as it does today. In fact, the general understanding by many was that if a writer didn't have his notebook out, it was off the record. As a result, the Skywriter dinners were a natural time for relationships to be built and friendships to develop, and less about grabbing quotes for the morning column.

In addition, at least at the outset of the tour, the number of newspapermen covering SEC college football was rather small, perhaps about thirty in total. It was a manageable number, both for coaches and the conference, and the coaches could be more available with their time, unlike today's environment. As Dooley recalled, the passing of this era, not to the mention the growth of the media, intimated that the SEC Skywriters Tour had a shelf life.

"There was a closeness there that will never be there again. The writers were always very discreet about what they wrote, and I think it's because the coaches felt comfortable with them and knew that they would be treated in the best way," Dooley said, adding that even when the number of writers on the tour grew from about fifteen to about thirty, it was still manageable. "But then the media got so big, the SEC couldn't accommodate them all in one of those old 404's."[22]

The sheer growth of the media covering the SEC in the early 1980s, as well as the slowly changing relationships between coaches and reporters, contributed to the end of the SEC Skywriters Tour in 1983. It was replaced with what is now called "SEC Football Media Days," a preseason conference the SEC organizes in Birmingham, Alabama. Instead of groups of reporters traveling across the South, coaches and writers gather together in a much more formal forum at SEC headquarters.

As both writers and university officials recall, however, the Skywriters Tour certainly had its moments, many of which came as a result of putting a large group of sportswriters together on the road for a couple of weeks straight every August. This was also the days of more regular and heavier drinking among the sportswriting fraternity, and there would be times when writers were simply unable to finish their stories, let alone start them. With so many writers around, the solution seemed logical enough. As veteran *Tampa Tribune* columnist Tom McEwen recalled matter of factly, "We would write their stories for them. I remember doing that several times. It wasn't somebody from the same town as you, so nobody would know the difference back in that guy's hometown."[23]

McEwen also remembered another time on the Skywriters Tour when he cobbled together a quick article for a writer from another town, although this time alcohol was not the contributing factor.

"He went to see his girlfriend in another town. He just skipped two cities and went to see her instead," McEwen laughed. "Back then you didn't think twice about it. He said, 'Would you cover for me?' I said, 'Yeah, sure.'"[24]

Even beyond the sportswriting shenanigans that occurred, many of the more humorous Skywriters Tour stories had little to do with football, such as one account of a former Atlanta United Press International writer who had a tendency to sleep in the nude. After a poorly timed episode of sleep-walking, he ended up locked out of his hotel room on a balcony overlooking the hotel parking lot. He knocked and knocked on people's doors, and someone eventually let him in, but only after his Skywriter colleagues let him walk around for a while.[25]

"Some of the funniest things I've ever gone through were with the Skywriters group," recalled former Florida Sports Information director Norm Carlson, who hosted the reporters when they would arrive each summer to cover the Gators. "They were on this old plane, this old propeller-driven thing someone had nicknamed 'CRASH,' and they'd be on the road for about ten to twelve days. They'd party all night, write their columns at some point, and then fly out in the morning. They were a bedraggled-looking bunch."[26]

One evening stood out in particular for Carlson—the "phone-bill night."

"It all got started when a guy named George Smith, who was sports editor of the *Anniston* [Alabama] *Star*, started trying to call Richard Nixon in San Clemente from the hospitality room," Carlson recalled with a laugh. "They finally did get somebody at Nixon's place—it wasn't Nixon, of course—and they said they'd be sure the message would be passed on to the President and Patricia.

"Then one of them wanted to see if they could reach Queen Elizabeth," Carlson added. "So they started to call London. Man, when I got that damn phone bill...trying to explain that to our AD, I was like, 'Well, they had to make a few phone calls.'"[27]

Transitioning to the "Honors Court"

The SEC Skywriters Tour was not the only college football initiative that Fred Russell was affiliated with in the 1960s. Just as his impressive list of contacts and college football relationships from the 1940s and 1950s had served him well when he was on the road each August across the South, another opportunity within the sport that could benefit from his knowledge and connections developed for Russell. The opportunity was with the National Football Foundation, and it became a legitimate possibility in the early 1960s when, for a variety of reasons, the popularity of the *Saturday Evening Post* started to decline. A significant factor was that journalism's competitive landscape was changing dramatically with more and more media outlets available to writers. The luster of being a lead writer for papers such as *Collier's* or the *Post* slowly diminished as reporters were able to write elsewhere and make equitable if not more money while doing so. In 1962, Fred Russell wrote his final installation of the "Pigskin Preview" for the *Post*, and it marked the end of his twenty-three-year history with the weekly magazine.

As his relationship with the *Post* came to an end in the early 1960s, Russell had an opportunity to stay involved with college football through the National Football Foundation. The NFF was established in 1947 with a mission of promoting amateur football in America with an emphasis on academic excellence as well. The NFF is still in existence today, and one component of the organization is its College Football Hall of Fame, the group responsible for determining college football's All-American players each year. The Hall of Fame Honors Court governs this process and is one of the more influential groups within college football with regard to the sport's annual awards.

"The Honors Court is the most powerful group in college football," noted Dick Philpot, a member of the NFF and former president of its Middle Tennessee chapter. "The members of the court studied the portfolios of every candidate, and that's how you get to be in the Hall of Fame."[28]

It was within the Honors Court that Fred Russell established himself as a leading champion and voice of the College Football Hall of Fame. From 1964 to 1991, Russell held the prestigious role of Honors Court chairman, and it was a role perfectly suited for him. The position required significant experience within college football, an appreciation for the game's rich history, and relationships with its coaches and administrators around the country. Importantly, the role of chairman required an instinctive sense of fairness and prudence in order to guide to court so it would make well-informed decisions and nominations for college football's highest individual awards.

In Fred Russell, the NFF Hall of Fame found all of these things, and it was Russell's integrity that allowed him to chair this court for almost thirty years, commanding respect from its members as he did so.

Robert "Bob" Casciola served as president of the NFF from 1995 to 2004 and remembered Russell well for his efforts within the Hall of Fame organization, especially when it came to Russell's leadership and sense of fairness.

"He was the guy who pulled it all together. He would sit down and say, 'We want geographical distribution. We don't want everyone from Tennessee. We don't want everyone from California. And we want positional distribution. We don't want four quarterbacks. We have to have lineman, receivers, and running backs,'" Casciola recalled. "That influence he carried had a profound effect for many years. It legitimized the whole process."[29]

To oversee the Honors Court, Russell drew on the countless relationships within college football that he had cultivated over the years. Whether he was covering games in the South for the *Banner* or touring the country each summer as he worked on his "Pigskin Preview" for the *Saturday Evening Post*, Russell effectively built up one of the more impressive rolodexes of coaches, former players, athletic administrators, and sportswriters. From Paul Bryant to Archie Manning, Frank Broyles to Lee Corso, Johnny Majors to Lou Holtz, Russell had relationships and friendship with all of them, and countless others. This "reach" into the college football community, coupled with his strong character and laid-back personality, put Russell in a perfect position to do well with the Honors Court.

"When you see the pride and delight the people take when they are elected into the Hall of Fame, you realize the impact he had on so many people," veteran coach Lou Holtz said of Russell. "And yet he did this unselfishly, and he made the Hall a very worthwhile thing so that other people, whether coaches or players, could enjoy it."[30]

The "Keeper of the Gate"

"Russell was never opinionated as the chair of the Honors Court," current Honors Court chairman and former coach Gene Corrigan commented. "[Russell] was just very fair. I'm sure he had his favorites, but we never knew who they were necessarily."[31]

Not surprisingly, decisions were not always easy, and certainly there were interesting ones that faced the court over the years. Casciola recalled one in particular, when LSU's 1959 Heisman Trophy-winner Billy Cannon was scheduled for induction to the Hall of Fame in 1983. In July of that year, Cannon pleaded guilty to involvement in a remarkable counterfeit scam, one that resulted in close to $6 million dollars in fake $100 bills.

"This story broke just around the time he was to be inducted, and Fred Russell was running the Honors Court at the time," Casciola recalled, remembering how it presented Russell and the court with a difficult decision. "There was no better college football player than Billy Cannon, but they rescinded his honors. Russell knew how big an honor this was, but he stuck to that decision."[32]

It was from situations like the Billy Cannon incident that earned Russell the nickname of "gatekeeper" within the Hall of Fame and Honors Court fraternity. Bill Wallace is a retired sportswriter from the *New York Times*, and, like Russell, he covered sports for multiple generations. Wallace was familiar with Russell's work in the South, and knew of his reputation within college football.

"Russell *was* the 'keeper of the gate,' regarding the College Football Hall of Fame as head of the selection committee for many years," Wallace argued. "He would not allow any pressures to ease the way into the Hall for the unqualified."[33]

In addition to his tough stances on matters of integrity, Casciola appreciated Russell for his ability to work a room, to quietly and modestly be the largest figure in the room, the one who commanded attention and respect. "He was the boss, and he was a highly respected individual, but Fred Russell was also a very funny guy. On his feet, he could entertain a room very easily," Casciola recalled.[34]

Dave Campbell from the *Waco* (Texas) *Tribune-Herald* was a strong advocate of Russell's and the way he handled his role as chairman.

"He was utterly fair, a wonderful writer, and well spoken. Fred was one of our leading lights at that time, and on the Honors Court, he was always good for two to three really good stories, to break the ice and get things started each year," noted Campbell.[35]

"Fred was comfortable everywhere. He was comfortable with presidents and bums, and he was one of the great joke-tellers of all time, some of which were repeatable, and some of which were not," added current chairman Gene Corrigan. "We just loved having our annual meeting so we could get together with him."[36]

Nowhere was this skill of Russell's more evident within the National Football Foundation than at its annual Hall of Fame weekend, which is highlighted by the celebrated college football awards dinner. The event is held each year at the historic Waldorf-Astoria hotel in New York, and just as when Russell was chairman of the Honors Court, the banquets attracted celebrities from across the sports spectrum.

Lee Corso has been involved in college football one way or another for over fifty years, and the Hall of Fame dinner continues to be a regular stop for the current ESPN football analyst. Corso's memories of Russell's day at the helm are vivid.

"I attended all of those dinners, and Russell was always one of the guys that everybody wanted to go up and be around," Corso recalled, noting that part of what made Russell so effective within the NFF was his character. "Everybody respected him, he had unquestionable integrity, and you could tell him something and not see it in the headlines the next day."[37]

It wasn't just sports celebrities who were drawn to Russell, either. One of Russell's close Vanderbilt friends was Art Demmas, who played football for the Commodores in the mid-1950s and was an NFL official for almost thirty years. Demmas joined Russell at the Hall of Fame dinner on occasion, and one year in particular, Demmas was left speechless.

"As we walk through the Waldorf lobby, here comes General William Westmoreland," Demmas recalled of his encounter with the famous American military hero from the Vietnam era. Westmoreland was one of the speakers that year at the Hall of Fame dinner, and as Demmas replayed the memory, the general needed Russell's advice.

"He said, 'Freddie! Am I glad to see you. I've got to do a talk to the media in about half an hour, and I'd like you to look over my notes, see what you think, and make any corrections that you need to,'" Demmas recalled the general saying. "That just shows you the respect Russell had in all areas of his craft."[38]

Dick Philpot had a similar memory, when he and Russell were in South Bend, Indiana, for the opening of the Hall of Fame. Casciola was giving Russell and Philpot a late night private tour of the building. On one of the walls were special awards, plaques, and photos. Philpot started scanning through photos from prior events and dinners in New York.

"I looked up on the wall, and there was a picture of Fred Russell...and Ronald Reagan," Philpot recalled, still shaking his head years later. "I remember saying, 'Well, Mr. Russell, it doesn't get much better than that, does it?'"[39]

Philpot has strong memories of Russell at those Hall of Fame dinners in New York, especially when things were often slow prior to the main dinner.

"The NFF would have a luncheon the day before the regular event, and these things could get pretty dull. As Fred used to say, it was a 'sunshine enema,' and they got longer and longer," Philpot joked. "But in the middle of all this, when the time was right, Freddie could always get up and tell a joke. It would just lighten the mood. He would keep everybody awake, and he kept it alive. When he left, well, they went back to sleep."[40]

Russell's popularity within the close-knit college football community did not go unnoticed by his employer, either. In 1980, Brownlee Currey became part-owner of the *Nashville Banner*, and he too had the opportunity to join Russell on occasion for the Hall of Fame dinners during Russell's reign as Honors Court chairman.

"I don't know of any member that was more revered than he," Currey acknowledged. "[Russell] was just worshipped by all these people, and I was sitting there with my jaw dropping, with all these people, these titans of the football world, would come up and say 'Hello, Freddie!' and talk to him for a long time."[41]

Of course, the reason people were there in the first place was to see the players and coaches being inducted into the Hall of Fame. It was the inductees who respected Russell more than anyone. Philpot remembered seeing this firsthand during his time with Russell in New York.

"These All-Americans were just so in awe of him. We'd be having breakfast and they'd come over to him, and be so unbelievably humble and quiet, almost whispering, 'Mr. Russell. What an honor,'" Philpot recalled. "Players, coaches, everybody: they knew they wouldn't be there if it weren't for Mr. Russell. He wouldn't say much, but when he did, boy, did everyone listen."[42]

Russell's years as Honors Court chairman reaffirmed his role as one of the leading influential voices within the sport. When he stepped down from the National Football Foundation Hall of Fame after thirty-one years, there was an article in the 1991 Hall of Fame program that summarized Russell's impact. The program read: "It is not often it can be said without impunity that a man 'becomes a legend in his own time,' but it is an unchallenged fact when it comes to describing Fred Russell."[43]

The *Banner* Part 2: Happy Days

"I grew up reading the *Nashville Banner,* down in Lynchburg, Tennessee, and I don't remember when I didn't know Fred Russell. Not only did he cover sports for us locally, he exposed us to so many other things: the writings of Grantland Rice, notary people from all around the country like Joe Louis, and football players and major leaguers."[1] —Johnny Majors, college football coach

In 1953, *Banner* publisher Jimmy Stahlman organized a "who's who" banquet of the sports world, in which sport celebrities, journalists, and politicians alike descended on Nashville to celebrate Fred Russell's twenty-fifth year in the business. Not surprisingly, the party essentially began once the banquet was over, and as current Tennessee sportswriter Joe Biddle explains, it led to one particular anecdote being passed down from one journalistic generation to the next.

"There's a great story about that banquet, because Red Smith had come down to it as well. During the night, they made plans for the next day that *Banner* reporter Waxo Green would go by the hotel and pick Red Smith up, because he had never seen the Hermitage, and Waxo was going to take him out there. As Mr. Russell tells the story, General Neyland was in town for the banquet as well, and that night at the hotel, it just turned into one big party that went on into the wee hours of the morning, with all sorts of people coming in and out. They got into some great stories and arguments, and there was a lot of drinking, as you might imagine back in that era. So Mr. Russell went home about three or four o'clock, took a shower, and then went to the paper to write a column for the day.

"Well, the rest of the writers come in later that morning, and Waxo shows up. He had been supposed to pick Red Smith up at 8 o'clock, but Red didn't show. So Mr. Russell and Waxo call the hotel and get connected to his room. It just rings and rings and rings. Finally, a real weak voice comes on, and slowly says, 'Yes?' Russell then goes, 'Mr. Smith? This is Jimmy down at Jimmy's Pool Hall. Sir, you left your hat down here last night. Would you like me to bring it by the hotel? Or do you want to come down here to pick it up?' At that point, there's a long silent pause on the other end of the phone, and finally Red Smith stammers out, 'Is there a head in it?' Long story short, Red wasn't in much shape to go see the Hermitage that day."[2]

* * *

After establishing himself in the 1930s and 1940s as a legitimate editorial voice at the paper, Russell built on that foundation in the decades that followed. His goal was to develop and lead a sports staff that out-hustled the competition for the best stories, and then out-wrote that competition once the stories broke. Through the 1950s, as his annual work with the *Saturday Evening Post* brought Russell's name into the national context, the *Banner* sports department became an attractive paper for which to work. Despite the relatively small-market size of Nashville, the opportunity to have a mentor in Russell was appealing to many writers, and by the 1960s, he had assembled a strong department of writers and columnists. Edgar Allen, Dudley "Waxo" Green, C. B. Fletcher, and George Leonard were Russell's primary writers, with other young staffers coming along the way, such as Joe Caldwell, Bob Witt, Delbert Reed, and Harold Huggins, to name a few.

Russell led by example. He was a perfectionist who paid attention to the daily details necessary to develop and cultivate a strong team. For the daily "Sidelines" column, Russell's staff would see their boss make the extra phone call, conduct the additional interview, make second and third trips to the library, or labor over just the right words to use. Whatever was necessary, Russell's approach was to make it perfect, or at least get it close. Adherence to the fundamentals is what positioned Russell and his staff to excel, and he made others aware of how important the basics were in making the final article come together. Being on time, well dressed, not settling for a first draft when a second or third would certainly be better—these were some of the basic principles Russell not only preached but practiced day after day, year after year at the *Banner*. If Russell thought a different word should be used, he'd call that writer in or be out there telling them at their desk. Staffers learned that Russell would not tolerate mistakes, and if he found one in an early copy of the section, writers could count on their boss yelling their name from his office, followed quickly by, "Get in here!"

In the process of establishing a leading sports staff, Russell continued to enjoy personal success as well during these years. Accolades and notoriety from his *Saturday Evening Post* efforts poured in, and Russell's growing national presence made him an even larger player in Nashville and in the South. Without abusing the popularity, Russell artfully leveraged this presence to make a difference in the community. As the title of this chapter indicates, these were good times for Russell and the *Banner*. The setting for the fictional television show "Happy Days" was 1955 to 1965, and it enjoyed a ten-year network run from 1974 to 1984. For Russell, it was all of these decades—from the '50s into the '80s—that represented the prime of his career.

1953 Banquet

The year 1953 was a watershed for Russell, a year in which he was able to reflect on twenty-five years at the *Banner* and at the same time eagerly anticipate what the years ahead might bring. His tenure at the paper was a noteworthy accomplishment, and given the reputation Russell had established within the sportswriting industry and the Nashville community, *Banner* publisher Jimmy Stahlman deemed it worthy of celebration. Given the contacts Russell had made and the relationships he had developed in that quarter century, the idea for a reception quickly morphed into a full-blown banquet. Sportswriters and editors from around the country were invited, as well as athletes, coaches, university officials, even politicians and members of the community who knew Russell. The banquet was held Monday, 8 September 1953, at Vanderbilt University's Memorial Gym. More than 600 people attended, including coaches and athletes from across the country, the commissioner of the Southeastern Conference, two congressmen, and a United States senator.

A notable absence that night was Grantland Rice, who was in his seventies at this point and in declining health. He sent Russell a personal note of regret, along with a poem entitled "To Fred Russell" that was read at the banquet and which honored Russell's contributions to the profession they both shared and loved. Even without Rice's presence, it was a marquee event in Nashville and for the top sports figures and writers across the nation—it was one of *the* hot tickets for the year.

The program was a testament to Russell's reputation and popularity within the sports world. National sports figures such as boxing legend Jack Dempsey, golf great Bobby Jones, and football icon Red Grange not only attended but delivered speeches celebrating Russell. Big name coaches within the Southeastern Conference, such as General Robert "Bob" Neyland (Tennessee) and Wally Butts (Georgia), spoke as well, as did national-level journalists Red Smith and Bill Corum.

Furman Bisher from the *Atlanta Journal-Constitution* attended the banquet, and one particular memory he had was those three icons of their sports coming together that day, quite literally, in fact, to help Jones, who was crippled at this point in his life, to the podium for his speech.

"[Jones] got to the steps with his crutches, and he sort of paused and looked around, not sure exactly how he was going to work it," Bisher recalled. "A real big fellow grabbed him on one side, and another man on the other side, and they hoisted him up on the podium. It was Red Grange and Jack Dempsey. I'll never forget that: two immortals giving another immortal a hand."[3]

Corum wrote of the evening's events in his column the following day for the *New York Journal-American*. Corum thought often of Vanderbilt's first famous sportswriter alum, Grantland Rice, and his column was written as if it were a personal note to Rice, since he was unable to attend. The standing ovation that Jones received gave Corum the material he needed for a fitting conclusion to his column: "Handclapping drew to as close to cheer as the clapping of hands can come. Tears jumped to sting a little behind your eyes," Corum wrote. "It was a fine thing, Granny. A very fine thing. I wish you could have seen it. Not many men, whatever they may have done, ever got a tribute so truly spontaneous and touching."[4]

The night itself, however, belonged to Russell. After all celebrity speakers had their turn at the podium, Russell spoke at the event himself. When thanking his friends who came to honor him that night, Russell was his usual humble self. "I'm honestly dreaming, and I don't know when I am going to wake up."

In his own "Sidelines" column the following day, Russell reiterated that sentiment, but also took the opportunity to thank his loyal readers.

"Not in one column or ten columns or a hundred columns would I be able to express adequately my heartfelt gratitude for the warmth of friendship which I experienced last night. That Bobby Jones would be here, that newspapermen Red Smith and Bill Corum would come down from New York, on their own, I can't take it in.

"But mainly, that home town friends would treat you so wonderfully—that's what gets next to you. Nashville, to me, is the best place on Earth. My heart and spirit are here. I ask no more than just continuance of the ability to write this daily piece—doing what I'd rather do than anything in the world, for the people I'd rather work for than anybody in the world."[5]

Russell treasured the letters he received from those unable to attend, in particular the aforementioned note from Rice. "I'd give a lot to come down with Red Smith and be with you and the bunch. I am still hoping faintly something may happen so I can make it," Rice wrote in an early September letter from his home in East Hampton, Long Island. "But I guess you can't fool around with the old ticker."[6] (Sadly, Rice's words were far more accurate than anyone would have wanted. He suffered a massive heart attack on 14 July 1954 and died at the age of seventy-three.)

Just as the banquet itself attracted some of the largest names in sports, the scrapbook the *Banner* put together for Russell, filled with telegrams and letters of those unable to attend the roast in Nashville, had a similar "who's who" feel to it.

Legendary pitcher Dizzy Dean wrote warmly of his friend. By the 1950s, Dean was off the pitcher's mound, but not out of the game, as he had transitioned out of baseball and into a career of broadcasting.

"Whether he knows it or not, his book, *I'll Try Anything Twice*, is one of my favorites," Dean wrote in a letter to the *Banner*. "It might have had some bearing on my taking up broadcasting, despite the fact my English leaves much to be desired. I felt like if he could try anything...well, so could I." [7]

Russell also received letters from many football coaches who could not make the September celebration due to the college season. Letters from Red Sanders (UCLA), Bobby Dodd (Georgia Tech), and Paul Bryant (Kentucky in 1953 and then later at Texas A&M and Alabama) are just three examples of notes collected in the commemorative scrapbook.

Letters from peers in the journalism business filled the pages of this book as well, as men such as Arthur Daley (*New York Times*), Si Burick (*Dayton Daily News*), Mel Allen (broadcaster), and Ralph McGill (*Atlanta Constitution*) all sent letters or telegrams passing along their congratulations to Russell. One telegram in particular had the dry sense of humor that Russell himself favored so much. Ed Danforth, sports editor with the *Atlanta Constitution*, had this to say on that September day in 1953: "I can never forgive you for coming along and keeping me from being the best in the business. Why don't you retire?"[8]

Jokes aside, because he had started so young with the *Banner*, some wondered if retirement was an option for Russell in the 1950s. He had been running full-speed at the paper since the late 1920s, and with his presence growing nationally due to his work at the *Saturday Evening Post*, it was not out of the question to wonder if Russell would step away from the daily newspaper grind. Even the *Banner* itself had some fun with their sports editor, running this cartoon the day of the banquet.

But Russell loved the grind. It's what got him up every morning: the competition and the desire to build the best sports department in the country. In retrospect, Russell was just getting started in 1953. His twenty-five years at that point were not even half of the years he would ultimately spend at the *Banner*. He had almost a half-century more to go in the business.

Roughly twenty-five years after the 1953 banquet, the *Banner* hired a young sportswriter from Daytona Beach, Florida, named Joe Biddle. He was in Russell's office one day and saw a picture of Russell with Bobby Jones, Red Grange, and Jack Dempsey.

"I asked him, 'Good grief, Mr. Russell, how did you get those guys together?' and he said very nonchalantly, 'Oh, they gave me a luncheon when I had been here twenty-five years,'" Biddle said. "Just think about that picture for a moment. Those guys knew him on a personal basis. That was the cream of the crop in the sports world, and those were the circles he ran in."[9]

Even today, more than fifty years later, there are many who still appreciate Russell and the sportswriter genre he championed. George Steinbrenner, the longtime contentious owner of the New York Yankees, and one whose dislike for the media is legendary, was almost wistful when commenting on Russell and that bygone era.

"Those days are indeed gone forever. We try to get back to those days, with relationships between players and writers. But they all have agents now, and agents have really hurt it," Steinbrenner lamented. "But the great ones of the game, they had a great respect for Fred Russell, believe me when I tell you that."[10]

Roy Kramer, Vanderbilt's athletic director from 1978 to 1990 before running the Southeastern Conference from 1990 to 2002, shared similar sentiments as Steinbrenner.

"Fred talked about Jack Dempsey a lot," Kramer commented. "Dempsey had everything in the world going for him, as far as being a notorious person, and the fact that he was there [at the 1953 banquet] and wanted to be there to see Fred, this gives you an example of how Fred could bridge that gap between writer and world famous athlete."[11]

Before the Fame, the Daily Grind, and the "Railroad Treatment"

Just as Russell spent years earning the admiration of sports figures and peers in the industry, he also spent those same years building respect inside the *Banner*. He did so one staff member at a time, one story at a time, and one afternoon edition at a time. Russell was fair, but demanding.

Harold Huggins joined the paper in 1969, and he learned early on just how much Russell expected as an editor. Huggins had written an article on the potential strike by the Dixie Flyers, a minor league team in Nashville from 1962 to 1971, and the edits he received from Russell sent a strong message. Longtime copy editor Bill Roberts was the messenger, and he handed the now-bleeding article back to Huggins for a second draft.

"It had red lines riddled through all my grammatical errors, misplaced commas, and the like from Russell," Huggins wrote years later. "I learned quickly that Russell demanded excellence, perfection, brevity, and accuracy when any story appeared in that sports section."[12]

Russell made his staff work hard, and over the years, it became an honor (not a right) to work on the *Banner* sports staff. Not everyone made it. Delbert Reed wrote for Russell in the mid- to late 1960s, and he recalled a colleague coming out on the losing end, someone who in the end did not pass the test for Russell. The day it happened, Russell broke the news in his office, a place that folks rarely wanted to be summoned.

"You never wanted to be called into his office, and this one time, Russell called a reporter into his office," Reed recalled. "Well, he came out of there, head down, and just looked bad. I asked him what had happened, and he told me that Mr. Russell had said, 'I just think you need to find a new job.' He was an okay writer, but you know, he was somewhat of a phony. And I think Mr. Russell saw through that. He didn't want that on his staff."[13]

Another manifestation of Russell's tough stance inside the sports department was his well-known "railroad treatment." This was the term Russell's staff coined for their boss when he was inside his office and needed to end a conversation on his terms, albeit in a generally indirect way without explicitly kicking you out. The expression itself, known throughout the *Banner* and certainly by any sports department staffer, had more to do with logistics than anything else. The *Banner/Tennessean* office building at 1100 Broadway in downtown Nashville was just a block west from the historic Union Station railroad yard. In those days, Russell's office had windows that overlooked the switching station for the L&N railroad, where the cars and trains would switch constantly throughout the day. If there was a conversation or a topic with a staffer that Russell did not want to entertain, he would turn around in his chair and just look out the window until that person left.

The "railroad treatment," as it became known, was something that Reed remembered learning about almost as soon as he joined the *Banner* staff in the mid-1960s. The veteran members of the sports department— men such as Waxo Green and C. B. Fletcher—quickly passed on the details to new *Banner* employees, and knowing Russell's mood from day to day was often a key component of whether or not one was likely to receive the treatment. If Russell happened to be in a particularly dour mood, perhaps if the *Banner* had been beaten on a story by the *Tennessean*, then it was even more likely, especially if a staffer went to Russell to discuss something as sensitive as compensation.

"We'd ask each other about Russell and what his mood was that day," Reed remembered with a laugh. "Sometimes that's all anyone would talk about, and if you ever went in there to ask Mr. Russell for a raise on a bad day, he'd just turn around and look out the window until you left."[14]

Over time, the net effect of Russell's demanding presence was that he was able to put together a staff over which he had direct control, both from a hiring and firing perspective, as well as with regard to daily editing and mentoring. The *Banner* held its own against its *Tennessean* rival, and the sports section was a key reason. As big a stick as Russell had and was willing to use, he also knew when to use the proverbial carrot. Huggins recalled one such moment, when Russell brought in the staff for an impromptu meeting.

"I remember sitting around with Bill Roberts, a wonderful copyeditor, Edgar Allen, George Leonard, Waxo Green, Joe Caldwell, C. B. Fletcher, and Louie Guinn," Huggins recalled. "Russell told us we comprised the best Monday-through-Saturday sports department in the country. I felt ten feet tall. I never forgot that."[15]

In addition to the well-timed and well-earned compliments to his staff, Russell had another secret weapon for leading his team: his sense of humor. For all his "work-hard" toughness, there was no getting around Russell's "play-hard" tendencies, which were equally part of the culture he developed within the *Banner*'s sports department. As Russell worked hard and demanded the same of his staff, this played perfectly into the sports editor's tendency for a good joke to keep his team honest. Commenting on the important role of one's sense of humor, longtime Dallas sportswriter and friend Blackie Sherrod said, "Freddie had one of the very best, supporting a longtime theory of mine that the longevity of a sports columnist is in direct proportion to his sense of humor. Of course, his practical jokes were legendary."[16]

As Russell proved over the years, the *Banner* sports room was fertile ground for building that legend. Just as Reed had witnessed the firing of a colleague, he knew firsthand how tough Russell could be when running the sports department. Early in his *Banner* career, Reed was still in the process of getting to know the veterans, and figuring out the roles of everyone on staff. One day, about a month into his new job, Reed saw the temper side of Russell firsthand, and he unwittingly became part of the fallout.

In his own words, Reed recounted the story:

I was just trying to get to know people. Back then, if he called you in his office, it was doom. You did not want to go in there. One day, the first edition paper came out, and Russell got the copy off the printer and as soon as he got back to his office, you hear him yell out, 'Roberts, get in here!' [Copyeditor Bill] Roberts goes charging in his office, with his head down, not knowing what's going to happen. Well, Russell starts yelling, telling him the headlines are terrible, tears up the paper, throws it on the floor, and tells Roberts to get out because he's done. Everybody's cowering in the corner, and I couldn't believe it was happening. So Roberts took off his apron that he wore when working with the copy, threw it down on the counter, got his coat and hat and went out the door. Everyone was silent.

As Roberts left the office, Russell yelled, 'Delbert, get in here!' I go in his office, and he says, 'I want you to take over the desk, remake this paper, and write new headlines, and lay it out better. Roberts did a lousy job, and you're it now.' I just said, 'Oh, uh, okay, sir.' I didn't know what to do, so I went over to [veteran reporter] Edgar Allen. Edgar said, 'Well, if I was you, I would go do it.'

So I proceeded to put on Roberts's apron, get behind the desk, and start looking at the paper, rewriting headlines, doing new layouts, and moving everything around. Nobody is saying a word. I'm thinking I'll be getting fired next. Well, the paper comes out, and Russell goes, 'That's better. That's a good job, Delbert.'

So I go home and then the next morning, Roberts is back in there, whistling and doing his job, as if nothing has happened. And when I show up, everybody got to laughing, because they knew Russell had pulled one over on me. It was just a practical joke.[17]

A Simpler Time

Compared to the 1940s dominated by World War II and the upcoming 1960s, arguably one of the most turbulent decades in American history, 1950s America was a quieter, more relaxed time. Newspaper work generally reflected that spirit. Access for sportswriters during this time was, by modern standards, nothing short of remarkable.

Writers and columnists would build relationships and friendships at the same time, and more often than not, writers would give their subjects the benefit of the doubt. As has been well documented over the years, there was an unwritten rule that off-the-field actions were off limits. In the days when friendships were the key to access, nothing could hurt a writer's ability to get information more than by bringing up the off-the-field behavior of his subjects that was morally questionable. Sportswriters generally gave a pass on such behavior, choosing to focus almost entirely on the events on the field. If off-the-field activities were discussed, chances were it was something positive, something that improved the image of the player or coach.

While the differences between modern sportswriting and that from the middle of the twentieth century are many, one notable aspect of 1950s sportswriting was that leading sportswriters were often identified with one city. Similar to Russell's years at the *Banner*, Dave Campbell spent more than sixty years in Waco, Texas, making his name part of Texas sportswriting history.

"The writers of that era became members of your family, and Freddie Russell was the epitome of that," Campbell noted. "You woke up with them and read their columns."[18]

In crafting his own daily columns, Campbell was fond of occasionally quoting other writers from different cities. Fred Russell often made that list for Campbell, something current *Houston Chronicle* reporter John McLain remembered from his early days of growing up and reading Campbell.

"All I knew about Nashville was that's where Minnie Pearl lived, but Campbell kept quoting this guy Fred Russell," McLain recalled from his Texas youth. "Dave always quoted him as the authority on college football and the SEC. It was the gospel. If Fred wrote it, you knew it had to be true."[19]

Another legendary "Dave"—Dave Anderson of the *New York Times*—began his sportswriting career not long after Campbell did, and recalled how important a reporter's access was back in the 1950s and 1960s.

"The biggest difference is that you were writing for people who never saw the game; the only ones who saw the game were those in the stands," Anderson noted. Still active with the *Times*, the veteran reported added that the advent of television, mass media, and cable changed the simple interactions between reporter and subject. "Years ago, after the game, the star would stand near the field and just talk to the media, answer all the questions. Now, he is surrounded by everyone who just wants their own sound-byte. You can't get the same conversational manner today."[20]

For Fred Russell, his personality and style were perfectly suited for the sportswriting generation in which he grew up. Through the middle decades of the twentieth century, his list of contacts was a veritable inventory of coaches and players now viewed as legendary or described as "Hall of Famer." This applied both at the local level for his hometown roots in Tennessee and also at the national level. In elevating his presence beyond that of just the *Nashville Banner*, Russell became somewhat of a civic icon for Middle Tennessee. He became more than just a sportswriter for Nashville. Russell became a man of influence in the 1960s, leading to one of the more interesting chapters of his life in Nashville.

Tennessee State and "I'll get back with ya"

During the 1950s and 1960s in Nashville, Russell's rise to prominence coincided with the similar success of the Tennessee State women's track team. Tennessee State University (TSU) is located in downtown Nashville, and up until 1968, the school was called Tennessee A&I. A predominantly black school, A&I's athletic program had enjoyed notable success in the late 1950s with multiple National Association of Intercollegiate Athletics championships, but it wasn't until the women's track team dominated the 1960 Olympics that the school jumped onto the national stage. Under the guidance of veteran track coach Ed Temple, the A&I women won a gold medal in the 4x100-meter relay at the Rome Olympics. The team was led by Wilma Rudolph, who brought home three gold medals, one for the relay victory and one each for the 100-meter and 200-meter events, respectively.

Before the breakout success in Rome that summer, Temple spent the 1950s building his program. He had recruited Mae Faggs from New York to run at A&I, and Faggs represented the United States on the 1952 Olympic team. Her success is what first connected Temple and Russell, as the sports editor wanted to learn more about Faggs and the program. It was the beginning of a lifelong friendship between the two men, as they were part of several remarkable developments that benefitted Temple, the women's track program, and the school during those turbulent civil rights years.

"Mr. Russell had a major impact here," Temple acknowledged. "He opened up the door for a whole lot of things, things that most people never knew how they happened, except for me and a few people out here."[21]

One of Temple's main recollections of Russell was a common expression the sportswriter used. "Something he always said was, 'I'll get back with ya.' If I ran into a problem," Temple continued, "I could always call Mr. Russell. And he would say, 'I'll get back with ya in a day or so,' and he would."[22]

Perhaps most remarkable of all is that Russell's involvement was intentionally behind-the-scenes and unbeknownst to almost everyone except Temple. On two notable occasions, Russell even called on the governor of Tennessee for assistance. It wasn't until years later for this biography that Temple spoke openly and candidly of Russell's involvement, of how the sports editor of a predominantly conservative newspaper during the segregationist 1950s and 1960s had gone out of his way to step in on behalf of a predominantly black state school.

It started when Russell went to the school track in 1953 to interview Temple and talk about the upcoming season for the team, which was led by Faggs. Temple recalled that when Faggs first came down from New York, she took one look at the old cinder track full of potholes and cracks and was ready to head back East. Temple shared that story with Russell, and as they walked around the track that day, Russell told the coach he was going to see what he could do to let the A&I team practice a couple of days each week at Vanderbilt.

"It was a cinder track, but it was nice, fine cinder," Temple said of the Vanderbilt track that encircled the school football field. "I'll never forget it, because he talked with Vanderbilt's coach, and Russell called me back and said that he'd be happy to have us out."[23]

That gesture turned out to be merely the beginning of how Russell would help Temple and TSU.

Russell, Governor Ellington, and a
New Track for the Olympic Champions

Against odds that at times seemed both insurmountable and inevitable, Temple kept improving his team through the 1950s. They continued to make use of Vanderbilt's track when it was available, which became more and more necessary when state funds were never appropriated for a new track at the A&I campus. In the winter months, without the use of an indoor track, Temple kept his team in shape by practicing at the school's indoor basketball gym, despite having to practice 50-yard sprints that would start at one end of the court and end outside the gym in a hallway. More remarkable was that athletic scholarships were not available to Temple's team members. Rather, they were on a work-aid program, which meant that in addition to their studies and their practices, the members of the track team were obligated to complete at least two hours per day of work.

Through it all, the A&I team persevered, and by 1960, Temple had assembled what was arguably the best collection of women's track talent in the nation. At the Rome Olympics that year, the A&I athletes broke through for the USA, winning three gold medals. For Temple and the team, it was their highest possible achievement.

Temple, however, had just about reached the end of his patience with the university. Having succeeded at the collegiate and the Olympic level, Temple expected the administration to recognize the program's successes as well as his accomplishments as a coach. While most coaches received raises in July when school was out, Temple noted that a raise in January was also possible if they had done well at the mid-year point. In the months that followed Rome, however, it was not to be.

"The biggest disappointment in all my forty-four years was when we came back from Rome. January came, and I didn't get a cent," Temple recalled. "Well, I'm thinking that I know I'm going to get a good one July 1. July 1st comes and I didn't get a cent, not one single cent."[24]

When Russell stopped by the track later that summer, the coach shared with him his dissatisfaction with the school and that he just felt it was time to find a different place to coach.

"Russell told me, 'Look, don't you do anything until I make a phone call. And I'll get back with ya.' So he called the governor, Governor Buford Ellington, and told him that I was thinking about leaving,"

Temple said, still shaking his head more than forty years later that Russell would do that on his behalf.

Not long after he spoke with Russell, Temple heard that the governor wanted to meet with him to find out what problems needed to be fixed so Temple would stay. Within days, Temple was downtown at the governor's office, face-to-face with someone who could make a difference.

It didn't take Temple long to share with Ellington that not only were the track conditions abysmal, but his Olympic gold-medalists still were on work-aid programs because scholarships had not been set.

"I just think I've done all I can do," Temple told the governor. "The only thing I could say at the time was that it was time for me to pick up and leave. Well, the governor stopped me and said, 'No, you're not going anywhere.' He picked that phone up and called Howard Wharf, who was the superintendent of colleges and the commissioner of all the colleges back then."

As he sat in the governor's office, Temple enjoyed the next part of the conversation.

"The governor called Wharf and said, 'Look, I've got Coach Temple here from A&I. He's thinking about leaving, and we need to get him some scholarships out there, and we need to get a new track out there. Do you understand?'" Temple remembered Ellington saying. Ellington also told Wharf to contact the A&I president to make sure these things happened.

"I was sitting right there," Temple recalled with a laugh. "Ellington turned to me and said, 'I'm going to take care of all this. Don't you worry about anything.'"[25]

When Temple returned to the university, it wasn't long before he took some heat from the athletic director and the university president. Because Temple had not shared any of the details in which Russell was involved, the A&I administrators simply believed Temple had gone directly over their heads by going straight to the governor. Temple took the heat, because in the end, his program got what it needed.

"We got an asphalt track around the football field, and we got scholarships for the first time. That was a big, big move," Temple admitted.

As for Russell's role with the new track, Temple didn't hesitate to recognize how pivotal it was for Wharf to have been contacted directly by the governor.

"Wharf was one of them boys who, if he didn't get a push, he was not going to do it," Temple noted. "He had to be pushed, but we had the pushers in Fred Russell and the governor."[26]

Wilma Rudolph and the Pregnancy Cover-Up

Getting a new track and scholarship dollars appropriated to the school was not the only time Russell called on Governor Ellington to offer support on behalf of Temple's track program.

When they returned from the Rome Olympics, Temple admitted that the attention on three time Gold medalist Wilma Rudolph was intense. If it wasn't *Life* magazine or *Look* who had reporters in town, then it was someone from *Sports Illustrated* who wanted to learn more about Rudolph and the track program.

Temple remembered hearing a rumor that someone had called *Life* and *Sports Illustrated* to report that Wilma Rudolph had a child.

"You have to realize, this is 1960. This is taboo," Temple pointed out. "This is against the grain, black or white, but especially black. And back then, nobody knew. It was hush-hush. People up there in Clarksville [Rudolph's hometown] knew, but that was it."

Temple knew. He knew all too well. He had been to Clarksville trying to recruit Rudolph to A&I. At the 1956 Olympics, even at the age of sixteen, Rudolph had shown glimpses of her future promise by winning a bronze medal.

"When she had that baby, they kicked her to the curb up there in Clarksville," Temple remembered. "So she was determined. She wanted to prove to them that she could do it."[27]

Four years later, in 1960, once word started to circulate about this possible child of Rudolph's, the rumor made its way to the *Banner*. Nothing had been officially printed at this point, but reporters were trying to confirm the rumor. Temple remembered well the call he received from the *Banner* sports editor.

"I never will forget that Fred Russell called me up, and he said, 'Coach, I'm going to ask you a question.' I knew what was coming. He said, 'Does Wilma Rudolph have a child?' And I paused, not knowing what I was going to say," Temple recalled. "But, I said, 'Yes. She does.' And he said, 'Fine, that's all I wanted to know.'"

Years later, Temple smiled when he thought back to that conversation and what happened next.

In addition to several media outlets being aware of a possible story if they could confirm the Rudolph child rumor, so too was Governor Ellington aware of the potentially damaging story. Russell was aware that Ellington had heard rumblings of what was going on, so Russell called the governor.

It wasn't long before Temple received a return call from Russell, who reported back to him that he had spoken with the governor. The governor's message to Temple was simple: "Everything's going to be okay."

To this day, Temple does not know exactly what happened next. What he does know is that when reporters from *Life*, *Sports Illustrated*, and *Look* all descended upon Clarksville in the days ahead, no one was talking and there wasn't much to find at the hospital.

"Everything was gone. They went to the hospital, no records, not a single one. They couldn't write anything. They could talk about it, but they couldn't prove anything," Temple said.

As interesting as it is to speculate on exactly what conversations took place between the governor's office and the Clarksville hospital, what's more remarkable is how the reporters had the real proof literally right under their noses.

Temple recalled how the reporters went to Rudolph's house when they couldn't turn up anything at the hospital.

"Wilma came from a large family, and they had an old broken-down house, and the kids were all there playing on the floor," Temple said with a laugh. "She had sisters and brothers who had kids there playing that day. Reporters were there talking to Wilma, and there were so many kids there, they didn't even know that her child was right there with her."

Years later, reflecting on those times, Temple realized how times have changed.

"Nowadays, it's not that big of a deal. A woman can have a child today, run tomorrow, and make a million dollars the next day," the retired track coach noted. "But back then, this story was never known, and it certainly wasn't in the papers. Until she died, Wilma and I talked a lot about this, and she knew how it had really played out. She knew that I had told Mr. Russell, and that Mr. Russell had called the governor. She knew that and really appreciated it."[28]

While Temple speaks with unbridled passion and respect for Russell, he was not the only who remembered some of the behind-the-scenes actions that the sports editor felt compelled to do.

Eddie Jones was with the *Banner* for two stints of service, his first back in the 1950s, and his second from 1987 to 1998 as the paper's editor. Long before the events with Coach Temple and the TSU women's track program played out, Jones knew such things were part of Russell's character. He knew where Russell placed his priorities, regardless of political or social stereotypes.

"His interests went far beyond sports, and he was a very influential person in the power circles of Nashville," Jones said of Russell. "He cared about what kind of city we had, and wanted to know what the *Banner* could do to influence the future."[29]

As for Russell's involvement with the governor and TSU, working to make sure the right thing was done, that didn't surprise Jones in the least.

"That's the kind of thing Russell would do. The interesting thing about that is that the *Banner*, in the minority community, was perceived pretty much as being a redneck segregationist rag," Jones acknowledged. "And the *Tennessean* was the liberal champion of everybody's rights. So here was this newspaper pulling off a deal that their buddies at the *Tennessean* either wouldn't or couldn't do."[30]

Wally Butts versus the *Saturday Evening Post*

Not since the Chicago White Sox threw the 1919 World Series has there been a sports story as shocking as this one. This is the story of one fixed game of college football.

Before the University of Georgia played the University of Alabama last September 22, Wally Butts, athletic director of Georgia, gave Paul (Bear) Bryant, head coach of Alabama, Georgia's plays, defensive patterns, all the significant secrets Georgia's football team possessed.

The corrupt here were not professional ballplayers gone wrong, as in the 1919 Black Sox scandal. The corrupt here were not disreputable gamblers, as in the scandals continually afflicting college basketball. The corrupt here were two men—Butts and Bryant—employed to educate and to guide young men.

How prevalent is the fixing of college football games? How often do teachers sell out their pupils? We don't know—yet. For now, we can only be appalled.[1]

—*Saturday Evening Post*, story cover box (23 March 1963)

In no other period during his illustrious sportswriting career did Fred Russell's legal background and interest in the law serve him better than during mid-August 1963. Russell spent two weeks in Atlanta covering the sensational Wally Butts versus the *Saturday Evening Post* libel case. It just so happened that his old friend and golfing legend Bobby Jones had his own attorney's office near the courthouse.

"Bob Jones's office was between the hotel where we were staying and the old Hansley Federal Courthouse, about three blocks from there. His secretary called me and told me that if I got a chance to drop by, a couple of afternoons a week, he would love to keep up with the trial, and I didn't miss that. Tuesdays and Thursdays, I would stay about 45 minutes or an hour, because he wanted to know everything about the trial. The arthritis had hit him so hard, it was just impossible for him to hold a glass—but I wouldn't be there more than two minutes, and he would punch a button on his desk, and not say anything to anyone; but in about five minutes, his secretary would arrive with two double martinis, every time, which I loved."[2]

* * *

The sensational editorial quote that begins this chapter was a turning point in the twentieth-century history of the iconic magazine in which it appeared, the *Saturday Evening Post*. At the close of the nineteenth century and through the first half of the twentieth, the *Post* had risen to enormous popularity across the United States. The *Post* provided a balanced mix of current events, sports, politics, humor, and general human interest news to its readers, and it was a successful formula for many years. Writers asked to freelance for the *Post* gained instant credibility, not to mention a national audience for their work.

In the 1950s, however, with an increase in competition as well as additional media outlets (most notably, television) being available to its consumers, readership in the *Post* began to dwindle. By the early 1960s, new ownership was in place at the *Post*, and in an effort to increase its circulation, the *Post* adopted a new strategy, one based on risky, sensational journalism. The goal was to attract readers with splashy, shocking headlines, and its brazen new editor-in-chief justified it as "sophisticated muckraking." The facts would work themselves out in the end, according to this strategy, and in the meantime, the American public would be more inclined to buy the magazine due to its remarkable stories.

The approach could not have backfired more. It was a disaster. The *Post* faced multiple libel suits in the 1960s, as numerous subjects in the magazine's articles sought legal action to repudiate the *Post*'s accusations and to restore their names. When punitive damages in the millions of dollars were levied against the *Post*, the magazine slowly lost financial credibility, not to mention its journalistic integrity. In early 1969, the magazine announced that it would be ceasing publication after 148 years. While the *Post* would be revived in the 1970s as a bi-weekly magazine with a more nostalgic feel, its days as a leading weekly publication ended when it shut down in 1969.

More than any other singular event, it was a story within the 23 March 1963, issue of the *Post* that triggered its demise. The story alleged corruption in college football, and it involved two schools—Georgia and Alabama—from the Southeastern Conference. Specifically, the story alleged that Alabama's head coach Paul Bryant and Georgia's athletic director (and recently dismissed football coach) Wally Butts conspired in such a way that Butts gave Bryant inside, secret information on how Alabama could beat the Bulldogs. If true, the story would send shockwaves throughout college football. Not surprisingly, the football men in question, Butts and Bryant, quickly renounced the article and filed separate libel lawsuits against the *Saturday Evening Post*.

It took more than four months for the legal proceedings to play out, and in August 1963, a two-week trial in Atlanta captivated the nation, especially those interested in college football in the South.

Fred Russell: The Perfect Reporter to Cover the Trial

During the 1950s and early 1960s, there was no greater authority on college football in the South, especially in the SEC, than the *Nashville Banner*'s Fred Russell. Russell was intimately familiar with both programs, and had known Coach Butts and Coach Bryant for years, Bryant in particular since he had been an assistant at Vanderbilt in the late 1930s. Coupled with his background and interest in law, Russell was immediately fascinated by the story and its implications, if true.

The fact that Russell had strong ties to the *Saturday Evening Post* added an element of intrigue to his position as 1963 trial reporter. Russell penned his first feature story for the *Post* in 1939, and then from 1949 to 1962, he authored his nationally acclaimed "Pigskin Preview" for the *Post* each summer. In it, he previewed the upcoming college football season. By the time the Butts-Bryant story broke in March 1963, he had over twenty-five years of canvassing the college football landscape, building relationships with coaches across the country, and covering the gridiron at the collegiate level.

When it became obvious that a trial was going to happen, it was an easy decision for the publisher of the *Banner*, Jimmy Stahlman, to send Russell to Atlanta, where the trial would take place. Russell arrived in early August, and was there for two straight weeks. Whether by design or just good fortune, he stayed in the same hotel and on the same floor as the attorneys for Wally Butts. As the trial wore on, Russell befriended the attorneys—who knew how much Butts thought of Russell—and it wasn't long before Russell was able to gather inside information from the Butts camp regarding the case.

In short, when Butts's suit against the *Post* came to trial in August 1963, no journalist was better equipped or positioned than Fred Russell to cover the proceedings. He possessed legal instincts that allowed him to break the case down to its basics, he had unquestioned knowledge of the sport itself, and he had relationships with participants on both sides of the case. During his two weeks covering the case, Russell wrote daily reports of the proceedings, and wired them back to Nashville for the following day's paper.

For two weeks straight, the veteran journalist did not disappoint. In the 1960s, even with national radio and TV, the gritty details of major sports stories were still confined to the sports sections of newspapers. With his trial updates and sidebar stories as well as his "Sidelines" column, Russell showcased his skills as an investigative reporter, sports journalist, and effective columnist. Having already secured national recognition through his years as a writer for the *Saturday Evening Post*, he further cemented his name at the national level with his Atlanta courthouse reporting. Russell's articles were widely quoted in newspapers throughout the United States, and the private interview he obtained with one of the jurors at the end of the trial was picked up by major newspapers across the country as well.

During the course of the trial, Russell reported on the tense drama that existed in the Atlanta courtroom, from the testimony provided by Butts and Bryant through the final statements by both sides, up until the verdict itself. Along the way, Russell articulated the inconsistencies and contradictions of the case as well as posed insightful questions in his columns regarding the trial and the legal strategies employed by the attorneys on each side of the case. More than anything, Russell ultimately expressed an utter disbelief in the shameful, incomplete reporting by the authors of the story and the complete lack of editorial integrity on behalf of its editors at the *Post*.

The Butts trial remains a fascinating subject almost fifty years after the events took place. What also warrants attention is a closer look at the journalists who were involved with the story in the first place, and why the questions Russell asked then are still captivating today. Specifically, Russell honed in on several journalistic issues that troubled him throughout the trial, most notably the questionable reporting, the seemingly apparent lack of basic fact-checking, and an almost shameless commitment by the *Post* to run with a story that could have far-reaching consequences, regardless of whether or not the story was true. Because of the coaches involved as well as the reporters who pulled the story together, these issues still illicit passionate feelings in the twenty-first century from not only casual fans who remember the sensational case that summer, but from fellow journalists who also covered the trial and even some of the family members themselves.

Some of the more compelling questions regarding the reporting of the 1963 *Post* article are:

- Why did the *Saturday Evening Post* assign the story to a writer (Frank Graham, Jr.) who had no experience covering football, let alone college football in the South, where the sport is a religion unto itself?
- What was the level of involvement of Atlanta sports editor Furman Bisher? Why might Bisher still deny any involvement in the story, despite the fact that Graham not only provided sworn testimony in a 1963 deposition to the contrary, but also reiterated Bisher's involvement more than forty years later in a personal interview for this book?
- Why were several other journalists or former colleagues only willing to discuss details of Bisher's involvement off the record?

September 1962: The Season-Opener and an Overhead Phone Call Eight Days Prior

Needed first is background on the game of 22 September itself, as well as the famous conversation that occurred eight days prior to the contest. Activities during these eight days, coupled with overzealous reporting by men who may have wanted to make a story rather than cover one, ultimately led the *Post* to run its story the following spring.

In the infamous 23 March issue, the *Post* ran a story entitled, "The Story of a College Football Fix: A Shocking Report of How Wally Butts and 'Bear' Bryant Rigged a Game Last Fall." It was a scathing article, and its author, Frank Graham, Jr., and the *Post*'s editors accused Butts (Georgia's former coach but current athletic director) and Bryant (Alabama's coach) of conspiring to "fix" the September 1962 game between the two Southeastern Conference schools. In its editorial text box that opened the story, the *Post* compared the case to baseball's Black Sox scandal of 1919, calling the two coaches "corrupt" and accusing them of selling out the young people they were paid to teach.

The two teams had met in late September to open the season, playing at Alabama's Legion Field. Alabama won convincingly, 35–0. Although the Crimson Tide was a 16- to 17-point favorite in the game, it was nonetheless the first game for both teams, and it was not immediately known how much better Alabama would be than Georgia. As the season played out, Alabama ended up being one of the nation's best teams. Coach Bryant's team finished the 1962 season with a 10–1 record and was the number-five ranked team in the country. Georgia, on the other hand, had a mediocre seasons and finished 3–4–3 in 1962.

Was the season-opener fixed? Or, as the season records reflect for that year, was Alabama simply a more talented team that dominated its weaker, inexperienced opponent? And what could possibly have occurred within a year's time of that game that led the *Post* to publish such a story in the first place?

These questions would never have even been asked if it wasn't for an insurance man from Atlanta named George Burnett. More than three months after the Alabama-Georgia game, Burnett came forward in January 1963 with allegations that he had overhead a telephone conversation between Alabama coach Bryant and Georgia athletic director Butts. Burnett claimed that eight days before the game itself, he overhead Butts providing Bryant with inside information on how Alabama could more easily beat the Bulldogs. According to Burnett, on 14 September a telephone operator had inadvertently connected his call with one between Butts and Bryant. Burnett stayed on the line when he heard the two men discussing college football, and eventually made handwritten notes of the conversation when it appeared to him that the two football men were discussing strategy about the upcoming game between the two schools.

According to the article in the *Post*, Burnett was stunned and somewhat frightened at what he had just heard, and after consulting with a friend, opted to do nothing. He stuffed the notes in a drawer at his home, where they remained until Burnett felt compelled to share his story several months later. In January, he shared his story with a friend who had played college football years before with Georgia's current coach, Johnny Griffith. It wasn't long before Griffith took the information seriously enough to meet with Burnett. In order to discuss the validity and accuracy of what Burnett alleged, Griffith and other Georgia university officials met with the insurance salesman on several occasions. According to Burnett, the university's initial interest led to harsher questioning of his motives, in part because he had admitted to a history of financial troubles. As described in the *Post*'s article, in order to protect his side of the story, Burnett opted to obtain an attorney in the matter. A decision was made to contact the *Saturday Evening Post* about the notes he possessed, and by mid-February, the *Post* decided to send one of its New York-based writers, Frank Graham, Jr., to Atlanta to learn more about the story's potential. Within a couple of days, an agreement was struck between the *Post* and Barnett, and he sold the rights to his story to the magazine for $5,000. Four weeks later, the 23 March issue hit the newsstands, and true or not, the story was public.

It did not take long for both Butts and Bryant to deny the accusations. They admitted talking in advance of the game, which both admitted doing often with each other and other coaches around the conference leading up to a game. As far as Butts intentionally sharing confidential information to help Alabama, both coaches vehemently denied those allegations, and each almost immediately filed lawsuits against the Curtis Publishing Company, which published the *Saturday Evening Post*. The coaches filed individual lawsuits, and as the legal proceedings played out over the summer, Butts's $10 million libel suit was scheduled to be tried first. Opening proceedings in the case began 5 August 1963, and reporters descended upon Atlanta to cover the drama firsthand.

The Trial: Wallace Butts versus Curtis Publishing Company

Fred Russell was one of the many reporters who arrived in Atlanta to cover the once-in-a-lifetime trial. So was one of his peers, Edwin Pope from the *Miami Herald*, who remembered how his friend, known throughout the industry for his sense of humor as much as his sportswriting talent, approached the trial.

"There wasn't much humor in that trial, and he was very close with both Bryant and Butts. Fred took that trial much more serious than he took anything else," Pope recalled.[3]

On the first day of the trial, Russell's report in his *Banner* "Sidelines" column set the stage. The jury would be selected that first day, and Curtis Publishing Company would present its case first, with all signs pointing to its star witness, insurance salesman George Burnett, going to the stand first to testify. Russell closed his opening-day column by cutting to the heart of the matter:

"Most unusual, perhaps unprecedented, is the fact that the case is based on scratch-pad notes from an allegedly overhead telephone conversation. Butts and Bryant do not deny having talked by telephone about a week before the Sept. 22 game. They do deny having discussed any Georgia football secrets.

"In an issue earlier this summer, the Post in a full-page editorial repeated its belief that the game was rigged and that it had printed the truth. Whatever the outcome of this trial, it is in my opinion the most important sports story of the year.[4]"

As Russell reported the following day (Tuesday, 6 August 1963), when Burnett took the stand to open the trial, it became immediately clear to Russell that there were some significant holes in the *Post*'s story, starting with Burnett as the primary source for the story. Under cross-examination by Butts's lawyer, Burnett testified that the *Post* never actually saw his handwritten notes, and when he was questioned by Frank Graham, Jr., he spoke from memory of the overheard conversation, roughly four months *after* the Bryant-Butts phone call took place. Furthermore, Burnett testified under oath that he never made one of the lengthy quotes attributed to him in the *Post*'s story.

After these revelations, Russell's succinct summation in his column that day: "Where then, did Frank Graham, Jr., get such information—or misinformation? Graham will be asked that, I suppose, when he testifies."[5]

As Russell reported the following day, however, Graham would not be called to testify. In fact, in a surprising move, it became clear that no editorial representative of the *Post* would appear as a witness. It would be one of the *Post*'s more critical legal blunders. Instead, the *Post*'s lawyers opted to call Georgia coach Johnny Griffith to the stand.

The strategy blew up in their faces.

In the original March 1963 article, Griffith was quoted as saying to Burnett, after he had read Burnett's notes, that the Georgia coaching staff had figured somebody had given Georgia's plays to Alabama, "but we had no idea it was Wally Butts."[6]

Under cross-examination, as Russell pointed out in his daily column, Griffith testified that he never made such a statement to Burnett. More damning to the story was Griffith's denial on the stand that he had gone to university officials, as stated in the *Post*'s story, told them what he had learned from Burnett, nor threatened to resign if Butts wasn't fired as athletic director. Russell summed up his coverage on the Georgia coach's testimony with the following:

"The *Post* article quoted Griffith as saying bitterly to a friend after the 35–0 defeat by Alabama: 'I never had a chance, did I? I never had a CHANCE.'

"On the stand, Griffith testified: 'I never told anyone this.'

"And Griffith appeared in the trial as a witness for Curtis.[7]"

In his writings from Atlanta, Russell clearly was baffled by such developments in the trial. It almost seemed as if each time someone who was quoted in the story went on the stand to testify, he admitted inaccuracies in the story's quotes or that the quotes were complete fabrications. During the opening days of the trial, Russell continued to question the *Post*'s reporting, as he noted several times in his columns, "Where did the *Post* get this?"[8] and "Where did the *Post* get info on denied quotes?"[9]

Russell expected the author of the story, Frank Graham, Jr., to shed light on this question. Even though Graham was never called to testify, he nonetheless provided some startling information to jurors, lawyers, and reporters. Part of Graham's official deposition was read into the court record on the afternoon of Wednesday, 7 August. When he had finished recording and summarizing Graham's startling deposition comments, Russell labeled this section of his next day's column, "Shocking Revelations by Author."[10]

In his deposition, Graham detailed what happened after he arrived in Atlanta on 21 February 1963. He learned about the handwritten notes and began to negotiate with Burnett's attorney for their purchase. Graham interviewed Burnett, was promised that the notes would be rushed to New York, and then returned to New York to write the story.

The notes never arrived, however, Graham explained in his deposition. As it turned out, when Burnett had first gone to university officials in mid-January to explain the conversation he had overheard, Burnett gave the notes to an attorney, Cook Barwick, representing the University of Georgia Athletic Association. So all Graham had for his story was an interview with Burnett that was four months removed from the incident he claimed that was so damning to both Butts and Bryant.

In the final paragraphs of his Thursday, 8 August, column, Russell recapped additional key points from Graham's deposition. When the courtroom learned that Graham was not working alone, more pieces to the puzzle of how the original article came to be slowly emerged:

"Graham, back in New York with only the affidavit as a basis for the story, went to a library and from newspaper files copied names of leading players on the 1962 Georgia and Alabama teams. Obviously, it was a rush job.

"Meanwhile, another person was getting into the act, Graham revealed in his deposition. [Furman] Bisher, sports editor of the *Atlanta Journal*, heard about Burnett's notes from Barwick, Graham testified. He went to New York Feb. 24, and sought to interest the *Post* in the story.

"Advised that the *Post* already had the story, a deal was made for Bisher to assist Graham. The deposition states: 'Bisher said he would go back [to Atlanta], get more information, talk to more people.' And later: 'I decided Bisher would have a better chance to interview.'"[11]

The Perfect Storm: The *Post*, Bear Bryant, and Furman Bisher

When Graham's deposition at the August 1963 trial confirmed that the New York reporter was not working by himself on the Butts-Bryant article, Russell was able to connect a few more dots. Since the article had been published in March, speculation had been rampant within the sportswriting fraternity regarding the sources, authorship, and validity of the story. The *Post* had sent a Northern reporter unfamiliar with football into the college football-crazed South, and the story that came out of it was as sensational as the phone conversation upon which it was based. In his daily articles from Atlanta during the first week of the trial, Russell was already expressing disbelief and anger at the inaccuracies and misquotations that were prevalent throughout the *Post* article. When the Nashville sportswriter learned through Graham's sworn deposition that Graham had been assisted by Furman Bisher, an additional aspect of this case came into focus.

The name Furman Bisher was not an unfamiliar one to Fred Russell. The two sportswriters had both been covering sports in the South for decades. Russell was almost a dozen years older than Bisher, who had been born in November 1918. Just as Russell had done before him, Bisher procured additional freelance work with the *Post* when possible. The Atlanta sportswriter never obtained the lofty status or national following that Russell had with his annual "Pigskin Preview" for the *Post*, but Bisher did author a handful of feature baseball stories for the *Post* in the 1950s.

Then came an October 1962 article that Bisher wrote for the *Post* entitled "College Football Is Going Berserk." In it, Bisher commented on what he perceived to be an increasing trend in the "brutality" of the college game. Specifically, Bisher criticized the teachings of a particular SEC coach, claiming that this coach deliberately taught his players to be as violent as necessary, using whatever tactics on the field were needed.

Who was this coach? Paul Bryant, coach at Alabama.

Bisher's evidence was a vicious hit that an Alabama player (Darwin Holt) applied to a Georgia Tech player (Chuck Graning) the prior season, back in November 1961. Bisher wrote predominantly and favorably for Georgia Tech in those days, as did many reporters in that generation when they were covering their hometown teams. Because of the hit, Graning suffered a concussion and a broken jaw, among other injuries, and when no penalty was called, the Georgia Tech faithful considered it an atrocity. So did the Atlanta media, Furman Bisher included.

For Russell, as he sat in that Atlanta courtroom in August 1963, observing a trial that Bryant was knee-deep in the middle of, he could not help but think back to Bisher's October 1962 article. Complicating matters was that Coach Bryant had not ignored that article. Just the opposite, in fact: Bryant had sued the *Saturday Evening Post* and Furman Bisher for libel.

As Russell tried to make sense of all the connections, he artfully shared his concerns and thoughts in his daily writings from Atlanta. Once Graham confirmed in his deposition that Bisher was involved, Russell started to believe that the *Post* may have gotten in over its head by running too quickly with the Butts-Bryant "game-fixing" story. One week into the trial, Russell realized that the *Post* would need to act quickly to regain momentum in the trial.

"My assumption is that [Post lawyers] saw the Saturday Evening Post article which is the basis of this suit before it was published. Indeed, lawyers were in on the sale and purchase of the raw material, which turned out to be an affidavit from George Burnett recalling from memory an alleged overhead telephone conversation between Butts and Bryant.

The Post thought it was going to get Burnett's scratch-pad notes, but they were in possession of Cook Barwick, attorney for the University of Georgia Athletic Association.

Sitting here, I keep wondering how interested the Post would have been in buying Burnett's affidavit if it had not involved Bryant. Bryant had brought a $500,000 libel suit against the Post last Jan. 4 for an October 20, 1962, article by Furman Bisher, on grounds that he had been charged with 'condoning brutality among Alabama football players.'"[12]

Right or wrong, Bisher's October 1962 article cemented the status of his future relationship with Bryant, which is to say, there was no relationship. Bryant banned Bisher from ever attending another one of his practices, and did not want the Atlanta reporter anywhere near Alabama's campus or his football team.

As for the Butts-Bryant trial of 1963, the disclosure of Bisher's involvement in the story and his support of Graham in gathering information could not have helped matters for the *Saturday Evening Post*. Jurors learned that not only had Graham been paid $2,000 for writing the article, but Bisher had collected $1,000 from the *Post* for his role in it. The *Post*'s entire case was predicated on factual, unbiased reporting in the 23 March 1963 *Post* article that alleged corruption between Butts and Bryant. However, not only were there blatant misquotations and inaccuracies that emerged during the trial, but through Graham's deposition, the jury learned that the author's inside source for information for the article (Bisher) was the author of another article in the *Post* that had prompted

115

one of the coaches (Bryant) in this trial to sue the *Post* for half a million dollars.

Needless to say, as Russell painted the picture for his readers, there were concerns over multiple conflicts of interest with regard to the *Post*, its editors, and the writers of the 23 March story.

As the trial neared the end of its second and final week, Russell tried to step back from all that he had learned and assess where things stood before the case was handed to the jury. In his opening paragraph on Monday, 19 August, Russell acknowledged that remaining unbiased had not been easy. He had written thirty-plus stories for the *Post* and had known Wally Butts since 1939. As he pondered how the jury might rule in the case, Russell's legal instincts and journalistic integrity converged, and he pulled no punches:

"Most shocking, disturbing revelation during the trial, for me, would be the incredibly loose, slip-shod, careless, irresponsible job the *Post* did in preparing the story. To have published a routine, harmless *Post* article on such little proof and with such hasty, shallow preparation would have been surprising. To have printed such a story which could ruin the lives of two men was unthinkable.

"After listening to other *Post* depositions, by author Frank Graham, Jr., and editors Roger Kahn and Davis Thomas, I would be most puzzled why Furman Bisher, *Atlanta Journal* sports editor, wasn't put on the witness stand by the defense. Even Judge [Lewis] Morgan from the bench expressed puzzlement when excerpts were read from a Bisher deposition in which he denied supplying specific pieces of information.

"'Isn't this man here in Atlanta,' the judge asked. 'Couldn't he be brought to testify as to these things?'

"There were many conflicts in Bisher's deposition and those of *Post* editors. As a juror, I would wonder why no one who had a hand in preparing the *Post* article appeared in person to defend it or explain it."[13]

The Verdict and the Fallout

Attorneys for both sides wrapped up their closing arguments Monday morning, 19 August. In his column that day, Russell expressed his opinion on where things stood: "As a juror, I would vote to award both general and punitive damages to Butts."[14]

Deliberations began Monday afternoon and resumed the next morning. By mid-morning, 20 August, the jury had reached its verdict, and it was in favor of Butts. General damages were in the amount of $60,000. Punitive damages were in the amount of a staggering $3,000,000. As witnesses in the courtroom described the moment, there was an audible gasp, followed by joy and relief for Wally Butts, and complete shock for the lawyers for the *Saturday Evening Post*.

In his final two articles from Atlanta, Fred Russell shared an exclusive interview with one of the jurors in the trial (Tuesday, 20 August), and then summarized his final thoughts on the case in his "Sidelines" column the following day. The "juror interview" article was picked up off the wire and published nationally, and in it, readers learned that deliberations did not take long because of a debate over the *Post*'s guilt. It was the amount to tender in punitive damages.

Ultimately, what led the jury to levy such a significant sum was the reckless, unprofessional behavior of the *Post*. This was what had bothered Russell the most throughout the trial, the way in which the article's authors and editors had rushed this story to publication before thoroughly checking the facts. When asked about where the *Post* fell short in its legal defense of the case, the juror confirmed one of the other issues that had puzzled Russell:

Juror: "I never could understand why Furman Bisher wasn't put on the stand to testify as to some of the information the Post said he furnished which certain witnesses testified was inaccurate or misquotations."[15]

The following day, in his closing "Sidelines" column from Atlanta, Russell admitted that the two weeks of reporting was the most demanding experience he had known as a newspaperman, but also the most satisfying. Waiting for the clerk to read the verdict was one of his "all-time suspenseful moments."

At the same time, Russell offered his own theory on how a relatively innocuous 35–0 Alabama blowout of Georgia in September 1962 led to a $3,000,000 award the following August to the disgraced former Georgia coach. It involved Alabama football, but it began back in 1961, not 1962.

"As this tragedy in sports ended, I thought of another eventful moment, the moment when it at all started. The place was Legion Field in Birmingham, on November 18, 1961. Had that foul not been committed by Holt, I doubt if there ever would have been what's now known throughout the country as the 'Butts-Bryant' thing. It was the Holt-Graning incident which triggered an October 1962 *Saturday Evening Post* article on football brutality. Bryant sued for $500,000."[16]

The fallout from that 1961 game involved the same sportswriter who the judge himself had inquired about during the Butts-Bryant trial: Furman Bisher. And Russell's implication in his own closing argument was clear. If Bisher had never gone after Bryant in his "brutality" article, Bryant would not have sued the *Post*. If Bryant had not sued the *Post* for the October 1962 article, the *Post* may not have been so inclined to jump (perhaps too hastily) on the Butts-Bryant story when it first came to the magazine's attention.

Several years later, Bryant acknowledged how he let the October 1962 article get to him, and in retrospect, his reaction just added fuel to the fire.

"It was a mistake. If I hadn't sued the *Post* on that one, I don't believe there'd ever have been the second story," Bryant told *Sports Illustrated* in late summer 1966. "You challenge somebody on one pack of lies and you wind up with a bigger pack of lies. They must have started working on that right after we filed the suit."[17]

In the immediate aftermath of the August trial, the *Post*'s lawyers, as expected, appealed the verdict. While Curtis Publishing never won any of its appeals to re-try the case, a federal court ruling did lower the punitive damages awarded to Butts to $460,000. Butts agreed to the settlement, in large part because the alternative—having to go back to court on this subject—would have been too painful.

As for Paul Bryant and his two libel suits against the *Post*, one from the October 1962 article by Furman Bisher, and one from the March 1963 article by Frank Graham, the Alabama coach settled out of court, mostly to avoid having to go to court himself and further subject his team, the university, and his family to the distraction. As Bryant stated to *Sports Illustrated*, "I settled for $300,000, and after I paid all my creditors I had a little left over to buy Mother a new dress."[18]

The trial also brought closure to Fred Russell's relationship with the *Saturday Evening Post* as well. From 1949 to 1962, Russell had authored his annual college football preview, the "Pigskin Preview." When the Butts-Bryant story broke in March 1963, he started to have reservations about being affiliated with the magazine. Its new editorial slant, "sophisticated muckraking," as Editor-in-Chief Clay Blair liked to call it, ran completely counter to Russell's style of fact-based, respectful journalism. The events and disclosures during the two-week trial did little to ease Russell's concern about the magazine's new direction or his perception of its journalistic integrity. Upon his return to Nashville after the verdict, Russell vowed to family and friends that he would never write for the *Saturday Evening Post* again. True to his word, he never did.

Setting the Record Straight

Over the years, the sensational *Wally Butts versus the Saturday Evening Post* case has generated no short supply of opinions and articles. At the time, in response to his reporting of the trial, Russell received acclaim nationwide, even from the judge of the trial himself. Upon returning to Nashville, Russell sent copies of his daily coverage to Lewis Morgan, the U.S. district judge who presided over the Butts-Bryant proceedings. In a letter dated just days after the trial ended, Morgan wrote to Russell on 27 August 1963. "Your daily approach to this trial is the finest reportorial job I have ever been privileged to read," Morgan wrote. "If you should ever see fit to write a book on the trial, I am sure it would outsell any legal drama ever written." [19]

While Russell never did write such a book, players, coaches, reporters, and even family members who were present in the courtroom or knew the participants as well as Russell are still fascinated by the case. Interestingly enough, the subject that generates more discussion and elicits stronger emotions than any other aspect of the case is the 23 March story itself, who wrote it, and why it was published.

Most relevant to this book is how accurate and insightful Fred Russell was at the time of the trial, as he focused on the poor journalism done by the *Post*. That was the heart of the case, and for Russell—an editor known for his obsessive behavior regarding attention to detail, thorough research, and precise journalism—it was only natural for him to concentrate on the libel aspect of the case. Nothing bothered Russell more than learning of the shameless, reckless, and irresponsible reporting that occurred. Even though he had long-standing friendships with Butts and Bryant, Russell's concern was not whether or not they had conspired to fix the game. Sure, he had his opinion on that matter, but Russell's focus at the trial was on the lawsuit itself, the merits of which had to do with whether or not the *Post*'s article was factual or libelous. The fact that the article was not factual and that there were multiple inaccuracies, limited fact-checking, and numerous misquotations led Russell to focus his criticism on the article's writers and editors.

Years later, what remains a lightning rod for discussion and emotion is the *Post*'s shoddy journalism, its use of a reporter who knew almost nothing about football, and its seemingly blind reliance on information provided by an Atlanta sports editor with a clear conflict of interest.

In 1986, almost twenty-five years after the trial, James Kirby published *Fumble*, a personal account of the trial, the events that led up to August 1963, and the legal proceedings that followed. Kirby was the attorney from Vanderbilt appointed by the SEC commissioner's office to be its official observer of the trial, and he sat in the same courtroom as Russell for the two-week case.

As a lawyer himself, Kirby offered a detailed and thorough look at the legal aspects of the case, specifically focusing on the strategies employed by both Butts's counsel (led by William Schroder) and the *Post*'s lawyers (led by Wellborn Cody). For as much praise as he gives to Schroder and his team, Kirby levies an even greater amount of criticism on the legal team representing Curtis Publishing. In his final analysis, Kirby argued that the *Post*'s lawyers so fumbled the defense for the *Saturday Evening Post*, and made so many errors in preparation, strategy, and execution, that any new trial of the case would have resulted in a better outcome for the *Post*.

Just as Russell and many others had questioned during the trial itself in 1963, Kirby reiterated that the *Post* made a critical, tactical error in not calling several key witnesses, one of whom was Furman Bisher, the aforementioned sports editor for the *Atlanta Journal*.

As Russell had speculated during the August reporting, Kirby acknowledged that it was Bisher's connection to Bryant that was the basis for the *Post*'s actions (or inactions) at the trial. "The malice issue may account for the *Post*'s decision not to call Bisher," Kirby wrote. "Since he was a codefendant in Bryant's pending libel suit based on the brutality article, his incentive to discredit Bryant and lessen Bryant's chances of winning the first suit was undeniable."[20]

It seemed a logical reason not to put Bisher on the stand and subject him to cross-examination that could further expose a conflict of interest to the jury. As time has shown as well, the tension between Bisher and Bryant was real. Bryant never covered up the fact that he had little respect for the Atlanta sportswriter, and he never did allow Bisher to attend another one of his practices.

Years later, Delbert Reed, a veteran sportswriter for the *Tuscaloosa News* during the majority of Bryant's Alabama years, was working on a biography of Bryant and reached out to Bisher for his assessment of Bryant as a coach. The short reply from the Atlanta sportswriter left little doubt how things stood: "Del, if there is any person, dead or alive, about whom I would never comment, it is Bryant."[21]

Of course, Furman Bisher was not the only person directly associated with the story who did not testify at the August 1963 trial. What about Frank Graham, Jr., the person whose byline appeared with the infamous story? Why wasn't Graham called to the stand?

In a compelling interview for this book, more than forty years after the trial, Graham provided some insight on that matter. About a year after the trial, Graham met with Schroder. Graham himself was curious as to why he wasn't called to the stand, by either the *Post*'s lawyers or Butts's counsel, which had been led by Schroder.

"I said to him, I never understood why I wasn't asked to appear at the trial, or why I wasn't named in the suit," Graham commented. "Schroder said, 'Well, you know, we always thought that the *Post* had just used your name and that Furman had written the story. We just never believed that you had written the story.'"[22]

As Graham confirmed, Schroder's instincts were in line with the *Post*'s initial thinking.

"I didn't know very much about football at the time, let alone Southeastern Conference football. I was completely ignorant of anything that had gone on before, or any of the characters, knew none of that," Graham admitted. "The original idea was to have Bisher do it, but the lawyers decided that wasn't a good idea, because the *Post* was already being sued for something Bisher had done."[23]

As it was decided then, Graham would be the official author of the story, but he would need support from Bisher in gathering football information. He admitted to these facts in both his deposition in May 1963 as well as again when interviewed in 2006.

Graham rushed that first draft on 24 February, never interviewing a coach or a player in Atlanta, basing his initial article purely on the affidavit from Burnett as well as information he could find in the library on the game itself. Burnett later testified at the trial that he did not speak with Graham again once the *Post* reporter left Atlanta and returned to New York. Years later, Graham recalled the night he wrote that story and expressed his dismay at how quickly the *Post* wanted to get the story in the magazine.

"I remember I sat down and wrote the story overnight. I typed out the story on a stool in this apartment we had rented, and they were all excited about the story," Graham said, adding that he knew at the time that the *Post*'s editors had not thoroughly fact-checked the piece. The outline of the story was checked by lawyers, but that was it, not the detailed facts.[24]

Just as it was recorded in Graham's deposition, Kirby in his book confirmed that the *Post*'s sports editor, Roger Kahn, asked Furman Bisher to visit Athens, where the University of Georgia is located, and gather information, specifically from people not associated with Burnett. Kirby noted that Bisher spent a day in Athens interviewing players and Coach Griffith and then telephoned those quotes to Graham.

As for the *Post* getting confirmation on the contents of the story, even though Graham felt it had not been thoroughly checked, Kirby revealed why the *Post* may have felt comfortable with moving forward with the article. Bisher was in Florida for spring training, and the *Post* sent him an advance copy to proof.

"After Graham's article was in final form, a copy was mailed to Bisher for his corrections," Kirby wrote in his detailed account of the trial. "He had none."[25]

Emotions Still Strong Today regarding Butts Case and Furman Bisher

One of the more remarkable aspects surrounding Furman Bisher's involvement in the fateful March 1963 issue of the *Post* is that Bisher denied having any involvement. One fact that was on his side was that

Frank Graham's name was the byline associated with the story, not Bisher's. That part was true: Graham was indeed the author of the story.

To say he had no involvement, however, was a stretch. Not surprisingly, when the story blew up in the *Post*'s face and Curtis Publishing lost the Butts lawsuit, *any* reporter associated with the story would have retreated as much as possible. Despite sworn depositions read during the trial that confirmed Bisher was paid $1,000 to assist Graham, Bisher made specific efforts in the years after the trial to distance himself from the story, sharing with other colleagues that he had not been the source of the information that was fed to the *Post*.

A fellow veteran sportswriter, Edwin Pope, recalled talking with Bisher about the incident in the years that followed. "Furman always insisted that he did not, and I don't have any information to the fact that he did," Pope said in late 2005. "It's one of those things that will forever be clouded in mystery."[20]

Jesse Outlar, the longtime Atlanta sports columnist who eventually became editor at the *Atlanta Constitution*, was there for the trial and remembered discussing Bisher's involvement with Russell, wondering why Judge Morgan didn't just call Bisher to the stand himself, to find out once and for all.

"Furman always told me he didn't have anything to do with it, but there was no doubt he had a hell of a lot to do with it," Outlar said in 2006.

It wasn't just colleagues who had opinions on just how much Bisher was involved with the *Post* articles. One of Georgia's most famous football sons, Charley Trippi, is a member of the College Football Hall of Fame. He played at Georgia in the mid-1940s and then was an assistant coach for the Bulldogs from 1958 to 1962. At the August 1963 trial, Trippi testified on behalf of Coach Butts, who had hired him in 1958.

"It was very clear what transpired at that time. Furman Bisher was the instigator for getting all the information for Mr. Graham," Trippi stated in 2006. "When I was coaching at Georgia, he came around the dressing room and asked me a lot of questions about that Alabama game. I didn't know at that time that he was trying to gather information to indicate that Coach Butts fixed a game."

Despite almost fifty years having passed since the *Saturday Evening Post* articles, Trippi's feelings on the matter remain strong, specifically toward Bisher.

"I get the paper, but I completely ignore his column," Trippi said emphatically. "I have no respect for him."[27]

Clearly, feelings and emotions lingered for years after the *Post* articles, certainly much longer than Bisher could have ever imagined, especially for not officially even having his name associated with the article. The actual author, Frank Graham, recalled how this led to an odd request from the Atlanta sportswriter.

"Years later, he was still having a lot of problems because of it," Graham said of Bisher and the harsh feelings that still existed toward him regarding his role in the article. "He wrote me and asked me if I would write a letter to him, affirming that he did not have anything to do with writing the story."[28]

So what does Furman Bisher say himself?

In his 2005 book *Face to Face*, Bisher addressed the subject, but only so much as to deny that he was the author of the story. He referred to the accusations that he wrote the story as a case of "mistaken identity," and that because of the existing lawsuit that Bryant had filed against the *Post*, people came to erroneously believe that "Frank Graham, Jr." was merely a pen name for Bisher.[29]

When contacted directly in April 2006 to comment about any involvement whatsoever in the Butts-Bryant case, Bisher declined an interview on the subject, but did issue a final statement via email:

"I'm not interested in discussing the Butts-Bryant situation. I had no role," Bisher claimed. "I was never involved, dragged in by some lawyer who chose to keep me out of the courtroom, and uninvolved beyond that."[30]

Conclusion

Perhaps there is still an element of mystery to the Butts-Bryant case, after all. If nothing else, Bisher's consistent denials of involvement with the article have managed to fan the flames for those in the South who remain interested in a case that is half a century old.

The emotion still attached to Bisher all these years later, coupled with his denials, is a tangible reminder of what a sensational story it was that appeared in the *Saturday Evening Post* in March 1963. Things could not have gone worse for the *Post* in the months and years that followed, as the $3 million dollar award to Butts ultimately became a major factor in the magazine's demise in 1969. For Fred Russell, the trial was as gripping as the *Post*'s story was flimsy. His coverage during those two weeks revealed to the South and to college football fans across the country that the *Post*—once an iconic journalistic establishment of twentieth century America—had sold out to sensational, yellow journalism.

In his opening column, Russell had predicted that the trial would be "the most important sports story of the year," and it did not disappoint. What Russell could not have predicted was how accurate his speculations and reporting would be throughout the trial. Looking past whether or not Butts and Bryant did more than just share casual football talk on that infamous overheard phone conversation, Russell realized that the trial came down to journalistic integrity. Over the course of the two-week trial, Russell artfully revealed that the *Post* had abandoned such integrity in favor of a splashy headline to attract readers. In the fallout of this decision, not only did the *Post* lose big, but it became clear over time that a simple three-page article in 1963 had implications and consequences for the rest of the twentieth century for those involved.

The Elbows He Rubbed

"When I think of Fred Russell, I think it's a shame that everyone in sportswriting didn't have the same intelligence and the same class that he had. If you think of a sportswriter that had the interests of his subjects uppermost in mind, the welfare of his subjects, and above all else, honesty and accuracy in what he wrote about people in sports, all of that is the absolute definition of Fred Russell."[1] —Bobby Knight, former college basketball coach

"I think the first time that I went from being just someone in the office to having a different relationship with him was when he was going out of town and he asked me to take care of his house. I've never been more scared to death in my life, honest to God. He had a cat named Leo that he loved, and that was my responsibility, to take care of Leo. But I was petrified, thinking that the house was going to burn down. Basically, I just got a blanket and slept in this little den, because I didn't want to disturb anything. I didn't go to any other parts of the house, and I didn't want to touch anything. But there was this back sitting room, and he had these unbelievable collections of pictures. Him and Richard Nixon, him and Bear Bryant; basically anybody who was famous, especially from the South, from the 1930s on, there was a picture of them with Mr. Russell. That was fascinating."[2] —Buster Olney, former *Nashville Banner* employee, current ESPN baseball analyst

* * *

One thing that was true 100 years ago, is true today, and almost surely will be true 100 years from now is that sportswriters are afforded wonderful entrée into the lives and careers of the athletes, coaches, and teams they cover. What sets the great sportswriters apart from the rest of the pack is what they do with this opportunity.

Fred Russell made the most of his opportunity.

Outliving and certainly out-writing almost all of his contemporaries, Russell rubbed elbows with the greats of his generation, not to mention the stars of the next several generations. From the Golden Age of Sport with Jack Dempsey, Bobby Jones, and Red Grange to the more modern era of Archie Manning, Bobby Knight, and George Steinbrenner, Russell knew them all. In between, he established relationships with icons across a number of sports, whether it was football's Paul "Bear" Bryant or baseball's Sparky Anderson.

At Vanderbilt, Russell's alma mater and "home school" during his years writing for the *Nashville Banner*, he built relationships with coaches and players from the 1930s through the rest of the twentieth century.

"He had immediate entrée to coaches and others; it didn't matter who," former Vanderbilt basketball coach C. M. Newton said in 2005. "He could pick up the phone and call [Notre Dame coach] Ara Parseghian, and the call would get through. John McKay at Southern Cal, Paul Bryant at Alabama: these people knew him and trusted him and respected him. The same was true in the golfing world and the horse racing industry."[3]

How did Russell do it? During his prime, there were hundreds of sportswriters all over the country, yet Russell was in a class to himself. What set Russell apart from his peers?

Timing played a small part, but generally speaking, it was talent, tireless hard work, and respect for his profession and its cast of characters. What set Russell apart from so many of his colleagues was his ability to build genuine, respectful relationships with his subjects and then bring those relationships to life in the *Banner*. For decades, in the days before the 24/7, multi-media environment that exists today, newspapers were *the* way for the public to consume information. When readers picked up the *Nashville Banner* sports section to learn about their sports heroes (or villains), Fred Russell was there for them. And each morning they would read about the exploits of the athletes and coaches Russell covered. Many of them knew him simply as "Freddie" or, as the years went by, respectfully as "Mr. Russell."

Getting Started during the Golden Age

When Russell broke into the newspaper business in 1929, it was at the tail end of the decade often referred to as the Golden Age of Sport. Many of sports biggest names—from golf's Bobby Jones to boxing's Jack Dempsey to football's Red Grange—came to fame in the years leading up to Russell's start with the *Banner*.

As a youth, Russell's introduction to sports was with these men grabbing the headlines, and it had a profound impact. As Russell reflected in his autobiography on his developing interest in sports, any boy during those times "felt the impact of their dazzling performances and responded to their colorful personalities. I gladly attest that some of the gold rubbed off on me."[4]

Russell added that the enduring appeal of this great trio—Jones, Dempsey, and Grange—can be traced to "their humility and graciousness. I came to know them well. Each was as friendly and available to sportswriters in Nashville...as to those in New York."[5]

Jack Dempsey was the world heavyweight boxing champion from 1919 to 1926, and coming from a small town in Colorado, his fierce style inside the ring earned him the nickname the "Manassa Mauler." While Russell knew the ferocious side of the boxer, the sportswriter also became friends with Dempsey through their shared friendship with Grantland Rice. He came to know a side of Dempsey most wouldn't expect from the fighter he once described as "the deadliest killer outside the jungle."[6] Years later, in a television interview for a regular Nashville show, Russell described Dempsey as a "delightful human being," adding that "even being the savage fighter that he was, I have never known a gentler man than Jack Dempsey."[7]

Russell came to know football great Red Grange as well during his early years with the *Banner*. At that time, Grange had moved on to the professional ranks with the Chicago Bears from 1929 to 1934. In later years during the middle of the century, Grange was part of the Senior Bowl game festivities, and the two would spend time together each January at the close of the college football season. And in the 1960s and 1970s, when Russell would be in Florida for spring training, an annual visit with Grange was part of the sportswriter's trips. During those long spring days leading up to opening day, a short column on "Catching Up with the Galloping Ghost" by Russell was just as likely in a March

"Sidelines" column as a story on how the Yankees were looking before the season started. In the end, Russell's own words on Grange summed up his thoughts on the great football player: "A sportswriter's good times were enriched if he knew Red Grange."[8]

Russell had the strongest friendship with Bob Jones, which grew over the years through Jones's tournament in Augusta, Georgia—the Masters. Russell would attend the tournament almost every spring, and just as visiting Grange was part of spring training, a visit with Jones in August was a treasured ritual.

Russell and Jones remained friends until the latter's death in 1971. One of the more endearing elements of the Russell family archives in Nashville is the collection of letters from Jones that Russell saved. One of Russell's grandsons, Fred Russell Harwell, has retained these correspondences over the years, and their existence underscores the close relationship between Russell and Jones, even up to Jones's final years. When Grantland Rice died in July 1957, a letter from Jones later that month thanked Russell for mailing several of the columns written as eulogies about Rice. In the 1960s, as Jones's own debilitating illness confined him to a wheelchair, one of his letters to Russell referenced his struggles. And in late 1970, there was a friendly note regarding how he and his wife, Mary, were doing and that they hoped to see Freddie and Kay soon.

One of the more remarkable letters written by Jones was not to Russell, but about the Nashville sportswriter. The audience for this letter made for the remarkable part: the president of the United States.

In early 1958, it had been several months since the release of Russell's autobiography, *Bury Me in an Old Press Box: Good Times and Life of a Sportswriter*. Russell had sent Jones an extra copy, and Jones wrote on Russell's behalf to President Eisenhower. A few notable excerpts of the letter:

"Freddie is one of my most highly valued friends of long standing. After visiting down here with me a short while ago, he wrote and asked if I thought you would enjoy having a copy of his book. I told him that I felt certain you would have the pleasure in both reading and owning it.

Freddie has an understanding of sports, a remarkable sweetness in his appreciation of other people, and an irrepressible sense of humor which I know you will enjoy."[9]

—Robert T. Jones, Jr., 13 January 1958, letter to President Eisenhower

Jones died in December 1971, and his letters to Russell reflected his ailing health. Jones ultimately was confined to a wheelchair, and painful arthritis in his hands was one side effect of the disease that claimed his life: syringomyelia. Jones signed each of his letters simply "Bob," but as the years went by, it was evident that it became harder and harder for him to sign his name.

For Russell, Jones's dedication in maintaining their friendship in those final few years, despite his poor health, merely reinforced and strengthened his feelings for the golf legend and good friend.

College Football and the National Stage

If there was one sport which catapulted Russell from being a respected journalist at major sporting events to being a nationally known sportswriter in demand, it was college football. In the 1930s and 1940s, Russell had established himself as a leading sportswriter in the South, and through his hard work and talented reporting and writing, he put himself in a position to meet the leading sports figures of the day. Whether it was the Masters and Bobby Jones, or Red Grange and an NFL championship game, Russell slowly built his inventory of contacts one big event at a time.

As noted previously, Russell's work with the *Saturday Evening Post*, in particular his annual "Pigskin Preview" from 1949 to 1962, gave the sportswriter a national audience. Even after Russell ended his relationship with the *Post* and no longer wrote the "Pigskin Preview," his reputation as a college football authority and presence on the national stage had long since been established. When he continued his relationship with college football by serving as chairman of the Honors Court for the College Football Hall of Fame, his status was set in stone. Coaches in the second half of the twentieth century—men such as Lee Corso, Lou Holtz, and Frank Broyles, to name a few—came to know Russell not as a rising star, but as a well-respected journalist whom they could trust. For Corso and Holtz, they were just getting started, and they remembered fondly the veteran journalist who made them feel at home early in their careers.

"As a young coach, just to be in his presence, I was in awe of him," Holtz said. "I felt so much at ease with him, and he always had intelligent questions. When you picked up a national publication, it wasn't authentic unless Fred Russell was in there."[10]

Corso had similar experiences when he was an assistant coach in the 1960s before landing head coaching jobs with Louisville (1969 to 1972) and Indiana (1973 to 1982).

"The true test of a human being's character is how they treat people in their life they don't need," Corso, now a successful and popular college football broadcaster with ESPN, commented when asked about Fred Russell. "And I think of Fred Russell. When I was a lowly assistant and then struggling as a college head coach, he always treated me with respect and dignity."[11]

In Corso's opinion, one of the contributing factors to Russell's popularity and success was his approach to and respect for the game. With the benefit of experience coaching and broadcasting, Corso sees how that is rare in the twenty-first century.

"Russell was low-keyed, always put college football first and himself second," Corso praised. "That was rare then and unbelievable now. Nobody does that anymore."[12]

Frank Broyles coached at Arkansas during these years as well, from 1958 to 1977. Broyles served as athletic director until 2007 and is associated with Razorback sports in the same way that Russell is associated with the *Nashville Banner*. Broyles remembers how well Russell had established himself within college football during the twentieth century as well as the way in which he did it: through relationships.

"He had the most friends in the newspaper business, and I admired him and respected him more than any person in any profession," Broyles noted recently. "What he gave of himself to the game of college football was unequaled by anybody, and he did for the South what Grantland Rice did nationally."[13]

It wasn't just coaches who acknowledged Russell's positive impact on the sport. Many players, some of whom were in the SEC playing against Russell's Vanderbilt teams, still marvel at the presence the sportswriter had within college football.

Count Archie Manning among that group. The Ole Miss quarterback from the late 1960s was a two-time member of the All-SEC conference team, and when he continued his playing days in the NFL with the New Orleans Saints, Manning's relationship with Russell spanned three decades. When his sons Peyton and Eli followed in their father's footsteps to play SEC football, Manning stayed in touch with Russell a fourth decade, in the 1990s.

Jake Wallace was a good friend of Russell's in Nashville, and he recalled running into the elder Manning one time in the early 1980s. With ties to Vanderbilt (he graduated in the mid-1950s) and Augusta National, Wallace knew Russell well enough to know his impact in the world of football. Wallace found himself paired with Manning for a golf tournament in New Orleans and told him he was from Nashville.

"The first thing he wanted to ask me about was Fred Russell," Wallace commented, adding that Manning said Russell had meant a "great deal" to Manning due to the many flattering articles Russell had written about him and his family. "I thought to myself, how many sportswriters are out there today that anybody would go out of their way to say such a nice thing?"[14]

The answer is not many, but Russell was one of them. An interesting connection between Russell and the Manning family was the annual Player of the Year award within the Southeastern Conference. Russell first started awarding the conference player and coach of the year in 1933, when he noticed that the conference did not acknowledge its top player and coach. So the young sports editor used the *Nashville Banner* as a way to start the tradition, and over time, it became an annual ceremony in Nashville. The *Banner*'s Banquet of Champions event was one of the hottest sports tickets in town. Russell polled the head coaches of the conference each year and then distributed the awards at the banquet.

In 1969, Archie Manning was selected as Player of the Year, and in 1997, his son Peyton received the same honor. Both father and son acknowledged how special the award was, and for Peyton, it was a chance to be connected to his father's generation through Russell.

"I've always been a fan of history, so I enjoyed meeting him and learning about his legacy and tenure as a writer," Peyton Manning said in July 2005. "I remember my Dad telling me about how Mr. Russell covered him during his days down at Ole Miss, and how he had unique relationships with players. He was a legend off the field, and he did it the right way."[15]

Freddie and "The Bear"

When it came to college football and Russell's impressive reach within the sport, no player or coach serves as a better example than Paul Bryant. The Russell-Bryant relationship is a remarkable one, dating back to an initial train ride in 1937 and lasting close to a half-century. Remarkably, Russell had a hand in getting Bryant an assistant coach's position at Vanderbilt in 1940 before Bryant had head coaching opportunities around the country. The two men stayed in touch during Bryant's coaching stops at Maryland, Kentucky, Texas A&M, and ultimately back at Bryant's alma mater, Alabama. There were annual visits between the two men and their wives as well as countless golf matches when either Russell was in Tuscaloosa or Bryant was in Nashville. As described in chapter 7, there was the memorable but tumultuous Wally Butts-*Saturday Evening Post* trial in Atlanta in 1963, in which Russell covered the events of the two-week trial from start to finish, including the day his good friend Bryant had to testify. And in January 1983, on a day Russell would later say he would never forget, the *Banner* sports editor learned of his good friend's death. It was a friendship that had lasted almost fifty years.

Russell remembered first getting to know Bryant after the latter had graduated from Alabama and stayed on as an assistant coach. In 1937, the Crimson Tide went to the Rose Bowl, and with that game came a long trip west. Russell went to the Rose Bowl that year and had ample opportunity to visit with the young Bryant.

"On a train trip where it takes about four days to go from Birmingham to Pasadena, you really get to know people quite well," Russell recalled years later. "I was never so favorably impressed by a young coach as I was by Bryant. He just had so much personality."[16] What also made an impression on Russell was Bryant's personal path of growing up poor in Arkansas but using football as a way out of poverty.

In a "Sidelines" column dated 24 September 1981, Russell recapped these memories, noting that Bryant's eyes would moisten when talking about being four to five years old and on a mule-drawn wagon with his mother, peddling vegetables.

"I hated every minute of it," Bryant told Russell. "Just like I hated chopping cotton. Not a day passes that I don't say a prayer of gratitude for what football has meant to me."[17]

During their train ride, Bryant's humility coming out of these and other life experiences resonated with Russell.

"I remember him talking about his very first trip [to Alabama], when they were recruiting him. Coming into Tuscaloosa and seeing the university buildings and the campus, and the thoughts that went through his mind that he would never leave there."[18]

A few years later, Russell's and Bryant's paths would cross again, this time when a coaching position opened up at Russell's alma mater, Vanderbilt. After a dismal 2–7–1 season in 1939, head coach Ray Morrison left the Commodores abruptly to take the reins at Temple University in Philadelphia. It didn't take Vanderbilt long to hire Red Sanders away from Louisiana State, where he was a backfield coach.

Russell remembers what happened next very well, in part because it ends with a laugh, and in part because it resulted in Paul Bryant coming to join the coaching staff of his boyhood friend Red Sanders.

"I hadn't talked with Bryant in a little bit, and when it was announced that Red was the new head coach, I was down in Florida at baseball spring training," Russell said in an interview some years later when talking about his early connections to Bryant. "In talking to [Sanders] that night in Baton Rouge, I just mentioned to him, 'I know you certainly have got all your staff lined up, but there's a young fella at Alabama, if you should have any openings, I think he's absolutely one of the best I've ever been around, and his name's Paul Bryant.'

"Red said, 'Well, I don't know him. I'm going to get Murray Warmath as my line coach. If I don't get him, I'd like to talk to Bryant if we could get together.'

"So about quarter 'til 11 the next night," Russell continued, "[Sanders] called me down at Sanford, Florida. He said, 'I want you to say hello to my new line coach.' So I got on the phone and said something like, 'Murray, I sure hope you're going to like it in Nashville. You and Red will make a great combination.' And then a voice came through and said, 'This ain't Murray. This is Bear.'"[19]

Russell said the conversation ending with a good-natured laugh, given the fact that he had assumed Sanders had not had the opportunity to track down Bryant. In fact, though, when Warmath opted to stay at Mississippi State, Sanders followed up on Russell's recommendation. He was immediately impressed with the young coach at Alabama and hired him to be his new line coach at Vanderbilt.

Among other things, this story underscores the friendship and trust that existed between Sanders and Russell. Over the years, that same friendship and trust marked the relationship between Bryant and Russell as well. Interestingly enough, even to this day, not all sportswriters can get their head around the close relationships that Russell developed, relationships that made possible such things as a recommendation to a lifelong friend about an up-and-coming coach. In 2005, in his book entitled *The Last Coach: A Life of Paul "Bear" Bryant*, Allen Barra questioned the validity of Russell's account, writing that "None of this makes much sense...it just doesn't seem possible that Sanders could not have heard of him or that he would need the recommendation of a sportswriter."[20]

What Barra didn't realize, however, was that Fred Russell was not just another sportswriter. As a Vanderbilt alumnus as well as a trusted friend of Sanders, Russell *did* influence the Commodore's new head coach.

Years later, when Russell was named vice president emeritus for the *Nashville Banner* in 1981, the legendary Alabama coach was asked to comment. In doing so, he confirmed what had long been suspected.

"Fred Russell is one of my all-time heroes," Bryant said. "He helped me get an assistant coach's job at Vanderbilt. Our families have always been close."[21]

A fellow sportswriter, Delbert Reed, wrote for Russell in the 1960s and then covered Bryant for the *Tuscaloosa News* in the 1970s, putting him in as good a position as any to comment on how Russell could have influenced Sanders or Bryant.

"It's really insulting to Russell, to Bryant, and to the Vanderbilt coach," Reed said about Barra's speculation of Russell. "But [Barra] didn't know Fred Russell. Russell was a powerful person in the Vanderbilt picture, particularly in the athletic department. He had the ear of those people because he wrote about them every day."[22]

From his years covering the coach, Reed also knew Bryant well enough to know how he felt about Russell.

135

"Bryant and I talked about Russell often, because he was a mutual friend," Reed continued, "[Bryant] talked about Russell as if he was the greatest guy in the world, and there's no question that Russell was one of Bryant's best friends ever. He was a real confidante."[23]

When Bryant returned to his alma mater in 1958 to coach the Crimson Tide, his return to the Southeastern Conference meant an annual game against Vanderbilt and a chance to visit with his friend and confidante. Their friendship became more social as well, particularly during the summer months, when Mary Harmon and Kay would join their husbands on trips between the cities. The two golfed frequently together, and Russell remembers Bryant taking part in their weekly poker game as well, from time to time. "He wasn't a very good poker player, but he loved to compete," Russell recalled.

"On the Friday nights before the Vanderbilt-Alabama game, all through the 1960s and 1970s, he would eat dinner in our home that Friday night," Russell added. "We had a dog, a big black lab named Bear. He was just crazy about that dog."[24]

While their personal friendship matured, on the sidelines and in the papers, Bryant and Russell continued to excel respectively throughout the 1960s and 1970s, maintaining a trusted relationship inside college football. It was the natural evolution of an initial acquaintance into that of a trusted confidante over the years. One of Russell's former reporters, Tom Robinson, remembers a classic example of seeing the relationship between Bryant and Russell play out.

It was October 1978, and the Commodores were coming off back-to-back 2–9 seasons under head coach Fred Pancoast. Pancoast had already announced that this would be his final season as Vanderbilt's head coach, so speculation was constant as to who would take over as Commodore head coach. Robinson recalled being with Russell the day before the Tulane game at Rotier's Restaurant, a popular place just a couple of blocks from campus. Russell received a call from the *Banner* news desk saying that there was an AP story out that Bill "Brother" Oliver was going to be the new coach at Vanderbilt. Robinson recalled Russell questioning the story, thinking he would have heard something about it if it were true. Russell told Robinson they had forty-five minutes before deadline to confirm the story, or else the news desk was inclined to put it on the front page of the sports section.

When they arrived back at the *Banner* office, Robinson joined Russell in his office, where they shut the door and Russell picked up the phone.

"Remember, this is a Friday before game-day, and he just calls Coach Bryant at his office," Robinson added, still shaking his head at the recollection. "I'm thinking, 'Man, this is cool.' He gets the secretary, and he says, 'This is Freddie Russell. Is Bear there?' The secretary says that he's in a game meeting, and Mr. Russell says, 'Well, I understand it's the day before a football game. Tell him that Fred Russell needs him.'

"A couple of minutes go by, and Bryant gets on the phone.

"'Bear, sorry to do this, but I gotta ask you something,' Russell said. 'An AP story just came out saying Brother Oliver is going to be the next Vanderbilt coach. Is that who it's going to be?'

"The response from Bryant back to Russell was as unequivocal as it was quick.

"'I don't know who your coach is going to be, but it's not going to be Oliver. Don't attribute that to me, but it's not Bill,' Bryant told his good friend.

"Robinson sat dumbfounded as he listened to Russell finish his conversation with Bryant.

"I remember him saying, 'All right, well, how's Mary Harmon doing?...Yeah, ok...yeah, we'll have to get together soon. All right, talk to you later.' And he hangs up the phone, and I'm just bewildered," Robinson admitted. "I said, 'Mr. Russell, now that's impressive.' He just said, 'Bear's a good friend. Bear's a good friend.'"[25]

Confidentiality was the foundation for that type of friendship, and Russell was unwavering in his ability to keep his word. Johnny Majors was another SEC player turned coach who became good friends with his Russell over the years, much like Bryant. It was Russell's confidentiality that made its mark with the ex-Tennessee player and coach.

"Fred always had his sources, and people could trust him implicitly. You could talk off the record with him, and you knew it wouldn't be reported unless he cleared it with you," Majors said of Russell. "I would tell something to him that I didn't want anybody else to know at the time, which might not have been fair to all the media, but I wanted to share a few things off the record with him that I needed to get off my chest."[26]

The strict adherence to confidentiality was a critical component of Russell's success. Through his many years working within college football, Russell's approach resonated with Bob Casciola, whom he got to know through their work together at the National Football Foundation Hall of Fame. Casciola had coached at the Princeton University during the mid-1970s.

"He could be a confidante, and that made him very successful as a writer. If you told him something significant that needed to be kept quiet, he would not reveal that to anybody," Casciola said of Russell. "People knew he was not going to make headlines at your mercy, and he had a lot of character in that regard."[27]

This type of confidence and trust took years to nurture, and with men such as Majors and Bryant, it resulted in richer friendships for Russell. The sportswriter's friendship with Bryant was witnessed by many over the years, from regionally known writers, such as Blackie Sherrod in Dallas to Nashville's Larry Woody, who wrote for the *Tennessean*.

Sherrod recalled a time he received a phone call from Bryant, and it was on a day when Russell was in Bryant's office. The reason for the call, as it turned out, was because of a plaque that Sherrod had sent a few of his newspaper pals, Russell among them. Sherrod had come across an old saying that he enjoyed, and he arranged for the quotation to be made into a nice plaque. As it turned out, Russell happened to have his plaque with him when he visited Bryant, which led to the Alabama coach's call to Sherrod.

"Fred Russell is in my office," Bryant said, "and he just showed me that plaque you sent him. I am confiscating it. It will never leave this office." Sherrod came clean on what was on the plaque:

> When you have
> Them by the
> BALLS
> Their Hearts and Minds
> Will follow.[28]

Larry Woody's memory of the friendship between the two men is an interesting one, largely because Woody wrote for the *Tennessean*, not the *Banner*. Woody well remembered a particular moment with Bryant and Russell that occurred during the height of Bryant's success and popularity as Alabama coach. Bryant was in Nashville to speak at the Belle Meade Country Club, and Woody had to interview the coach. He remembered Bryant and Russell visiting in the corner of the ballroom when he approached the two.

Bryant mumbled and gave Woody the cold shoulder, even turning away from him in order to deflect the interview. However, a few minutes after Woody had returned to his side of the room, Russell showed up with Bryant at his side.

"Larry, coach is ready to talk now," Russell told Woody. "Go ahead and ask him whatever you want."

For Woody, that was impressive. It was the sports editor of the rival newspaper helping out a fellow journalist. "Whatever he said to Bryant, it was basically enough to have him come over and talk to me," Woody admitted. "If it had not been for Freddie Russell, I would not have been able to get that interview."[29]

The final chapter in the Russell-Bryant friendship came suddenly when Bryant passed away 26 January 1983. Bryant had announced that his retirement would be effective with the end of the 1982 season, and his last game was a 21–15 victory in the Liberty Bowl over Illinois. Less than a month later, he suffered a heart attack, just twenty-eight days after his last game as coach.

Russell's column on 27 January 1983 tells of his conversations with Bryant, especially one just a month before he died. They were eerily foreboding.

"I cannot remove from my mind the conversations about retirement—not recently, but four and five years ago—wherein Bryant, more than once, commented: 'I would go nuts. I'd have too much time on my hands. I wouldn't live a month.'

"And in mid-December, saying to him: 'The next few years, free of so much pressure, should be treated as the happiest of your life. Living, that's the thing. Dying is no big deal.'

"He just grunted."[30]

For Russell, it was more than the death of a great football coach; it was the shocking loss of a dear friend.

"That morning, knowing he was in the hospital, I talked to his chief assistant, Sam Bailey," Russell recounted several years later. "[Bailey] said, let me tell you, I just went to the hospital, and he was sitting up and laughing. I think he got this whipped. That was about 11 o'clock. I got home, and it was about 1 o'clock, and I got the phone call from Tuscaloosa that he had died.

"I couldn't believe that he had gone," Russell continued. "I thought for sure that here was a man who would be around for twenty years or so."[31]

What Russell remembered even more vividly was the funeral that followed. It was more of an event, actually, as there was a motorcade from Tuscaloosa to Birmingham, with people out in their yards at almost every home as they left Tuscaloosa.

"I've never seen anything like it," Russell noted. "The minute you hit the edge of Birmingham, the streets were lined. The most memorable tribute I've ever known for a sports figure."[32]

"How's Mr. Russell?"

While Russell's friendship with Paul Bryant is one of the more notable and prominent relationships the sportswriter had, it was by no means the only one. Russell's reach within the broader sports community was as diverse as the sports he covered and as deep as the old filing cabinet in his office where he kept index card after index card of contacts.

Through the years, Russell built his reputation one contact at a time, one sport at a time. It did not go unnoticed.

ESPN baseball analyst Buster Olney was a member of Russell's staff at the *Banner* in the 1980s and witnessed firsthand how his mentor devoted a significant amount of time to getting to know people in sports.

"When things would come up, he was always the guy with the phone number," Olney commented. "If there was an issue, he was the person who had cultivated phone numbers, and cultivated contacts. That was strongly reinforced to me at the time."[33]

Prior to Olney joining the *Banner* staff, Joe Biddle had arrived to work with Russell in the late 1970s. It was the beginning of a thirty-year friendship for Biddle, and he attributed at least part of Russell's impressive list of contacts to the events he was able to cover.

"He seemed like he was everywhere, because he was," Biddle said. "It wasn't like today, where you often hear, 'Oh, we don't have the budget for that.' Back then, he could go anywhere he wanted to, and he did. And he never met a stranger: he would go up and introduce himself to anybody and anyone."[34]

What Biddle noted about Russell's relationship skills was what he did *after* the events he covered.

"He would write letters, keep in touch, call periodically," Biddle noted. "I think people did a lot more of that back in those years, and that doesn't happen anymore. But he always followed up with phone calls or letters, and then when they'd see each other again, they'd talk in person."[35]

Biddle wrote for the *Banner* for twenty years until the paper was sold in 1998. He stayed in the same office building, however, making the move over to the *Tennessean*'s sports staff. Having been affiliated with Nashville sports for more than thirty years, Biddle knows Russell's reputation and legacy as well as anyone.

"Everywhere I went in the 1980s and 1990s, whether it was a Super Bowl, a Final Four, the Masters, it didn't matter what the event was," Biddle remembered. "When I would tell someone I was with the *Nashville Banner*, the automatic words out of their mouth were, 'How's Freddie Russell?'

"I could have been in Bangledesh and met somebody and that's what they would have said," Biddle concluded with a laugh. "He was a household name."[36]

"Everybody knew him, and it didn't have to be just in sports," noted George Plaster, one of Nashville's leading sports broadcasters since the mid-1990s. "Most of us who are in sports, we know just those people, but it appears that with Russell, he seemed to have ties with everybody, and everybody had ties with him."[37]

Plaster recalled one specific incident in Houston when he ran into Tommy Lasorda at an Astros game. Upon hearing that Plaster was from Nashville, Lasorda's first words were, of course, to inquire about Russell.

From all the years he spent in baseball, Lasorda had good reason to remember Russell. The two would see each other annually at baseball's spring training, as the Dodgers trained in Vero Beach from 1949 to 2008.

Over the years, as did so many others, Lasorda came to enjoy Russell's company and was willing to help out his sportswriter friend if needed.

"There was a sports club in Nashville, and he asked me to speak there," Lasorda remembered. "I told him I would, and I went down and spoke there, and it was only because of Fred Russell that I did."[38]

Within every sport Russell covered, there are stories of his connections, his reach, and his reputation that preceded him. One particular example within Russell's football circle was shared by Mark McGee, a *Banner* staffer from 1981 to 1994. In 1985, McGee was planning to be in New Orleans in late January to cover a basketball game and wanted to find a way to the Louisiana Superdome for the Super Bowl. Biddle had the *Banner*'s official pass, and McGee was calling friends and contacts to track down a personal ticket. All efforts led to no ticket. Reluctantly, McGee went to his last resort.

He went into his boss's office and told Russell that he hated to ask this of him, but he was hoping to go and was willing to buy a ticket if he could just find one. He talked with Russell for a few moments, and then Russell reached into his book of contacts and started dialing.

"Paul, this is Fred. I've got a guy here who needs a Super Bowl ticket," Russell said with McGee there in the room. "I wonder if you can help him out?"

McGee watched Russell write a few things on his paper and then hand him the paper, saying, "This will be mailed to you tomorrow by Federal Express."

Dumbfounded, McGee started to walk out of the office, but then stopped because of his curiosity. He had to know who Russell had just called.

"I don't mean to be nosy, but who were you talking to?" McGee asked Russell. "He told me it was Paul Brown, who was with the Cincinnati Bengals at the time. Well, I had a seat on the 50-yard line, in about the 30th row. It took him five minutes to do what I had been trying to do for what seemed like three months."[39]

If you talk long enough to people who knew Russell, stories such as this are commonplace. He created a network that was founded on trust and friendship, with both colleagues and those he covered. Interestingly enough, when you combine Russell's personality with the sheer volume of years that he worked and the diverse events that he covered, it makes for some great storytelling. In fact, for those who remember Russell well, the storytelling sessions themselves become memories.

Plaster remembers a luncheon he had with Russell, Biddle, and Vanderbilt's basketball coach at the time, C. M. Newton. They gathered at Swett's, a Nashville tradition much like Rotier's, and one of Russell's favorite restaurants for Southern homestyle cooking. Plaster recalled how the lunch turned into a storytelling affair for Russell, sharing with the group practical jokes from the old days as well as the differences in sportswriting, when writers and athletes traveled by trains, not planes.

"I remember watching Coach Newton and Joe, and we just stopped talking," Plaster said. "He was holding court. And what probably should have been an hour-long lunch lasted a couple of hours."[40]

Newton coached at Vanderbilt from 1981 to 1989, and was followed by Eddie Fogler. Fogler was at Vanderbilt for four seasons, long enough to have a few luncheons of his own with the historic sportswriter. Fogler was impressed, to say the least.

"It was like listening to history speak. The recall of the past, as far as he went back, so when he remembers DiMaggio and gives you the date and the score, you could just be mesmerized," Fogler said. "I don't know what you would pay to just listen to him talk about where he's been, what's he's done, what he's seen, who he's covered. You didn't talk. You just had your mouth wide open."[41]

Of course, as Russell aged, the ability to recall the minute details of events every time he told them sometimes blurred. So goes the story from C. M. Newton himself, who shared an additional connection to Russell. Newton's first cousin, Nancy, married Tom Siler, a longtime sportswriter for the Knoxville *News-Sentinel*. Siler and Russell had been friends since before World War II, and Siler served as either columnist or sports editor at the *News-Sentinel* from 1949 to 1979. Newton fondly recalled a night in the 1980s during his years at Vanderbilt when the Silers visited. Fred and Kay joined the two couples for dinner at the Hermitage in Nashville, and the two sportswriters shared stories of all the major events they had covered over the past four to five decades.

As the night wore on, Newton remembered laughing at how Siler and Russell would finish each other's sentences, oftentimes struggling with a name here, a location there.

"Fred would be telling a story about a heavyweight boxing fight in Chicago, and he would stop and say to Tom, 'Now who was so-and-so fighting? It was old, oh, what's his name?'" Newton recalled. "And Tom would remember, and then Fred would go on and finish the story. Then Tom would start telling one, and he'd say to Fred, 'Well, remember that Kentucky Derby when so-and-so was running and won with the funny-looking jockey—you remember that horse, right?' And Fred would, and then Tom would finish his story."[42]

Finally, after about two hours, Newton turned to Russell and Siler.

"You guys HAVE to get a tape recorder for this sort of thing and collaborate on a book, or make audios or something. This is just unbelievable what I am hearing," Newton said to the two men. "Why don't the two of you get together and do a book?"

Without batting an eye, Nancy Siler jumped in with, "Well, I've got a good title for the book: 'You Remember: Old What's His Name.'"[43]

Russell at his desk in his *Nashville Banner* office (ca. 1950s)

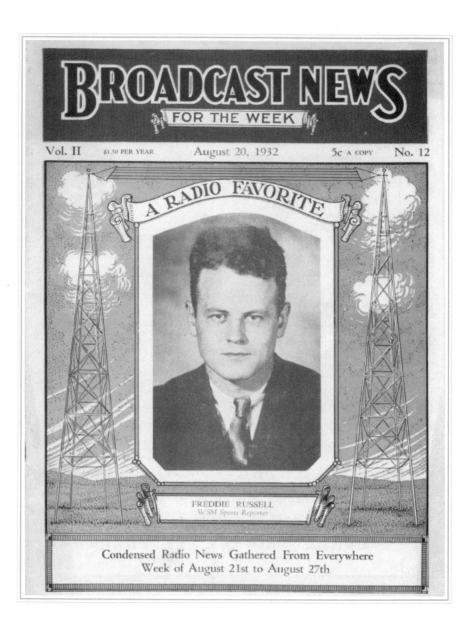

A 1932 photo of the young sports reporter
when he had five-minute radio spots on WSM in Nashville, Tennessee

September 8, 1953 *Nashville Banner* cartoon,
celebrating Russell's twenty-fifth year at the paper (artist: Jack Knox)

Russell with heavyweight champion Muhammad Ali

Book-signing for Russell's 1957 autobiography *Bury Me in an Old Press Box*
with Nashville Vols manager Dick Sisler (right) and
Vanderbilt football coach Art Guepe (middle)

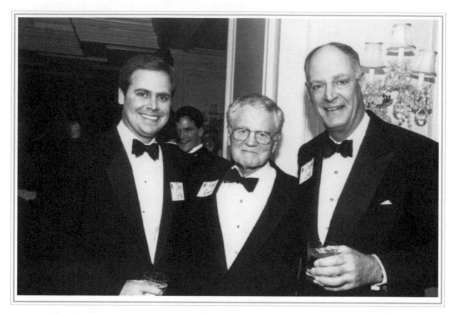

Russell with former TRA president and patron for Russell-Rice sportswriting scholarship, Charles Cella (right) and his son, John Cella (left)

Russell and Grantland Rice in St. Petersburg, Florida during spring training

Russell with Japanese star Sadaharu Oh and Cincinnati Reds manager
Sparky Anderson in Japan in the mid 1970s

Russell with mentor Grantland Rice and former Vanderbilt football coach Red Sanders

UNIVERSITY OF KENTUCKY ATHLETICS ASSOCIATION

LEXINGTON, KY.

August 22, 1953

Mr. Fred Russell, Sports Editor
The Nashville Banner
1100 Broad Street
Nashville, Kentucky

Dear Fred;

I received an invitation to attend the banquet in your honor on September 8, and it is with deep regret that I find that I will be unable to attend due to the fact that we will be in the middle of practice for our first game.

Fred, you certainly deserve this honor for the great work you have done for the Southeastern Conference and football in general in your particular field during your many years of service It is only just and certainly wonderful that you receive recognition from the people with whom and for whom you have worked. I want to extend to you my heartest congratulations and deep felt regard for your work. May the future years bring you the even greater success that you so rightly deserve.

Again may I say that I regret my inability to attend your banquet, and with best wishes and warmest personal regards, I am

Sincerely yours,

Paul Bryant
Paul Bryant

From his 1953 banquet scrapbook,
the personal letter from Kentucky coach Paul Bryant (1953)

Aug. 31, 1953

Mr. Jim Elliott,
The Nashville Banner,
Nashville, Tenn,

Dear Jim:

Freddie Russell is one of my favorite persons and I am indeed sorry that I can't be with you to pay tribute to him. Nashville is lucky to have him and luckier to hold him, because he has wit and charm and personality and writing skill, one of the most delightful fellow it's ever been my privilege to know.

Confidentially, I'm very glad that Nashville is clinging fast to him. Competition is tough enough in New York as it is now. Freddie would drive all the rest of us to cover if he ever operated up here. I must confess that I love the bum - in a manly way, of course. So treasure your prize because a prize he is.

My very best to him on this notable occasion.

Sincerely,

Arthur Daley

"ALL THE NEWS THAT'S FIT TO PRINT"

From his 1953 banquet scrapbook,
the personal letter from acclaimed *New York Times* writer Arthur Daley

1953 banquet: Russell with legends Red Grange, Bobby Jones, and Jack Dempsey

1953 banquet at Memorial Gymnasium on the campus of Vanderbilt University

Russell with Georgia football coach Vince Dooley at an NCAA football banquet

Russell presenting *Nashville Banner's* SEC Coach of the Year Award
to Alabama's Paul "Bear" Bryant (ca. 1970s)

Russell presenting NCAA Coach of the Year Award to his good friend,
Alabama head football coach Paul "Bear" Bryant, with Walter Cronkite looking on

The sportswriter and his wife Kay in Nashville, 1968

Two of Vanderbilt's most famous sons: Fred Russell and Grantland Rice.

Russell with his portable typewriter at his home in Nashville, Tennessee;
a photo of Grantland Rice is over his shoulder on the wall

Russell with hall-of-famer head coach Bud Wilkinson (Oklahoma)

Russell with New York Yankee pitching coach and Tennessee native Jim Turner (ca. 1950s)

Russell's acceptance speech at the Grantland Rice Memorial Award in 1955
(with Bobby Jones in the foreground)

Russell speaking on the campus of Vanderbilt University
(with Chancellor Harvie Branscomb in foreground)

At the age of eighty, Russell speaking at the Liberty Bowl in 1986

Russell in 1981 at a spring training game in Tampa, Florida,
with *Dayton Daily News* sports editor and lifelong baseball friend Si Burick

Russell at home with his four daughters: Kay, Ellen, Lee, and Carolyn

STORY OF

Tennessee's Neyland

by

FRED RUSSELL

SPORTS EDITOR
of the

BANNER

in the

DECEMBER 30 ISSUE OF THE

Saturday Evening Post

Nashville Banner newsstand advertisement promoting Russell's 1939 article
on UT's Bob Neyland in the *Saturday Evening Post*

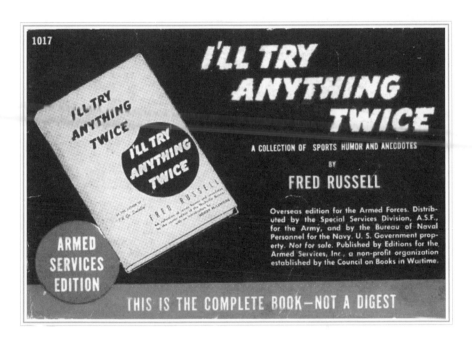

Advertisement for *I'll Try Anything Twice*, Russell's 1945 book
that was distributed widely to troops overseas fighting in WWII

Nashville Banner awards dinner photograph with Russell,
VU athletic trainer Joe Worden, and former VU football player Art Demmas

Russell with Vanderbilt chancellor Harvie Branscomb on the campus of Vanderbilt University

At the National Sportscasters and Sportswriters Association (NSSA) in Salisbury, North Carolina, Russell with Frank DeFord and Bob Costas

A promotional shot for the *Nashville Banner* of eighty-year-old Russell keeping busy

Russell in his office at the *Nashville Banner* with his classic Royal typewriter (ca. 1970s)

The *Banner* Part 3: David versus Goliath

"They used to have a joke in the sports department. We all parked out in the back of the newspaper, so we were going to work generally in the afternoon, when the *Banner* guys were going the other direction. Out in the parking lot, many times we'd run into Mr. Russell, who was coming out having written his column for the next day. If he was friendly to you, spoke to you with a smile, maybe even inquired as to your well being, you had to figure that you hadn't had a good story in weeks. Now, if he passed you by with just a grunt, then you knew you were doing your job."[1] —Jimmy Davy, former sportswriter, the *Tennessean*

In a two-newspaper town, competition gets fierce. In Nashville, when the *Nashville Banner* and the *Tennessean* were going head-to-head and shared the same building while doing so, that ferocity led to some remarkable situations. One such instance, as shared below by former *Tennessean* editor John Seigenthaler, resulted in story-swiping allegations from the *Banner* side of the office.

"The two sports departments were close in proximity, of course, and the *Banner* would always be working Saturday on its Monday paper. Freddie came to me once and said, 'One of your beat reporters is coming into our office on Saturdays and lifting material, stealing it, and you are beating us on Sunday unfairly.' I said, 'Freddie, if that's true, obviously I'll take some action about it.'

"I investigated it and had absolute denial on the part of the staff member. I went back to Freddie and we went to lunch. I said, 'I've looked into this, and I've talked not only with the reporter but a couple of sports figures, coaches, who were involved in the material, and both of the coaches say they had conversations with both reporters.' Freddie just said, 'John, you know how coaches are. They like reporters and they'll help them anyway they can, and my guess is this is what's happening.'

"So, a few weeks went by, and we'd see each other at various events, and nothing happened. It seemed as if the problem was solved, which made me a little bit uncomfortable. Well, sure enough, not too long after that, Freddie came in one day and said, 'Okay, now look, this is what happened last week.' Again, I went back, and John Bibb was the sports editor, and John stood by his reporter because he believed him. So I told Freddie that, and walked in his office, and I told him that both John and I had looked into this. He told me that he certainly trusted my word and John's word, but he also said that he thought it was just too coincidental. This time, a month went by. Then he came in one day and just said, 'Gotcha.'

"What he had done, they had the *Banner* reporter who was competing with us write a dummy column with false information over the weekend and leave it on his desk. Well, we [the *Tennessean*] had run that information in the paper that Monday morning. At this point, it was so clear. I brought Bibb in first, and I said, 'I don't want to see him [the guilty reporter]. I don't want him around here. Tell him to get his stuff out of the office.'"[2]

* * *

In this relatively small Middle Tennessee town, the "competition" for the *Nashville Banner* was clear: it was the *Tennessean*. The 1937 Joint Operating Agreement between the two papers had made things both easier and harder for the *Banner,* and Fred Russell lived the latter far more than he did the former. The most notable example of this is that without a Sunday paper, Russell had the unenviable task each and every week of covering two-day old events in his Monday sports section, the same events the *Tennessean* had covered in its Sunday paper. However, Russell's toughness and demanding presence as an editor made the competition between the two papers very real and very heated.

Russell's reputation and talent certainly had something to do with the rivalry as well. In the early 1960s, Russell was at the peak of his national stature and popularity. He had authored the nationally acclaimed "Pigskin Preview" since 1949, and that annual appearance in the *Saturday Evening Post* brought Russell recognition and credibility from coast to coast. In Nashville, as a Vanderbilt man at heart, Russell's decades of covering the Commodores favorably—some might say too favorably—had resulted in a filing cabinet full of contacts and

146

relationships at his alma mater. With Vanderbilt athletics still the number one sport in town, Russell was well positioned to garner top stories from his many sources within the athletic department. If he wasn't getting information from the athletic department, Russell was providing it *to* folks at Vanderbilt. He drew on his extensive network within the sports world and shared things as needed. The rationale was simple: Russell leveraged his contacts and experience to help his alma mater whenever possible, built or expanded relationships inside the department along the way, and positioned his paper for inside information and lead stories in the process. It was a good arrangement for both the *Banner* and Vanderbilt; it was a great arrangement for Russell.

Over time, Russell's influence at Vanderbilt bred a healthy but bitter rivalry between the *Banner* and the *Tennessean*. The latter did everything it could to keep up with Russell, his staff, and their slew of contacts inside the athletic department. For decades, the competitive tension between the two papers was palpable, as the sports staffers would go up against one another night in and night out. From the 1960s through the 1980s (and even up until the *Banner* folded in 1998, to some degree), this competition made for better sports sections within both papers. Years later, many of the writers from both papers still have vivid memories of this ultra-competitive time, in particular of Russell's role in the competition, and how he set the tone for the rivalry with his actions and his own desire to win.

Russell the Athletic Director?

To be factual, Fred Russell was never an employee of Vanderbilt University, let alone put in charge of its athletic department. Despite staying true to his call to journalism, however, there were plenty of people in and around Nashville who felt otherwise. As one rival sportswriter from the *Tennessean* said, "The truth was that for many years, Fred was Vanderbilt's phantom athletic director."

In hindsight, one of Nashville's more interesting sports rumors revolved around Red Sanders's hiring of Paul Bryant as a Vanderbilt assistant coach in 1940. As Sanders filled out his staff, he had an open assistant coach's position that he needed filled. Sanders followed the advice he received regarding the young, ambitious graduate assistant coaching at Alabama, and Bryant coached two years with the

Commodores before serving in World War II and then taking his own head coaching positions at Maryland, Kentucky, Texas A&M, and, of course, Alabama.

So who gave that tip to Sanders in 1940? Was it another coach? A former player? A member of Vanderbilt's athletic department? Perhaps someone in Bryant's own family? The answer was none of the above.

It was Fred Russell.

Russell had first met Bryant when Bryant was a player in the 1930s at the University of Alabama. He saw something in Bryant that made him take notice, and several years later, Russell recalled that feeling and passed along the idea to his friend, who needed another coach for his staff. Who knew that Bryant would go on to win six national championships in twenty-five years at Alabama, not to mention thirteen conference titles?

All luck and coincidental hirings aside, one thing was for certain: by the end of the 1940s, after ten years as *Banner* sports editor, Russell had clearly established himself within the Nashville community and at Vanderbilt as *the* go-to contact for sports information. His tireless work ethic and talent as a reporter and sports editor, coupled with his love for the Commodores, made for a natural connection to the athletic department. In those days, the head football coach served as the school's athletic director as well. Vanderbilt was no exception, and it wasn't until Jess Neely in 1966 that someone other than the football coach served as athletic director. When Sanders came to Vanderbilt in 1940, therefore, he also assumed the role of athletic director until 1948. As a result, for almost a decade, Russell had the ear of the athletic department in his good friend, Red Sanders.

During the same time Sanders was head coach, Russell was further establishing himself as one of the nation's rising stars in journalism. He quickly became more than just a local sports editor, and around Nashville and throughout the Vanderbilt community, Russell's stature and, connections made him an easy choice as someone to consult.

And make no mistake, when it came to important decisions related to its programs, Vanderbilt did its share of asking, and Russell did his share of consulting. Over the years, it was common knowledge that if university officials needed to make a decision, especially on its football coach, it made sense to speak with someone who knew the conference and the nation better than anyone else.

"Frankly, Mr. Russell for a long time ran the athletic department," former *Banner* reporter Joe Biddle commented. "He ran it because all his buddies were on the Board of Trust, and when it came time to change coaches, Mr. Russell was the one they asked, 'Well, who should we get? Who should we hire for this job?'"[3]

Biddle's recollection of his boss's stature is not an overstatement. It's a sentiment shared by many. John Rich, who played baseball and football in the 1940s for Vanderbilt and has been on the university Board of Trust since 1987, went one step further.

"He ran the sports world behind the scenes at Vanderbilt," Rich stated simply of Russell.[4]

The Fred Pancoast Hiring

One particular incident that highlighted Russell's involvement occurred in the mid-1970s with the football program. It also showed that Russell wasn't always on the right side of the decision. In the case of the Fred Pancoast hiring prior to the 1975 season, history shows that Vanderbilt probably should have gone in a different direction.

Pancoast was coming off three strong seasons at Memphis State from 1972 to 1974, and when the current Vanderbilt coach, Steve Sloan, left for Texas Tech in early 1975, Pancoast's came up as a potential replacement in Nashville. Asked years later how that originally developed, Pancoast admitted that it was Russell.

"Fred Russell's the one that really started the movement," Pancoast said regarding his candidacy for the Commodore coaching position. "My record at Memphis State was such that he took note, he called me, and then he ran an article in the paper about me. That's what started the ball rolling for me."[5]

When it came time to interview for the position, the interview took place in Washington, D.C. The annual football coaches meeting was taking place in the nation's capital, and word had already circulated that Vanderbilt officials would be in town to interview Pancoast. Also in D.C. to cover the proceedings were Butch Brooks, a sportswriter from Memphis who covered the Tigers, and Jimmy Davy, the Vanderbilt beat writer with the *Tennessean*. Davy still marvels to this day at the conversation he had with Pancoast that day.

Pancoast had told Davy that after he met with Vanderbilt officials, he would join Davy and Brooks in the hotel lobby and tell them how the interview went.

"When he arrives, Pancoast has this great smile on his face," Davy recalled. "We asked him how it went, and he goes, 'Well, you know, it's a strange thing. There was a sportswriter in that interview.' And it was Russell!

"He had gone with several Vanderbilt people on the board, and had actually participated in the interview of the next football coach," Davy noted, still shaking his head at that fact more than thirty years later.[6]

Pancoast ended up landing the job, and he remembered Russell's role very well.

"He was right in the middle of this one, and if there's anyone I can point to who had the most to do with my job change, it was him," Pancoast said of Russell.[7]

As it turned out, Pancoast was not the fit for Vanderbilt that Russell and others imagined or had hoped for. Despite going 7–4 in his first season, Pancoast coached only three more years, each season going 2–9. Looking back at that period of his life three decades later, Pancoast still has a sense of humor about Russell.

"Sometimes I wish he had never made that call," Pancoast said of Russell with a laugh. "Goodness gracious, I was on top of the world in Memphis. And my good friend was the SEC commissioner at the time, Boyd McWhorter. Between him and Fred Russell, they felt like that was the right move for me to make professionally."[8]

While it's clear that this was not the case, what was interesting about the Pancoast hiring, to say nothing of the fact that Russell had been intimately involved with his selection, was who Vanderbilt looked past to get to Pancoast.

At the time, Bill Parcells was a developing assistant coach working for Steve Sloan while Sloan was at Vanderbilt. Ultimately, when Sloan left Vanderbilt to coach at Texas Tech, he took several assistants with him, including Parcells. Before that move became final, however, Parcells had made it to the short list of candidates to succeed Sloan at Vanderbilt. So, too, had a young up-and-coming coach from West Virginia named

Robert Bowden, who had expressed an interest in the Vanderbilt position when Sloan departed.

In the end, though, the committee chose Pancoast. Parcells spent three years in Lubbock before taking the defensive coordinator position with the NFL's New York Giants. Four years later, he was named the Giants head coach in 1983 and went on to win two Super Bowls (1986 and 1990). John Rich recalled how the Pancoast selection had come as a surprise to Parcells.

"Parcells came by my office a couple of years later and said that he had been told he was the priority for the coach," Rich said, thinking back to what might have been if Parcells had been hired instead of Pancoast. "He was a little mystified about what had happened, as were a lot of other people. That would have changed a lot of things."[9]

As for the West Virginia candidate, "Bobby" Bowden stayed on as Mountaineer head coach just one more year, and then went on to Florida State. Bowden coached there for over thirty-five years, compiling more than 300 victories for the Seminoles, including two national titles (1993 and 1999) and twelve conference titles. Clay Stapleton was the Vanderbilt athletic director at the time, and recalled looking past Bowden.

"Bowden was no big deal back then, but he wanted an interview, so I gave him one," Stapleton said. "I didn't really think he was serious. I thought he wanted to stay at West Virginia, and that he was using the Vanderbilt interview to get more out of West Virginia. So I turned him down."[10]

It is remarkable that Vanderbilt and Russell both looked past Parcells and Bowden before settling on Fred Pancoast, but ultimately, what was most memorable of this particular story was Russell's direct involvement. How many coaches go through interviews that include the sports editor of one of the city's biggest papers? Not many, of course, and therein lies the fact that Russell's power and influence within the athletic department was significant. Larry Woody joined the *Tennessean* staff in 1966 and has marked the turn of the century with that paper. He remembers those days well, when Russell carried such a big stick within the athletic department.

Woody pointed out that his former boss, John Bibb, even suggested one time that Vanderbilt consider hiring Russell. During a time when

Vanderbilt was in between athletic directors, Bibb suggested they look at Russell.

"A lot of people misinterpreted it, they thought Bibb was being sarcastic," Woody recalled. "But he was serious about it. Russell was so knowledgeable, he loved the school, and he had so much influence around the city and around the country."[11]

Russell stayed with the *Banner*, never really contemplating a position at his alma mater. His calling was journalism, and even if he didn't have endless fun in the business—which he did—Russell was too talented a writer and editor, and too competitive, not to wake up every day and battle against the mighty *Tennessean*.

Russell's Influence Stoked the Rivalry Fire

The simple fact that there were two daily papers in a medium-sized city such as Nashville was enough to guarantee stiff competition. Fred Russell and his connections around the city, in particular at Vanderbilt, merely fanned the rivalry flames.

In the first half of the twentieth century, and even throughout the 1950s, the Commodore football program was one of the stronger ones in the South, unlike most of the past fifty years. Without major professional sports to compete with, Vanderbilt athletics dominated the Nashville headlines. So when coaching changes happened, or other news of significance within the program surfaced, the competition between the *Banner* and the *Tennessean* to get those stories first was very real.

The Fred Pancoast story was just one example, and Davy and other *Tennessean* writers endured the impact of Russell's influence at Vanderbilt for years. From the 1960s until 1984, Davy was at the *Tennessean*, toughing it out against Russell and the *Banner*. Davy first worked for sports editor Raymond Johnson and then later for John Bibb, both of whom took their turns against the iconic sports editor from the *Banner*.

"Particularly in the '70s, it was more heated with Russell. He didn't like get to beat," Davy noted, adding that Russell's deep connections inside Vanderbilt took its toll on the staff at the *Tennessean*.

"That kind of influence drove us crazy over at the *Tennessean*. That he was so inside with everything," Davy added. "It was very difficult for

Johnson and Bibb, who was a Vanderbilt graduate himself, to deal with Russell as far as breaking stories. We knew he had information."[12]

"Freddie absolutely had a lock on sports information coming out of Vanderbilt," former editor, publisher, and chairman John Seigenthaler commented. "If there was going to be a new coach, Freddie knew it first and quite often had a role in determining who among the competing candidates was the favorite, largely because Freddie's contacts with sportswriters and others around the country was much wider than Raymond's."[13]

Seigenthaler stressed the importance of Vanderbilt's Board of Trust placing great confidence in Russell. *Banner* publisher Jimmy Stahlman was a board member, and not a quiet one either. From Seigenthaler's perspective, it wasn't a coincidence that from the board room to the bylines, it was usually Russell's name attached to breaking sports news within Vanderbilt.

"Stahlman was inside every Board of Trust meeting, and he was a very dominant influence inside that board," Seigenthaler explained. "Anything that came out of that meeting about Vanderbilt athletics, everybody at that university knew where it was supposed to go."[14]

There's no disputing these claims, even from the former *Banner* staffers themselves. Russell provided a definite competitive advantage for the *Banner*.

"Russell basically knew everything before it happened, and it used to drive John Bibb and Raymond Johnson up the wall," Biddle acknowledged. "He got the stories just by being who he was and being associated with Vanderbilt for all those years. If you look at it, it wasn't really fair, but that's the way it was."[15]

Seigenthaler had his share of memories of hearing about this from Bibb. The longtime editor of the *Tennessean* admitted that Bibb held Russell in high regard, but that didn't take away the sting of losing stories to his counterpart at the *Banner*.

"When John Bibb became sports editor and succeeded Raymond, our situation did improve, primarily because John was an alum," Seigenthaler noted. "But when John got beat, I'd hear about it Monday morning when he'd come in screaming about Russell's contacts."[16]

For Russell, the end game was clear: win. Get the story, protect your sources, and beat the *Tennessean* at all costs. And, especially from

Saturday afternoon until Monday morning, make sure nothing leaked before the *Banner's* first edition hit the stands Monday afternoon.

Through the decades, Russell never wavered from this position, and former *Banner* reporters remember his competitive spirit well. Pat Embry joined the *Banner* sports staff in 1979 and eventually worked his way to the editor position in the late 1990s, up until the *Banner* folded in 1998.

"Other than the warm embrace of his wife, daughters, and assorted grandkids and great-grandkids, Mr. Russell knew no better joy than when we beat the *Tennessean* to a story," Embry said. "The ultimate compliment was for Mr. Russell to come out of his office with the paper in front of him, beaming. His response was invariably 'Great! Great!' like he was the Southern version of Tony the Tiger."[17]

Buster Olney, now with ESPN, joined the *Banner* after graduating from Vanderbilt in the mid-1980s, and he cut quickly to the chase.

"There's no doubt that the primary motivation of Mr. Russell was that he wanted to kick the shit out of the *Tennessean* every day," Olney said with a laugh. "That's what it came down to. That was the primary moving force for him."[18]

Harold Huggins wrote for Russell and the *Banner* from 1969 to 1988, and he learned from Russell his first week on the job that "Beat the *Tennessean*" was objective number one. Objective number two was to repeat objective number one.

Huggins eventually wrote for the *Tennessean* after he left the *Banner*, and he had the opportunity to get to know John Bibb better than when he had worked for Russell. Before Bibb passed away in 1999, Huggins recalled talking to him one time about the intensity of the rivalry when both he and Russell were in their prime. Bibb shared one story of a game they were covering.

"They were seated *right next* to each other with very little space between chairs," Huggins shared. "Bibb said Russell never said a word and the icy atmosphere was evident and you could cut the tension with a knife."[19]

Of course, a rivalry doesn't exist, however, unless the competition is shared on both sides and each team gets it share of victories. Throw in a couple of body blows to the competitor's leader, and the heat gets turned up a notch. The *Tennessean* certainly had its moments against Russell, and one such story involved Davy, who endured the underdog status against

Russell longer than any other *Tennessean* writer. If he wasn't going head-to-head with Russell during the 1960s, Davy was up against Russell's top reporters who had earned the coveted "Vanderbilt beat."

This particular story involved Peabody College and its potential positive impact on the Vanderbilt athletic department. For much of the twentieth century, Peabody College was located across the street from Vanderbilt, and its focus was on education and human development. By the late 1970s, however, financial strains forced the college to choose to either close or become affiliated with Vanderbilt University. In 1979, that merger took place, and the Peabody campus has been a vital part of the Vanderbilt undergraduate and graduate experience ever since.

From an athletic perspective, the importance of this merger could not be overstated. Peabody College offered additional class choices that provided all students—in particular, student *athletes*—with a more diverse selection of undergraduate programs. For a university whose sports teams (most notably, football) had suffered tremendously in the second half of the twentieth century, this development was seen as a potential watershed moment. With additional curriculum options, Vanderbilt could attract more students and potentially better athletes to its revenue-producing programs. Before the merger took place, there were rumblings around Vanderbilt that something was in the process of being worked out between the two schools, but nothing concrete enough to print. Jimmy Davy recalled being at a Commodore Club meeting in which Chancellor Alexander Heard and Vice Chancellor Rob Roy Purdy were among a group of about fifteen discussing Vanderbilt athletics, ways to improve the programs, and things that people should be expecting or looking out for in the future.

Davy remembered the evening well, especially the statement from Dr. Purdy indicating that "There [was] going to be a wonderful announcement coming in a couple of days, and everyone was going to be very happy."

Generally speaking, such Commodore Club meetings were informal, "off-the-record" types of gatherings. But technically, nothing could prevent Davy, or any other reporter who may have been there, to act on information overhead.

When Davy overheard Purdy's comment, given the recent rumors surrounding Peabody, he felt pretty confident he knew what the vice chancellor was intimating. However, before the meeting was over, Davy was approached by a Nashville attorney named Lew Connor who was hosting the meeting and cautioned about writing anything yet in the paper.

In Davy's words, Connor sought him out and said, "Now, Jimmy, you know you can't write anything about this. This is a secret."[20]

Undeterred, Davy decided to write about the merger. "I took my career in my hands and wrote a story that basically said, the only logical thing this could all be is the Peabody integration with Vanderbilt," recalled Davy.[21] Not surprisingly, the day that Davy's story broke in the *Tennessean*, there was nothing about it in the *Banner*.

Equally not surprisingly was the fact that this did not sit well with Fred Russell.

Davy remembered a column by Russell a few days later that questioned Davy's journalistic ethics by taking advantage of Dr. Purdy's comments, which had been made in a generally accepted off-the-record forum.

From Davy's perspective, though, Purdy had slipped up, and Davy still had a job to do.

"There wasn't any secret after that many people knew about it," Davy noted. "But Mr. Russell was horribly upset, and the reason was because he knew the story was true. He already knew it, but he was just waiting for Vanderbilt to say, 'Go ahead, Fred, write the story.'"[22]

Battlefield Logistics and High Expectations

Through the years, for every "Peabody College" story that the *Tennessean* had first in the papers, Russell and his staff had at least one or more "Vanderbilt" scoop in the *Banner*. Ultimately, the everyday battles made for healthy competition, which resulted in more aggressive reporting and better writing. The net effect of the competition was that both papers were better off with the rivalry in place than the alternative: a one-paper city.

When discussing the rivalry between the two papers, regardless of the names on the bylines, the simple operational logistics raised the stakes even more. You couldn't talk about the wars between the *Nashville Banner* and the *Tennessean* if you didn't mention the fact that they worked side by side. This co-location arrangement, which may have made business sense for the two papers, was a daily reminder from publishing down to advertising, from the news room to the copy room, that personnel from each paper worked in close proximity with their archrivals. Given the numerous hours during the day and night required to make a paper function, one could say you were sleeping with the enemy.

Ever since 1937, when the two papers signed their Joint Operating Agreement, the *Banner* and *Tennessean* staffs had shared office space in downtown Nashville. The *Tennessean* had been purchased out of receivership that year, and its new owner, Silliman Evans, worked it out with the *Banner*'s Jimmy Stahlman for both papers to cut down on operating expenses by sharing office space, printing expenses, and other operational costs.

"There was a wall between the two news rooms that was psychologically as impenetrable as the Berlin Wall," Seigenthaler pointed out. "We didn't go over there, and they didn't come over on our side."[23]

The sports departments were no different, and Biddle's memories are vivid. When he arrived in 1978, tensions were high enough at that point. What he heard about the decades before him were legendary.

"At one point, the sports departments in that building were right across the hall from one another," Biddle said. "During the time of Jimmy Davy, Waxo Green, Bill Roberts, Edgar Allen, and all those guys, the competition was incredibly fierce. I wasn't a part of it, but I've talked to all those people who were, and it was so bad, that they wouldn't even speak to each other."[24]

Larry Woody joined the *Tennessean* in 1966 and was there for many of those years of tension. "Both papers dreaded getting scooped, and every afternoon, we'd pick up the first edition of the *Banner* and quickly glance through it to see if they had beaten us on anything," Woody remembered. "And the *Banner* would do the same thing in the morning, checking to see if they had missed anything the night before."[25]

When it came to beating the competition, what was arguably the most challenging thing for Russell and his sports staff was dealing with the fact that the *Banner* had no Sunday paper. This was particularly painful during football season. Games would be played Saturday afternoon, and the *Tennessean* would have its Sunday section filled with game coverage. The *Tennessean* would also have its Monday morning paper out before the *Banner*'s first edition of the week arrived Monday afternoon.

Russell's approach to this challenge was to make the extra time between editions a positive thing. He refused to dwell on the fact that his competitor had two full editions before he even had his first opportunity to report on the game.

Delbert Reed wrote for Russell in the late 1960s, and he learned early on in his *Banner* career that Russell expected his staff to out-work and out-hustle the competition. The *Banner* couldn't afford to take any other approach. Reed remembered Russell's weekly pep talk that reinforced this strategy.

"Don't tell me about the play-by-play. Everybody knows who won by the time this afternoon paper comes out. Write something special. Have a different angle," Reed recalled Russell saying early and often during his tenure at the *Banner*.[26]

Without a Sunday paper, it was no surprise that the *Banner* took its lumps that day. But as Reed reflected on his years with the *Banner*, he remembered how Mondays would typically turn out.

"We'd have all these follow-ups, and all these after-the-fact stories and quotes," Reed remembered. "During the week, we had all these stories that would just wipe them out."[27]

Tom Robinson started working for Russell in 1976 and has similar memories of football weekends in Nashville working for the underdog *Banner*. Robinson would catch up with Russell Sunday mornings to talk about the game and then stop at the coach's show on Channel 4 before heading over to the university training room. As Robinson remembered, Russell was always interested in knowing who might be in the training room or the whirlpool Sunday afternoon trying to heal up from the Saturday game.

Russell also made sure Robinson and his staff were selective in what they asked the coach during a press conference or after the Sunday television show. He also instructed to get as much private time with the coaches as possible.

"I'd go out there and Jimmy Davy would be out there, and Russell would tell me, 'Pull coach aside when Davy's not around and ask him such-and-such.' That was part of the fun of being on the afternoon paper," Robinson recalled. "Deadline-wise, you were the underdog. But if you could scoop them on something, nobody enjoyed that more than Russell did."[28]

In the 1970s and 1980s, there was another element of everyday *Banner* life that should not be overlooked: typing up Russell's column during the latter years of the veteran's career. For over four decades, Fred Russell sat at his own old-style Remington typewriter and banged out his daily column, one click at a time. Over time, of course, technology advanced and computers became the easier tool to write and store one's work. The term "easier," however, was in the eye of the beholder. For Russell, it was *considerably* easier to use his tried-and-true Remington than learn to use a computer. Thus was born one of the more unenviable tasks around the *Banner* sports office.

"The responsibility of typing his column into the computer system was regarded with enormous fear," Buster Olney stated without a hint of humor in his voice. "You had to be very precise, and Mr. Russell would be very upset if the thing didn't turn out the way that he had written it."[29]

Olney recalled how it typically would work if you happened to be in the office on a day Russell's column needed to get entered. Russell's column was published on a weekly basis by the 1980s, and he would bring it down to the office on Tuesday or Wednesday.

"The sports editor would come over to you to dole it out, and the look on his face, it was like the Grim Reaper," Olney recalled. As he remembered his share of columns to enter, Olney added that the assignment usually went something like this: "Guess what, loser? You drew the short stick. You get to type in Mr. Russell's column this week."[30]

Mark McGee was a *Banner* reporter during the 1980s as well and had his share of "Russell column" assignments. "If it got put on your desk, you were like, 'No.' You were hoping that you had something else that you could do," McGee admitted.[31]

For all the humor former staffers find in the assignment, when they look back on it years later, there was a silver lining to the task of typing up Russell's column. It was something Biddle stumbled upon when he had his share of Russell columns to enter. Even as sports editor, if he happened to be the only one around when Mr. Russell dropped off his column, Biddle would take his turn. Through that process, he was reminded of how sharp his mentor stayed and how solid Russell's writing remained, even as he was almost eighty years old.

"I took great pleasure in doing it, because for one thing, I'd be the first person to read his column that week," Biddle admitted, adding that part of the process was printing it out and giving it back to Russell for review. "You didn't want it to come back with that red pen mark on it. Very rarely did you ever have to question him about a fact or a name or a spelling. He was as close to perfect as I've ever seen in this business."[32]

From Johnny Majors to Ron Mercer

When it came to the lows, if the *Tennessean* had a story before the *Banner*, you could see it in Russell's face and hear it in his voice. The only thing worse than getting beaten on a story, which was bound to happen from time to time anyway, was getting beaten on a story because of a screw-up. When that happened, the reactions were legendary.

"Russell had a temper on him. Don't let anyone tell you he didn't," Biddle noted. "You didn't see it very often, but you knew exactly where you stood if you messed up really bad."[33]

One such story involved former player and coach Johnny Majors from the University of Tennessee. Runner-up for the Heisman in 1956 when he played for the Volunteers, Majors returned to coach at his alma mater from 1977 to 1992. In 1987, Majors was being considered for induction into the National Football Foundation Hall of Fame for his efforts as a player (not a coach). At the time, Russell was still the chairman of the Honors Court at the National Football Foundation, which is the body that elects the annual inductees into the Hall of Fame. Russell had been serving on the Honors Court for almost three full decades and was as popular a leader of that organization as it had ever had.

Once the Honors Court made its decision on the class of 1987, there was a small window of time, maybe a day or two, in which the inductees were known to only a few inside the NFF. The court had selected Majors as one of its inductees that year, and Russell wanted to take full advantage of the inside information so that his paper could get the story first.

Biddle and Mark McGee both were with the *Banner* during this time and remembered the episode well. In his decade of coaching the Volunteers, Majors had elevated his status from legendary player to coaching icon. Majors was almost bigger than the Tennessee program

160

itself, and the story of him being elected to college football's highest hall of fame honor was a significant one.

At the *Banner*, Russell approached one of his new employees, a gentleman from Las Vegas—whose name will remain anonymous to protect the guilty—whom Russell had hired as his executive sports editor. It was a position more about operations, and was designed to run the day-to-day aspects of the sports section in the early morning and get the paper out for the afternoon. Russell wanted to hand his executive sports editor this "can't miss" top story, so the story would show up in the *Banner* one afternoon before the official press release was even announced. The *Banner* would beat the *Tennessean* on a story that the competition didn't even know existed.

That was the plan, at least.

Biddle remembered Russell coming in and talking to the young reporter about how it would all shake out.

"Now here's this story, and it has to run this day, because they are going to have the press release this next day," Russell told the reporter.[34]

Unfortunately, the importance of the scoop was lost on the new staff member.

"He got the note from Mr. Russell, and I guess he just didn't think much of it," McGee recalled.

"The guy forgot it. He *forgot* the story," Biddle echoed, adding that the story didn't run when it was supposed to, in the afternoon slot where it was guaranteed to beat the *Tennessean*.

What was the sport editor's response?

"Russell...went...nuts," Biddle said.

Russell knew what his counterpart at the *Tennessean* (John Bibb) would do once his staff got their hands on the official Associated Press release. Biddle and McGee still marvel at the attention the story got from the *Tennessean*.

"When John Bibb at the *Tennessean* realized what had happened, he just went all out for the next morning's edition," McGee remembered. "There was a two-page section with big pictures and headlines, honoring Majors like it was a 'lifetime achievement' or something."[35]

"They treated him as if he had just been elected president of the United States," Biddle said of the *Tennessean*'s coverage that day. "I have never seen Russell as mad as he got then," Biddle remembered when his boss saw the paper that morning.

As it turned out, the executive sports editor Russell had hired from Las Vegas was not doing too well at the paper anyway. This episode was the proverbial straw that broke his boss's back. "He was gone the next week," Biddle recalled. "He was there one day and then he wasn't, and I haven't heard from him since."[36]

"Did Mr. Russell have anything to do with it?" McGee asked with a smile. "Who really knows, but we always thought that he did."[37]

McGee also remembers a time when *he* was the subject of Russell's wrath. McGee wrote for the *Banner* from 1981 to 1994, eventually working his way up the ladder to be the Vanderbilt beat writer, a coveted position within the *Banner* sports staff.

"That was the top beat of the paper before we had pro teams," McGee recalled. "That's what everybody worked for, but if you got that beat and screwed up, oh, he was not a happy person."[38]

McGee remembered one particular incident in which Russell's attention to detail, especially with Vanderbilt news, caught up to him. There was a casual press release from the athletic department about Vanderbilt's basketball team being selected to play Georgia in the Kuppenheimer Classic the upcoming season. As McGee remembered, it was a one- to two-paragraph press release that came across the wire on a day when he was out of the office. McGee called the sports desk and had a staff member type in some of his notes for his column. Ultimately, the "Kuppenheimer" story did not make it into his column. The former beat writer still remembers the phone call he received from Russell the following night at his home.

"Have you seen the *Tennessean* today?" Russell asked McGee.

"Yes, sir."

"Vanderbilt's in the Kuppenheimer Classic."

"Yes, sir."

"Why don't we have it?" the veteran sports editor inquired.

"Well, I called the desk and told them to put it in there, but they just didn't get it done," McGee tried to explain.

"They? They?! *You* are the Vanderbilt beat writer. Why don't you just quit?" Russell said, and hung up the phone.[39]

McGee didn't quit, of course, knowing that his boss was just frustrated and needed to make his point. Russell demanded attention to detail, no matter how big or small the story might appear to be.

"With that beat, you had to be on top of things. He was a very competitive person, and he wanted us to be competitive," McGee said. As for the Kuppenheimer story and how close he came to leaving, McGee knew that wasn't really what his boss wanted.

"He never brought it up again. And that's important, too," McGee admitted. "Once Mr. Russell got it out of his system, it was over."[40]

As with any strong leader, Russell knew when not to pile on. Even though criticism served a purpose when delivered at the right time, Russell knew that what really motivated his people was recognition from the top. Despite all the short-temper episodes or moments of frustration, there was no bigger cheerleader for the Banner sports staff than Russell. He would often walk the sports room, and sometimes it was the simple pat on the shoulder or a nod of his head to one of the writers. Such gestures indicated Russell's satisfaction with his team, and it lifted spirits within the Banner year after year. At other times, he was animated, with one of his well-known expressions of approval.

"I can still see him pumping his fist," McGee recalled, "and he's saying 'That's just great, just great!' He really reveled in that, standing there in his seersucker suit, with a big smile on his face. You lived for and worked for the 'That's great!'"[41]

The Banner didn't always beat the Tennessean, but there were some memorable victories, especially the ones that came during the Banner's final years, when the uphill battle against the Tennessean was a harsh, consistent, and daily reality for the underdog Banner staff.

A prime example was the "Ron Mercer" recruiting story in spring 1995. In the early 1990s, Mercer played at Nashville's Goodpasture Christian School and was named "Mr. Basketball" twice. For his senior year of high school, Mercer transferred to the highly acclaimed Oak Hill Academy in Virginia. By early 1995, Mercer had narrowed his college choices to Vanderbilt and Kentucky. Kentucky was used to landing blue-chip prospects based purely on its tradition and history, ever since the days of Adolph Rupp. Vanderbilt, on the other hand, rarely landed such a coveted play-maker as Mercer, someone who could step in immediately and make a good team great.

At one point, the recruiting rumor mill reported that Mercer was Vanderbilt's to lose. The local basketball star wanted to play close to home and help elevate the Commodores to the upper echelon of the conference. Standing in the way, however, were Mercer's poor grades and academic scores that were just above NCAA minimums. The story turned into whether or not Vanderbilt would lower its academic standards and make an exception for Mercer in order to increase its chances for athletic success on the basketball court. As winter wore on, it became increasingly apparent that Vanderbilt would not sacrifice its academic standards.

Eventually, Mercer made his own decision, and then it was just a matter of which paper learned first. The *Banner*'s Greg Pogue was in the right spot at the right time. In his early days on staff, Pogue served as the prep editor managing the local high school sports scene. When Mercer was at Goodpasture Christian School in the early 1990s with fellow standout Drew Maddux (who did attend Vanderbilt, coincidentally, and had a successful Commodore career), Pogue covered the school and its star players extensively.

"I developed my relationships, and he had told me all along that whenever he decided, he would give it to me," Pogue said of Mercer. "That was the biggest story of the time, whether he was going to go to Kentucky or Vanderbilt. In the end, his decision was to attend the University of Kentucky."[42]

Mercer called Pogue late one night, around 11 P.M. The copy deadline for the morning edition of the *Tennessean* was still a couple of hours away, and Pogue and sports editor Joe Biddle had to sit on the story as long as possible that night.

The reason for this was simple logistics and the co-location of the two papers in the same building. Operationally, due to the Joint Operating Agreement that existed between the *Tennessean* and the *Banner*, there were shared services that existed, one of which was technology. Stories were entered into what amounted to a shared system, and Pogue remembered the lack of trust that existed during those years. Reporters and staff on both sides could navigate through the system to read their competitor's material if they were savvy (and bold) enough.

"We never trusted the *Tennessean*, so we certainly wouldn't put any breaking news in there," Pogue admitted.[43]

The night Ron Mercer called his old contact at the *Banner*, Pogue knew he couldn't risk submitting the story in case it got lifted. So he waited. And he waited some more.

"I did not start writing that until 3 o'clock in the morning," Pogue admitted, adding that he waited until every edition of the *Tennessean* had cleared before he started.[44]

"When we found out they didn't have it and that we were going to get the break on it, we were high-fiving and jumping up and down," Biddle recalled. "Mr. Russell wasn't there at 3 A.M., of course, but he was very excited the next morning. His competitive juices never quit flowing, and he really loved sticking it to the *Tennessean*, even in those final years."[45]

From Rivalry Friendships to Chinks in the Armor

In an odd twist of fate, the circumstances over the years that led to so many legendary battles, week in and week out, between heated rivals, also resulted in camaraderie and meaningful friendships. Reporters would join one staff or the other, spend one season after another staying in the same hotels, cover the same teams, talk to the same coaches and players, and in the long run, the things that united them were far more common than that which separated them. For the writers who stayed for years with either the *Banner* or the *Tennessean*, the bravado of youthful competition often gave way to respectful rivalry.

Bill Roberts was the longtime copyeditor at the *Banner*, working there from 1949 until the mid-1990s. Roberts remembered the tough feelings that existed between his boss and Russell's counterpart at the time across the hall, Raymond Johnson.

"Even though we were fighting each other for every bit of news we could get, Raymond and I got along well," Roberts recalled. "And his guys that worked for him in the press box, I got along with all those guys as well."[46]

Larry Woody began at the *Tennessean* in the 1960s and was there through the most heated years of the rivalry. But Woody can't talk about his counterparts at the *Banner* without talking about the friendships. The *Tennessean* veteran remembers when he and *Banner* writer Joe Caldwell would travel together to cover auto racing and games within the Ohio Valley Conference. He remembers his boss, John Bibb, for years traveling with the *Banner*'s Waxo Green to report on a variety of sports that both papers covered extensively.

"The papers were archrivals, but at the same time, a lot of the staffers were best friends," Woody said. "It was like playing golf with a good friend. You both want to win and beat each other, but after it's over, you go to the clubhouse and have a beer together."[47]

Through all the years, the competition was heated. In the latter stages of the twentieth century, however, the cracks in the *Banner*'s business model were starting to show. Advances in technology, primarily with television, began to offer the American consumer additional ways to obtain information. In the first half of the century, it may have been common for big cities to have five or more papers. But even cities such as New York, Chicago, and Los Angeles started to see a dip in newspaper consumption. For the *Banner*, which once boasted of circulation in excess of 100,000, those numbers were in rapid decline. In the early 1990s, circulation was hovering above 60,000, and by early 1998, it was just over 40,000.

In a two-paper town in a small market such as Nashville, it was unclear if both papers could survive with circulation so low. The *Banner* had been the stronger paper in the first half of the twentieth century, but the situation had changed. The *Tennessean*, with its Sunday paper and morning circulations, became more financially solvent in the second half of the century. When Gannett purchased the *Tennessean* in 1979, the strength of that publishing giant was almost too much to bear for the family-owned *Banner*. It became increasingly apparent that coupled with the *Tennessean*'s financial strength, the *Banner*'s primary disadvantages— no Sunday paper and only an afternoon paper during the week—would be their undoing.

For Fred Russell, a man who had worked and written for the *Banner* for almost seven decades, it was impossible to think that the *Banner*'s demise was even possible, let alone probable. Friends, colleagues, and family members of Russell merely hoped that the long-running conservative newspaper could somehow outlast its legendary sports editor.

In February 1998, unfortunately, it was not to be. Not only would there be no more heated competition between the *Tennessean* and the *Nashville Banner*, there would be no more *Nashville Banner*.

10

Memoirs of a Practical Joker

"Freddie's delivery was very calm, as he told a story. His voice would drop, and when he was in a crowd, you'd see people leaning over to hear him. He'd tell these wonderful stories. You could not help but listen, and the more he'd lower his voice, the more people would lean in, and then everybody would just burst out laughing."[1] —Earl Beasley, Jr., son-in-law

For all the stunts Russell pulled over the years, it was only natural to expect that others would make the legendary prankster the subject of one of their own gags. As his youngest daughter recollected, on at least one occasion, the culprit came from a place he least expected: his own family.

"One time, there was a new preacher at the church, and he was coming to visit. Well, they were Methodist, so of course nobody was 'supposed' to drink. Mother called me one day at work, and said, 'People have told me we can serve him wine. Do you think we should?' I said, 'It doesn't matter, Mother. Go ahead.' I hung up and remember thinking, 'Hallelujah, this is the greatest day of my life. The preacher is coming to their house, and there's going to be the biggest delivery from Belle Meade liquor ever.'

"My friend Bob Goidel did it, and he did the most wonderful job. It was a huge box that had the big bottles with the handles. I had filled them with water, and Bob delivered it. Russ Montfort, the new preacher, was sitting there, and Bob went in the house. Keep in mind, Bob had never met Mother and Daddy, but he went right in and cheerfully announced, 'Hello, Mr. Fred! Belle Meade Liquor!' Daddy was standing at the mantle facing the front door, and Bob saw the back of the preacher's head in the wing chair. And then Daddy said to the preacher, 'I know nothing about this!'

"But Bob kept going, and started pointing to the kitchen. 'Mr. Fred, you want me to put it in there, in the regular place?' And Daddy just said to the preacher, while pointing to Bob, 'Never seen him in my life!' Mother, who was always just friendly with everyone, came out from the kitchen and said, 'Oh, hey, there, darling!'

"When he turned to leave, just to add the final touch, Bob went, 'Okay, Mr. Fred. I'll see you same time next week.'"[2]

* * *

In June 1986, Russell met with William Harper, a professor at Purdue University who was writing a biography of Russell's childhood idol, eventual colleague, and close friend, Grantland Rice. Russell was just two months shy of his eightieth birthday, and the veteran sportswriter was lamenting a project he hadn't been able to pull together.

"I've been working on a book thing myself, but no self-discipline at all," Russell told Harper with a laugh from his Nashville home. "It's called *Memoirs of a Practical Joker*. I've got all this material, but I just can't get the time."[3]

Only Russell could genuinely want to write a book at that age *and* be sincere in his assessment that he didn't have the time for it. He would continue his sportswriting craft for another full decade until the *Banner*'s demise in 1998, and Russell remained in touch with a myriad of people within the sportswriting business. He was a busy man, to say the least.

Unfortunately, the "memoirs" book never did get written, just as Russell predicted in that interview almost two decades prior to his death in 2003. But if ever there was enough material for a book to be written, it would be around the long list of stories and gags attributed to Fred Russell.

Russell was the ultimate prankster. What made him stand out in a crowd, both figuratively on the pages of newspapers, and literally when he was among friends, was his sense of humor. Whether they were reading his column each morning, working alongside him at the *Banner*, or just happened to be in the right place at the right time, Fred Russell made people laugh. What was his secret? Simply put, Russell took his job seriously enough to know that he should never take himself too seriously. He had a keen awareness that the sports world could get a little dull from time to time, and he seemed to take it upon himself to lighten the mood whenever possible.

Roy Kramer, former Vanderbilt athletic director, SEC commissioner, and friend of Russell's, summed it up best: "What a legacy it is to make people laugh, and that truly is the legacy of Fred Russell's world."[4]

As a result, where there's a story about Russell, there is inevitably a story of either a prank he pulled or helped to organize. In the same breath that someone describes the talent that Russell possessed as a sportswriter, the interview can't end without referencing a favorite Russell prank or a memorable joke he shared. A telling example of this occurred in mid-September 2005, in an interview with Bob Broeg, longtime sportswriter for the *St. Louis Post-Dispatch*. At the age of eighty-seven, Broeg was in failing health but wanted to comment on his old friend. His voice was shaky, and at times, barely audible, but Broeg believed Russell was the top writer in the South during his day. At one point during the brief interview, Broeg apologized for not being able to recollect more. He had recently undergone surgery and still had a broken leg, while confined to a nursing home.

"I probably disappointed you, but my memory is a little fuzzy," Broeg admitted, then paused, as if to gather additional strength to ask one final question. "You do know about the fat lady, right?"[5]

The "Fat Lady" joke is one of the Russell classics, told and retold enough times that while the subtle details change each time, the punch line is always the same. It was remarkable that Broeg made this one of his final comments about Russell. Just six, short weeks later on 28 October 2005, Bob Broeg passed away. The fact that Russell's sense of humor came to mind for Broeg, during his final weeks, sums up how and why people remembered Russell.

Former Vanderbilt vice chancellor John Beasley knew Russell for many years in Nashville, in part because of his association with Russell's alma mater, but also because Beasley's brother, Earl, married Russell's eldest daughter, Kay. Beasley was privy to Russell's gifts as a storyteller and jokester.

"He never demanded the stage, but always took it and did it with such style," John Beasley recalled. "Over the years, I must have heard him tell the same story maybe fifty times, and it was as fresh the fiftieth time as the first. You knew where all the pauses and punch lines were going to be, but you longed for them, and you laughed uproariously when they arrived."[6]

Important to note is that Russell's pranks were never mean-spirited, and it is within that context that Russell is so favorably remembered when it comes to his sense of humor. As his friend and legendary sportswriter Red Smith once said, "He is the only practical joker who never hurt anybody with his practical jokes."

Getting Started Early with Red Sanders

As Russell's family remembers, he got started young, with some of the more memorable gags occurring during his college years at Vanderbilt. In the mid-1920s, one of Russell's buddies was Henry "Red" Sanders, who would eventually coach football at LSU, Vanderbilt, and UCLA. Carolyn Russell, the fourth of the four Russell daughters, remembers growing up hearing about the troubles Sanders and her father would cause during their academic years as Commodores.

"They would go to silent movies and one of them would pretend to be blind, walking in and stumbling with a cane," Carolyn recalled with a laugh, when repeating a Sanders-Russell story from the 1920s. "The other would read the subtitles as they came on the screen, and purposely describe in great detail everything that was happening on the screen. They would do this until people in the theater would get annoyed and move away from them."[7]

Sanders became Russell's target on more than one occasion later in life, especially once the former had garnered coaching success at the collegiate level. Perhaps the most well-known stunt that Russell pulled on Sanders occurred on the grounds of the Belle Meade Country Club in 1941, with the aid of a barefoot caddy known for his ability to deftly pick up a golf ball with his toes. Russell and Sanders were part of a foursome that day, where money was on the line, so the rules were strict: no "winter rules" would be honored. Each player would have to play his ball wherever it was found. Belle Meade golf pro George Livingston and *Banner* golf writer Waxo Green rounded out the foursome with Russell and Sanders.

Describing the joke decades later, Russell noted how Sanders's confidence on the golf course was practically begging for a prank.

"Sanders took his game so seriously, and he would always strive for an edge in strokes," Russell said in a late 1990s interview when talking about his good friend. "And when he thought he had the game locked up on the first tee, he would say, 'Sun in the air, blue sky, isn't life wonderful?'"[8]

As the Belle Meade golf pro, Livingston's instructions to his caddy were clear: give Sanders the worst possible lies that could happen on the course. When it was all said and done, the prank went over so well that eventually Russell included a summary of the gag in his "Sidelines" column years later, not to mention recording it for posterity in his 1944 book, *I'll Go Quietly*.[9]

Following Livingstone's orders to perfection, the caddy made sure tee shots that looked stellar off the tee somehow managed to find the only divot in the middle of the fairway, or perhaps inconceivably rolled up behind a rock next to a tree just off the fairway.

"Sanders hit a great drive on the dogleg number one there at Belle Meade, and he felt great about it. But he got down there, and the only hole around, it looked like a brick had been cut out of the ground, and he was in that," Russell laughed. "Now, the caddy did not overdo it, but I tell you, he had him crazy by the seventh hole. Sanders was doubling, and cursing all the time. It was great."[10]

After the first nine holes, Sanders was beside himself. "Have you ever known anybody as snake-bit?" Sanders said to Russell and the rest of his foursome that day. "Somebody hold my hand when we go back across the bridge so I won't fall in."[11]

The back nine was no better for the Vanderbilt coach. After a seemingly good tee shot on the eleventh hole found yet another miserable lie, Sanders declared, "There must be prairie dogs on this course." After another head-shaking lie, Sanders had this to say to his caddy: "I'll say one thing, boy. You are the most honest caddy I ever saw."[12]

The final straw came at number eighteen, where all bets were doubled.

"Sanders was $14 down, and he wanted to play for the $14," Russell remembered. "I said, 'You must be insane. I'm not playing for all that.' I wanted to be as stingy as I could, and it just incensed him, because we ended up playing that last hole for three dollars and a half. So Waxo hit first, and he intentionally hit about five inches behind the ball, and topped it so that it just trickled out there. And Sanders just said, 'You choking bastard.' And he meant it. He was so disappointed."[13]

When it was Sanders's turn to hit on number eighteen, Russell noted that his partner hit one of his best drives of the day. Which made it all the more unfortunate for Sanders when that great drive found yet another unlucky resting spot.

"How in the world the caddy gave him this lie I don't know, but when Red walked up and saw where it was, he threw his driver overhand into the tenth fairway," Russell added, describing it as "the most horrible lie in the history of golf. Honestly, the ball was in sort of a trap-door, or grave."[14]

Subsequently, Sanders closed with an eight on the final hole and stumbled to the clubhouse with a score of 112. When asked by his helpful caddy what to do with his clubs, a dejected Sanders offered a final reply: "Break 'em up for kindling. Do anything, I don't care."[15]

The BMCC Was Fertile Grounds for Russell

As it turned out, the Belle Meade Country Club made numerous guest appearances in the practical-joke-playing world of Fred Russell. One such occasion was an April Fool's joke that Russell pulled on the Middle Tennessee community in 1965 when he splashed a story on the front page of the sports section that new legislation would extend the Natchez Trace Parkway directly through the golf course. The *Nashville Banner* that day spared no detail in their coverage of this story, as there was a map of the new road going straight through the course and a number of its holes.

As Russell's youngest daughter recalled, it was a big hit. "There was a diagram and quotes from city officials, who were proud that there was even going to be a rest-area for tourists," Carolyn Russell remembered. "A lot of people went crazy, they believed it."[16]

Years later, Russell laughed at the story and how many people fell for the gag, even though it ran on April 1st. "I spent the better part of the next day fielding irate phone calls from some of Belle Meade's most prominent citizens," Russell recalled in 1996.[17]

If it wasn't the golf course as the subject of good humor, it was the sport itself. From his own years of enjoyment as well as frustration with the maddening game, Russell once crafted a list of golf's "cardinal principles" to help guide players on appropriate etiquette on the course.

With tongue firmly in cheek, he documented fourteen such rules to live by, with several notable examples:[18]

1. After making a poor shot, register surprise and examine your clubs carefully.
2. Before pocketing a ball lost by another player, it is well to wait until it has stopped rolling.
3. Never argue with your opponent over his score—ask him first and you have every advantage.
4. After your best drive of the season, turn around disgustedly and say, "No distance."

On the course itself, though, Russell had his most fun when setting up his friends. Red Sanders wasn't the only coach who became a victim to Russell's shenanigans on the golf course. Paul "Bear" Bryant, a Russell friend since the two met in the late 1930s, would often play golf with Russell when he visited Nashville during the summer months.

One particular time, Russell and Bryant played golf in the afternoon at Belle Meade and then retreated to the Russell home for dinner with their wives. As they were getting settled, Russell snuck out the back door and went over to the neighbor's house. He had already told his wife Kay that he'd be calling on the phone. When the call came in, she was to be busy and ask Coach Bryant to pick up.

So the phone rings, and Kay says, "Paul, will you answer the phone?"

He answered the phone, and Russell put on this strong accent and goes to work. He says, "Is Mr. Russell there?" and Bryant goes, "No, he's not here right now."

"Well, who am I speaking to?"

"This is Coach Bryant."

"Oh, Coach Bryant. You're the one I was calling about, actually. I'm out here at the country club, and people have been saying you're a cheap sonofabitch. Well, I've been defending you, but when you were out here today playing golf, there were four of you in that group, and you're the only one who didn't tip the caddy. I just wanted to let you know that from now on, if anybody asks me about you, I'm going to say that yes, Paul Bryant sure is a cheap sonofabitch."

Russell wasn't expecting what happened next. Bryant slammed the phone down and stormed out the front door and went to get in his car. Acting quickly as well, Russell ran over from next door and intercepted him just in time. "Where are you going, Paul?"

"I'm going out to Belle Meade Country Club, and I'm going to kill every damn caddy until I get the right one."[19]

Vanderbilt Antics Abound

If it wasn't Russell's home golf course that provided the setting for some of his more memorable gags, there was a good chance it had something to do with his alma mater on West End Avenue. The "Drinking Referee" gag is one of the Russell pranks that has been told and retold over the years. It was spring 1974, just after new football coach Steve Sloan had finished his first year coaching the Commodores. Sloan was just one of the targets that evening; Russell also wanted to get the relatively new chancellor at Vanderbilt, Alexander "Alec" Heard, as well as a young man named Wayne Sergeant, who had joined the *Banner* as its new publisher. To set things up properly, Russell and his wife took advantage of a Saturday afternoon brunch they were hosting at their home in advance of a Tennessee-Vanderbilt men's basketball game. He employed the assistance of his good friend, Cotton Clark, and a family friend, Allen Wallace, who dressed up like an official.

In the words of Russell himself, here's how the story played out:

"Everyone had been there for about fifteen minutes, and there was a loud knock on the door. Here was a man in a striped shirt, had his basketball whistle hanging around his neck, and he was loud-talking. He said, 'I just wanted to come by and say hello.' I was watching Sergeant— he couldn't see me—he was whispering to his wife, and you could tell he was probably saying, 'Does this really go on in the South? A basketball official coming by a sportswriter's home before a game?' For the gag to go, only one person was in on it, and his responsibility was to maneuver the basketball official to where he could be heard. And Cotton Clark did a great job of that. So I told him, 'Listen, we love you coming by here. We're going to eat in about fifteen minutes, and we'd like you to stay and eat with us.' But he said, 'Oh, no. I never, never eat before a game.' But all the while, he was kind of eyeing the bar. Finally, he said to Cotton, 'I wouldn't mind having a little vodka on the rocks, though.' So Cotton really fixed him a load, and then he was walking around, talking to everybody, drinking his vodka, ready to officiate the game, and I saw Alec Heard leave and go into the library with Clay Stapleton, who was then the director of athletics. I got filled in later, but Alec said, 'Clay, even should we win, this is *not* good.'

"Then the official, he kept on conversing with everyone, he finally looked at his watch and said, 'I have got to get to the game. But Cotton, fix me one more for the road!'" [20]

Years later, Sloan remembered that afternoon well, even when he mentioned to Russell that it just didn't seem right what was going on. "The chancellor was getting concerned, and so were some of the other higher-ups, and this guy just kept drinking," Sloan said. "I thought it was one of the funniest and cleverest things I had ever seen. I was only twenty-eight, twenty-nine years old at the time, and everybody was sucked into that trap."[21]

The Classics

The "Drinking Referee" or the "Basketball Official" joke (those were two of the names given to that prank) eventually became one of the Fred Russell "classics," a prank that would get told and retold over the years. For every orchestrated gag such as this, however, there were plenty of simpler, more subtle instances of Russell's humor. One example was shared by fellow sportswriter Tom McEwen (*Tampa Bay Tribune*) in May 1988. When Russell was being inducted into the National Sportscasters and Sportswriters Hall of Fame, McEwen gave the induction speech, and he intermingled facts about Russell's prowess as a sportswriter with some stories from the "other side of Fred Russell."

McEwen commented that Russell had a way of opening up a speech with just the right amount of humor. He recalled how his friend had recently spoken at a "Daughters of the Confederacy" event and had opened his speech with the following:

"What an honor it is to be here, ladies. You know, my grandfather, Beauregard Lee Russell, was a Confederate general in the War Between the States. But he fell at Shiloh...he fell at Vicksburg...and he fell at Atlanta. He was considered the clumsiest bastard in the Southern Army!"[22]

Perhaps the most quoted and often remembered Russell joke is the "Fat Lady" at the hotel. As acknowledged earlier when renowned St. Louis writer Bob Broeg referenced it just six weeks before he died, the joke was typical Russell ad-lib humor. Humorous in its own right, the exact location of the joke has ranged from Lexington to Tampa, from Cincinnati to Chicago. Perhaps it was after a Kentucky Derby or one morning in spring training. In the end, those who remember the story don't sweat such details. What is for sure is that Russell had checked into a hotel on one of his many out-of-town trips, and as he sat in the lobby, his attention was distracted by a female guest at the front desk who was trying to check in to the hotel. She was loud almost to the point of being obnoxious, not to mention rude to the hotel staffer. In her case, it didn't help that she was a bit heavyset. As former *Tennessean* reporter Jimmy Davy recalled, what ensued next was classic Russell.

"So this rather portly woman continues to give the clerk a hard time, and as she leaves, she leaves a wake-up call for 7 o'clock in the morning. Well, Russell sets his alarm for 6:45, and a few minutes before 7 A.M., he calls this lady's room. The phone rings, and she picks up. Saying he's from the front desk, Russell says, 'It's 7 o'clock in the morning, the sun is shining, temperature is in the 70s, and it's time to get your fat ass out of bed.'

"Russell then hangs up the phone and runs down to the lobby, so he can see this lady run out of the elevator, charge the front desk, and raise hell in every direction."[23]

Gene Corrigan currently serves as the chairman of the Honors Court of the National Football Foundation Hall of Fame, the organization Russell was with for thirty-plus years. Corrigan recalled a classic Russell joke, one that was pulled on him and others during their annual gathering, and one that Corrigan still tells to new members of the Honors Court.

Corrigan recalled how Russell arrived one year with the following story:

Well, I had an interesting trip in here. I was on this airplane, and this fellow sat down next to me, and he seemed like a nice guy. We got to talking, and he asked me what I did, and I told him. And then I asked him what he did. He said to me, 'Well, I'm retired. I go around the country and whenever there's a city that has a different kind of name, I research it.'

"And I said, 'Well, isn't that something. And where have you been recently?'

"The man said, 'I've been to Ashtabula, Ohio.'

"'And is there a story about it?'

"'Yes, there's a wonderful story. That whole area was occupied by a huge Indian tribe, by the Iroquois nation, and there was a powerful chief there. He did something that most Indian chiefs did not do: he had two wives. One was Rose and the other was Bula. And when he went to bed at night, he used to sleep facing Rose.'"[24]

During Russell's decades as a writer, a common denominator associated with his classic pranks or jokes was that no matter when they occurred, the gags stood the test of time and were recycled often. Furthermore, it was not uncommon for fellow writers to enjoy the humor so much so that a Russell prank would show up in one of their own columns. One such example came in 1968 in the daily column by Orville Henry, a legendary Southern sportswriter in his own right. Henry was the sports editor for the *Arkansas Gazette* for forty-six years, and when he dedicated a January 1968 column to the fun and games of his friend Fred Russell, he felt compelled to include a Russell story from the rich history of Southern League baseball, the famous "Notes to the Rookie Umpire" gag from thirty years before.

As told by Henry in his 18 January 1968 column:

"There was one night in Sulphur Dell, the tiny, historic Nashville ball park, when the Birmingham Barons, managed by Fresco Thompson, met the Nashville Vols in a key game of the 1938 pennant race. Some 11,000 persons jammed the park. A new umpire was behind the plate, his first game up from the Sally League. For a baseball man, Fresco Thompson bordered on the intellectual. As things went against him early, he began verbally cutting the new umpire to ribbons. The press box in Sulphur Dell hung right over home plate; his words carried clearly to the scribes.

"Russell took this in. He scribbled a little note. He sent it to the Birmingham dugout. This was the note, written in feminine script, as best Fred could manage:

"'Dear Mr. Thompson: I drove all the way from Dothan, Alabama, to see my nephew work his first Southern Association game as an umpire. I would appreciate it very much if you would quit saying such ugly things about him. Miss Luella Brown.'

"Thompson read the note while sitting on the top steps of the dugout. His eyes slowly panned the box seats as he put the note away.

"For four innings, Fresco didn't let out a peep. Meanwhile, Birmingham went ahead. But Nashville rallied to tie. Birmingham put runners on first and second with none away in the eighth. A single to center sent the lead runner, John Glenn, to the plate. He was called out. Glenn exploded. The umpire thumbed him. Fresco came perilously close to ejection. With that, Russell penned another note:

"'Mr. Thompson: If you don't stop insulting my nephew, I'm going to come down and kick you right in the.... Miss Luella Brown.'

"Fresco clapped a hand to his forehead and tumbled over backward, out of the dugout, and onto the ground near the stands, apparently in a dead faint. Players rushed to his aid; so did the umpire. They called for a doctor. When they'd sat him up and brushed him off, he handed them the last note."[25]

Everyday Targets

As tough and demanding an editor as Russell was, for the members of the *Banner* sports department, their leader was famous for keeping things light, albeit at their expense more often than not. No one was ever safe from Russell's sense of humor, and he reveled in the stunts he could pull off at 1100 Broadway. In Russell's own words, he admitted that the well-planned practical jokes and gags were much more common during his early days than in his final decades. But there was an unwritten code that he applied to his pranks as well.

"You wouldn't think of pulling anything on someone you didn't like, or they didn't like you. It was always on someone you knew," Russell said in a television interview in 1986. "It was just part of the newspaper business, it went on all the time, and it was particularly part of sports."[26]

When it came to combining sports and practical jokes, for whatever reason, baseball season often turned into prank season for the leader of the *Banner* sports section. Perhaps it had to do with baseball's six-month-long season, and it was the infamous dog days of summer that led Russell to mix things up with his staff.

One such story involved longtime copyeditor Bill Roberts, an avid fan of the Brooklyn Dodgers. In the early 1950s, after Ford Frick had become the commissioner of Major League Baseball, the Dodgers were still in Brooklyn. The franchise didn't move to Los Angeles until 1958, and in summer 1953, the Dodgers were in the midst of their best season ever. They held a commanding lead throughout the summer, and their fans were hoping for Brooklyn's first-ever World Series title.

That's when Russell went to work on his unsuspecting copyeditor. He contacted one of his buddies who ran the Associated Press wire, which happened to be in the same building on Broadway. In the words of Roberts himself, the prank went as follows:

"The Dodgers were about eighteen games ahead, and Russell had it all set up with the Associated Press guy. One day, a bulletin comes across, and I was there for the city edition. Mr. Russell tells me to go check the bulletin, look for any late news coming in after the city edition for the final edition. I see this bulletin, it comes out on the teletype, and it says:

"'President Ford Frick has taken thirteen and a half games from the Brooklyn Dodgers for using an ineligible player.'

"I can't believe this! I come running in to Freddie, and he reads it. But then he goes, 'Aw, nobody cares about this.' I thought he was crazy! I said, 'What?!' And he tells me to go see if there's anything else. So I'm checking the machine, and the commodities are coming in, the news from all over is coming in, but nothing more on the Dodgers. Then one of the copy boys comes to get me and says Mr. Russell needs me back in his office. So I come rushing back in, and by that time, he was laughing too hard. All I could do was laugh with him. I thought about hitting him upside the head, but I couldn't do that, so I just laughed with him."[27]

Such was the sense of humor of Fred Russell. Good-natured ribbing that perhaps dented a man's ego, but only for a moment. Another baseball-related gag that Russell pulled on one of his own came in the late 1970s, when reporter Tom Robinson had a baseball beat for the *Banner*. A local player named Mike Wright had played prep baseball and football at Father Ryan High School and then at Vanderbilt in the mid-1970s. An all-around solid athlete, Wright was selected in the amateur baseball draft in 1978 by the Detroit Tigers and by the Cincinnati Bengals in 1980 as a potential quarterback. While he never made it up to the highest professional level in either sport, Wright was a local product who generated genuine media interest in the late '70s.

One day, Russell decided to ruffle Robinson's feathers and told him to call the player personnel rep for the Tigers at the time, an up-and-coming baseball man named Bill LaJoie. (LaJoie would eventually become general manager for the Tigers in 1984, the year Detroit won the World Series.) Russell's bait for Robinson was that he had heard through the media grapevine that the Tigers were going to be signing Wright, and Russell wanted to know how much the offer was going to be so he could get the scoop in the next edition of the *Banner*.

With that as the backdrop for the prank, here is Robinson in his own words about what came next:

> "So I jump on the phone, get Bill Lajoie, and he's real short with me. I tell him that I heard about them sending someone down to sign Mike Wright, and he says, 'Yeah, what about it?' Well, I asked if he could tell me what they were going to offer him. 'Well, that's none of your bleepity-bleepity-bleeping business, and you're a bleepity-bleepity-bleep to even call and ask me that bleepity-bleepity-bleep question, and if you do it again, I'll send that guy over to bleepity-bleep in your rear end. Don't ever bother me again,' and he slams the phone down.
>
> "Well, I thought, 'Crap, Mr. Russell wants a story and I have to tell him this. There isn't a word he said that I can print.' So I'm just sitting there thinking, and [veteran *Banner* reporter] C. B. Fletcher was there laying out the paper. He goes, 'Tommy, you gonna have that story?' I said, 'Man, I don't know, C. B.' He goes, 'Well, we got a deadline coming up.'

So about ten minutes after the phone call, Mr. Russell comes walking by on his way upstairs and comes by my desk. He says, 'Oh, by the way, did you call Bill LaJoie like I asked you to?' I told him that I did, and Russell asked what LaJoie had said. I asked if he really wanted to know what was said, and he said of course. So I'm there quoting him word for nasty word, and Mr. Russell's just standing there, nodding his head, looking at the floor. I said, 'And that was the sum of the conversation, and he slammed the phone down.'

Mr. Russell paused for a second, then looked up at me and said, 'Snooty bastard, ain't he?' And he walked off, didn't say another word. Well, Waxo Green is sitting nearby and he's just laughing. I didn't know what I was going to do, so I said, 'What are you laughing at Waxo?' He said, 'Russell hooked you. He's just been jerking your chain because you're so darn serious.' Well, Waxo and I had a good laugh after he told me that."[28]

As it became quietly known throughout the *Banner* staff, if you were new to the sports department, chances were that Russell would initiate you to the paper with a prank of some sort. It wasn't just *Banner* staffers who were everyday targets, though. So, too, were Russell's good friends. One such person was Max Benson, who was the public relations director for the General Shoe Corporation for years in the middle half of the twentieth century in Nashville. Benson was well positioned within Nashville, and he became a target on more than one occasion for Russell. One such gag became known simply as "The Hat."

Nashville's Jimmy Webb, who passed away in January 2009, remembered the story well. In downtown Nashville in the 1950s, one of the more popular men's clothing stores was Davitt's. One day, Benson purchased a top of the line hat from the store owner, Slick Welch. Russell and Welch were friends, and after seeing how proud Benson was of his new hat, Welch contacted Russell. Welch told Russell that the hat Benson had just purchased was a size 7 and 1/8th, and if there was anything Russell could think of, this might be an opportunity to have some fun. As Webb recalled, Russell's response was immediate: "I'll be right down."

Russell made his way over to Davitt's shortly after getting the call from Welch, and within minutes, the two had concocted a mischievous

181

prank. In Webb's own words that follow, it's hard to imagine the prank going any better than how events unfolded:

"Fred goes down there and gets the same hat, only size 7 1/4. He had the initials placed in the same place and everything. He got the folks at Max's office in on it as well. He stopped by his friend's office without Max knowing it, and had the secretary swap the hats off the rack. Russell also made sure that Max was available for lunch that day and arranged with Max's secretary for them to meet. So lunchtime comes, and out comes Max, and he puts on his new hat, and it comes down too far on his forehead. He looks inside, see that it's his hat all right, that it's the right brand, and it says that it's 7 1/8th. Well, he goes back in his office, takes out some paper, and puts it inside the sweat band, so it'll fit right.

"They go to lunch, and Russell had this all figured out. When Max leaves the hat at the coatroom, Russell had someone switch the hats again, this time taking the paper and putting it in the original hat that really is 7 1/8th. So when Benson gets up to go home from lunch, it fits way up on his head now, and he can't figure it out. He looks again, and sure enough, it's the same hat. Well, they kept switching hats on him, and this went on for weeks. True story, Max finally went to the see his doctor, telling him that he had this terrible problem with his head."[29]

Not Everything Was Fit to Print

While some of the aforementioned stories have been retold in various newspaper columns or magazine articles over the years, there were certainly a handful of Russell gags that were better left undocumented, at least from any official sense anyway.

One of Russell's less circulated gags occurred as a result of a visit in the mid-1950s from the Reverend Billy Graham. The target was Vanderbilt's head football coach, Art Guepe.

Longtime *Banner* news editor Eddie Jones recalled the story and noted that an important component of this gag was the use of a certain word that wasn't spoken too often in those days.

"Back in the late 1940s and 1950s, the F-word was a shocking word. It just wasn't used, nor was it printed," Jones began. "Well, Fred fit it into almost everything he did. Now, this was in 1950, and there was a Billy Graham crusade coming to town, and they were using Vanderbilt Stadium, which did not have lights. The crusade people worked out a deal with Vanderbilt that they would buy and install lights so they could have night football out there in return for the use of the stadium.

"It was Art Guepe who was coach at the time, and Fred had Bill Roberts on his staff," Jones continued. "Freddie would do up these scripts and have Roberts make the call. Our switchboard operator at the paper would patch in the favored few so we could all listen in. So Roberts calls Guepe, and says,

"'Coach Guepe, this is Dr. Sinclair with the Billy Graham team.'

"'Yes sir, Doctor. How are you?'

"'Getting along just fine, thank you. Now you realize the crusade is giving night lighting to Vanderbilt so you can have night football.'

"'Oh, yes, we sure do appreciate it. It's going to make a wonderful contribution to the athletic program.'

"'Yes, well, when it gets down to this point, just before a crusade is going to open, Billy gets all nervous and wonders about things, and he's now concerned about the lights. So, coach, he just wanted me to call you and find out if those f---king lights are going to work.'

"So there's this long pause at the end of the line," Jones says, himself in laughter at retelling the joke. "Coach Guepe finally says, 'I beg your pardon, Dr. Sinclair.'

"'You heard me. Billy wants to know if the f---king lights are going to work.'

"And then Coach Guepe just hung up on him," Jones concludes. "It was one of the funniest damn things I ever heard."[30]

An additional story that was better shared outside the margins of Russell's "Sidelines" column again involved Max Benson, this one occurring all the way back in 1942. As evidenced by this unpublished gag, Russell's "Hat Trick" on Benson paled in comparison to a new civic-minded "committee" that Benson was apparently interested in starting in Nashville.

Benson was at his desk one day when he received a call from Vernon Tupper, one of Nashville's civic leaders and a fellow vestryman at Benson's church, Christ Episcopal. Tupper got straight to the point, telling Benson that even though he had a number of good ideas in the past on community affairs, this time Benson had gone too far. Benson was dumbfounded and inquired as to what Tupper was talking about.

"This damn letter I just got in the mail," Tupper said to Benson. "You must be out of your mind."

Throughout that morning, Benson received multiple calls from dozens of prominent Nashvillians, with comments similar to if not stronger than Tupper's. It wasn't long before Western Union arrived at Benson's office with a copy of the letter sent to Tupper. Only then did Benson realize what his good friend Fred Russell had been up to.

Dated 28 May 1942, the letter itself was the practical joke, and it read as follows:

"Dear Mr. Tupper: As you have noticed in the newspapers, the Nashville Police, through authority of the Federal Government under the May Act, have taken steps to deal with the problem of prostitution in Nashville, it being with the Camp Forrest and Fort Campbell area. This has presented a most difficult situation which our committee is attempting to solve.

"Closing of the sporting houses here has affected an estimated 150 professional women, unfortunates who now do not know where to turn. The Federal government has suggested that the city of Nashville take it upon itself to absorb these women, to reclaim them into society. It is to this most delicate task that I have been assigned.

"We are launching a rehabilitation program, the first phase of which will be to place these unfortunates in private homes for a brief time, where they can begin their period of orientation on a sound basis.

"I am asking a selected list of Nashville citizens, my friends in whose care I consider these waywards free from temptations, to take one 'refugee' for this brief period.

"Please telephone or write me at your earliest convenience. And excuse this impersonal letter, as on work of this nature I am having to handle all my own correspondence.

"Sincerely, Maxwell E. Benson, Chairman, Prostitution Orientation Committee"[31]

The Benson "prostitution" letter was not the only such correspondence that Russell would craft on behalf of unsuspecting, honorable members of Nashville society. While not nearly as orchestrated and contrived as the Benson letter, Russell once drafted a correspondence to himself, congratulating himself on a recent book about Vanderbilt football that he had coauthored. It was August 1946, and while such a letter seems relatively benign at first, the catch was that Russell configured the note to appear to come from the desk of Duke University's Harvie Branscomb, the chancellor-elect for Vanderbilt University. Not only that, there was a rather remarkable postscript at the end of the letter that Russell felt compelled to share with others at the *Banner* and around Nashville. Not surprisingly, those who viewed the letter couldn't believe such a thing would come from their incoming chancellor, let alone the former biblical scholar and dean of Duke's divinity school.

What did the letter say? In all its formality, here is the "Branscomb" letter, dated 23 August 1946:

"Dear Mr. Russell: Many thanks for the copy of *Fifty Years of Vanderbilt Football*, which came in this morning. What an excellent idea which seems to me admirably carried out! I shall examine it with much enthusiasm. When I was growing up in North Alabama, the Vanderbilt team came down annually, trailing robes of golden Glory; and all the small boys as well as some older ones, shivered in admiration.

"The newspapers have certainly been magnificent in their handling of the announcement of my election, and I look forward with much enthusiasm to our future work together in the development of the university.

"Yours gratefully, Harvie Branscomb

"P.S. I sure hope we beat them Tennessee bastards this year."[32]

Beyond these two examples of "official" letters, there were a couple of other Russell pranks or jokes that stayed out of his column for good reason. One such example was the "Stuttering Basketball Coach," one of his favorite jokes told often at cocktail parties, golf outings, or sports events. To attribute the retelling of this Russell favorite to only one source would be an impossible task. But suffice it to say, the joke made its rounds, and as one close friend admitted, "Freddie told us he just never could find a way to clean this up enough for the paper."[33]

With that in mind, here is the "Stuttering Basketball Coach":

There's this assistant basketball coach at Western Kentucky who was a brilliant basketball mind. He had just one problem: he stuttered. Too often, when the game was on the line and things were getting exciting, the kids would come over, and the coach would ask the assistant to help out. Well, when he tried to tell the kids something, he would just st-st-stutter and not be able to say anything. After a while, the head coach finally said, "I just can't put up with this anymore." So after one game, the head coach is talking with his assistant, and he wants to help him. He says, "Look, you need to get away, do something else for a night. You're in need of some luck, and I happen to have some info on something that might help: Ellis Park—the horse race next Thursday. Take whatever you can muster and bet the fourth horse in the fourth race. Very easy, number four in the fourth, Ellis Park, next Thursday."

So the assistant thought about it and realized it was a chance of a lifetime, inside information on a big race. So he drew every dime out of his savings account, borrowed some more money, and went to Ellis Park. He bet it all on number four in the fourth race right before the window closed. He's watching the race, and as they come around the last turn, sure enough, old number four is right out in front. But then all of a sudden, that dumb horse ducked his head to the left and crashed right through the inside railing, throwing the jockey. Everybody went wild, wondering what the heck was wrong with that horse. Well, that poor coach, he just tore up his tickets.

He went down to the paddock, and after things calmed down, he asked the trainer, "What happened out there. Th-th-that horse just du-du-ducked his hea-hea-head and went rrrr-ight through the rrrr-ail out there into the in-in-infield."

The trainer says, "He had done that in training but never in a race. And I don't know what happened to that horse."

The basketball coach then says, "Well, I-I-I can te-te-tell you how to fi-fi-fix it."

And the trainer says, "Well, tell me. What would you do?"

"You ne-need to baaaaa-lance his head. You put some lead in his rrrr-ight ear, and it will br-bring his he-he-head stra-straight up."

The trainer gets this puzzled look on his face and says, "Put some lead in his ear? How the heck do you do that?"

"Wi-with a f---king pi-pistol."[34]

As often is the case for good joke-telling, timing is everything. Not only did Russell have that sense of timing, but he also realized that the use of a well-placed expletive, especially the most unexpected expletive, from a man who truly was a Southern gentleman, could turn a good joke into a great one. By not over-using profanity, Russell's employment of the occasional curse word elevated his sense of humor to another level. And when he incorporated that aspect of his humor directly into his pranks, the results were legendary.

Turning the Tables

While Russell was often the one pulling the strings, it wasn't unheard of for the sportswriter prankster to be victimized himself. Perhaps the most well-known example of this was the "West Point" gag that the Army coaching staff pulled off on Russell.

It happened in the early 1960s, shortly after head coach Paul Dietzel had left LSU to take over at Army. Dietzel coached at West Point from 1962 to 1965, and having befriended Russell during his days of coaching in the Southeastern Conference, the new Army coach invited Russell and several other reporters to their training camp prior to the start of the season. Russell landed at LaGuardia Airport and was picked up by one of Dietzel's assistant coaches. They made their way to the West Point grounds, and Russell was dropped off near a field and told that coach Dietzel was on his way to pick him up. As Russell recounted in his "Sidelines" column years later, he wasn't expecting what happened next:

"In this little clearing in the woods, I sat on a log reading the new NCAA Football Guide, received only that morning. I really hadn't noticed a couple of signs that read: DANGER AREA.

187

"Presently, a helmeted soldier passed in a jeep, driving up the dirt road toward a wooded hill. He returned shortly accompanied by a tall young man in combat fatigue apparel, who jumped out of the jeep and yelled to me: 'Sir, you are in a target area here. They fire live ammo.'

"I told him I was waiting for Coach Dietzel and had no idea where I was. Suddenly, the firing began. It was loud and sounded crackingly low.

"'Try to make that ditch!' the soldier shouted. 'Follow me!'

"My leader was fast, but I passed him in three strides, diving for cover."[35]

As it turned out, that tall soldier was Dietzel's assistant coach, Bill Battle, who eventually took over at the University of Tennessee in the mid-1970s. Battle had played his part well, first telling Russell to sit tight. Then the firing started, and Battle's not-so-calm reaction got Russell more than just a bit nervous.

Furthermore, unbeknownst to Russell, Dietzel himself and three other assistants, all armed with cherry bomb firecrackers, were in the woods near the trench Russell and Battle went running for when the so-called "firing" began. As Dietzel recalled all the "commotion" on the firing range, he still laughed at how fast his sportswriter friend went ducking for cover.

"There goes Bill running for the bunker and he jumps in there, and Freddie's running right behind him as fast as he can," Dietzel recalled with a laugh in 2005, more than forty years after the prank. "The guys who are hiding keep throwing firecrackers up in the air, and then they start throwing dirt up in the air, along with some gravel, causing just a huge mess."[36]

For good measure, just to make the prank complete, Dietzel had another assistant filming the whole thing on tape. Later that night, Russell was the guest movie star for all to enjoy.

"I had already made a lead-in to it, and here it comes on the screen: 'Freddie Visits the Academy,'" Dietzel recalled. "It showed those two diving into the trench, and all the dirt flying up everywhere, and we absolutely were hysterical laughing about it."[37]

Not surprisingly, within Russell's college football network of coaches and the National Football Foundation Hall of Fame, the "West Point" story was shared year after year, either by Russell himself or one of the coaches involved. Eventually, those within the Hall of Fame came to know it as one of the Russell classics, even though Russell was the victim this time. Bob Casciola served as the president of the NFF-HOF from 1993 to 2005, and Russell was one of his mentors within that organization in the 1980s. When recalling the West Point cherry-bomb prank, Casciola spoke of a conversation he had with Russell years later.

"It was a riot, and they loved it. But when he first found out it was all a hoax, I can't tell you what he called Dietzel," Casciola laughed. "He called him every name under the sun when he got in there. Mr. Russell told me later that he was 'scared shitless,' that's what he said."[38]

Beyond the Typewriter

"Growing up, I had two imaginary friends for a while—names were Pabby and Hollah—and you couldn't sit in a chair if they were in it. One day Daddy asked me what happened to them. I said they got run over by a truck in Texas. I must have been five or six. Well, here's how cute he was. When we began to walk down the aisle at my wedding, he leaned over and said, 'Pabby and Hollah are in the front row.' He did things like that all the time."[1] —Kay Russell, daughter

Away from his "Sidelines" column, Fred Russell had an equally, if not more, important role: that of father, husband, and friend. His respectful demeanor and penchant for following up with sports figures with letters, cards, and phone calls was not done simply to develop his business. Rather, it was part of who he was. It was part of Russell's fabric, and it was evident throughout his life with friends, family, and neighbors. One notable example occurred during the Christmas season during World War II.

As was the case with so many families at the time, the Russells had close friends who had personal connections to someone overseas serving in the armed forces. This was the case for Paul and Grace Stumb, longtime friends of the Russell family. Tragically, Grace Stumb's younger brother, Pete Cavert, was killed in the line of duty at the Battle of the Bulge. In its entirety, this "battle" stretched from 16 December 1944 to 25 January 1945 and was the worst battle of the war in terms of losses, as 19,000 Americans were killed. The Cavert and Stumb families learned of Pete's fate over the Christmas holiday.

"We were waiting for the answer to whether he had been killed, and we found out just before Christmas that he had been killed," Grace Stumb recalled. "Kay and Freddie were the first ones on Christmas morning to come out to our house, to grieve with us and share our heartache. They had such compassion and love, and that's the kind of friends they were."[2]

It is hard to imagine that Fred Russell's life as a sportswriter was anything other than busy. Quite simply, it was. Despite the fact that the sportswriting industry in general during his prime years was a much more relaxed business, Russell set himself apart by out-working his competitors. Putting in the long hours as well as the odd hours of the day or night that were needed within the newspaper business, that was part of the job. It would be understandable if Fred Russell had little time for anything other than sports. This was not the case, however. Part of what made Russell a respected and successful man within the sports business was how he lived his life away from the job.

Aside from the national reputation he built as a sportswriter, Russell's life was a relatively normal one. He wasn't perfect, nor did he ever make any claims to be. He had a temper, but did not abuse that trait. At times, he had more than the occasional drink, but rarely in excess. He endured the ups and downs of life, and in living as long as he did, there were certainly a fair share of both for Russell. Holiday events and neighborhood parties brought spirited memories to the Russell home, and the birth of their children and grandchildren were natural highlights. For every celebration of life that occurred and brought happiness to Russell, however, there were events that brought sadness as well. The deaths of close friends took their cumulative toll, and the respective passings of Henry "Red" Sanders in 1958 and Paul "Bear" Bryant in 1983 were particularly painful. Russell lost not only acquaintances from the sports world, but he lost friends he had been close with for decades. No death brought more pain to Russell, however, than when his wife, Kay, died in 1996, just a few weeks shy of their sixty-third wedding anniversary. Despite the clear fact that Kay had lived a long, full life, Fred Russell was alone for the first time in more than half a century. The events after his wife's death offer a somber but heartwarming glimpse into this part of Russell's life, a time when he was rightfully stepping away from the public eye and resigning to a more private time.

Courting Kay

What made it so hard on Russell when his wife died was that he lost the person with whom he had built and shared everything. In his life away from the *Nashville Banner*, the Russells were a strong, nuclear family that placed an emphasis on faith and family relationships. His

191

integrity and character as a journalist were merely a reflection of the man behind the typewriter. And as the cliché rightfully goes, like all good stories of a man who does well, the story starts and ends with a woman. For Russell, that woman was Katherine Early.

"The first time I remember seeing Kay, she was about 14, in pigtails and riding her pony, and I was 18 and a Vanderbilt sophomore," Russell wrote in his autobiography, adding that "There's no age gap as wide, I think, as between an 18-year-old boy and 14-year-old girl."[3]

Between college experiences for both, it would be another seven years before Russell would see Kay again. She gave her brother John and Fred a ride to the train station so they could join the Vanderbilt football team on a trip to Atlanta to play Georgia Tech in 1931. That singular car ride had a profound effect on Russell. He had not seen Kay since 1924. Now, at the age of twenty-two, she was a young woman with a cavalier, take-charge attitude. In an instant, she changed his life forever.

"From that moment, I knew she was the one," Russell wrote. "I think that's something you find out in the eyes, though I wouldn't attempt to explain it further."[4]

Kay Early felt it as well. Her youngest daughter, Carolyn, remembered a conversation she had years later with her mother about that initial meeting. Kay shared with Carolyn what she had told her own mother at the time.

"Mother told me that she had gone with her brother and Daddy. She came back and she said to Mumsie—that's what we called her mother—'I've met the man I'm going to marry.'"[5]

While he didn't divulge much in his autobiography, Russell did write a number of letters to Kay Early during these years, and as recalled by his eldest daughter, the letters displayed Russell's strong feelings for his future wife.

"I have read the letters, and Daddy was head-over-heels," Kay Beasley recalled of the courtship between her parents. "They are the most loving romantic letters. He would feel things deeply, intensely."

Two years after that chance meeting in 1931, at the ages of twenty-seven and twenty-four, respectively, Fred Russell and Katherine Early married 2 November 1933. In his autobiography, written more than two decades later, Russell intimated one of the secrets of their success.

"A woman marrying a newspaperman deserves to know what she's getting into—the odd hours, the sudden changes in plans, the necessity for adaptability," Russell wrote. "Some like it, some don't. She did."[6]

Russell expressed this in 1957, and little did he know that he and Kay would be blessed with four more decades of marriage. The couple was married almost sixty-three years, raised four daughters, and turned their house at 3804 Brighton Road in the West End area into a home of true warmth and family.

For Family and Friends,
It Was "Grand Central Station"

After their marriage in 1933, Fred and Kay Russell moved into an apartment on Belmont Boulevard and immediately began a family Within a couple of months, Kay was pregnant with their first child, Katherine Early, who was born 18 October 1934. Over the next twelve years, the Russells would have three more children, all girls: Ellen Fall (12 March 1937), Elizabeth Lee (8 July 1942), and Carolyn Evans (17 October 1946). After Ellen was born, Fred and Kay made plans to purchase a home near West End Avenue, and beginning in 1938, the Russells lived at their Brighton Road home for the next fifty-five years. As the girls moved out over the years, Fred and Kay remained at Brighton Road until 1993, at which time they moved together to Richland Place, a nearby retirement community.

While at the Brighton Road home, Fred and Kay made it a point to be involved in their neighborhood and their community. Members of West End United Methodist for decades, the Russell family became a fixture within the local community. Among their closest friends were Tommy and Dorothy Frist, a friendship that began years before either Russell or Frist (of Hospital Corporation of America fame and fortune within the Nashville healthcare business) had become known outside of Middle Tennessee. Within the community, the Russell home became known for its holiday events and neighborhood picnics, just to name a few.

One of Russell's good friends later in life was Art Demmas, who played on Vanderbilt's 1955 Gator Bowl team and then served as an NFL official for almost thirty years. Demmas and Russell also teamed up to run the Middle Tennessee chapter of the National Football Foundation

College Hall of Fame, and with these football connections, Demmas stayed in touch with Russell often.

"I loved going into their home," Demmas recalled. "It was very special, and it really was a home, not a place to live. When you walked through the front door, you could feel the warmth of that wonderful family."[7]

"They added on to that house twice, when they needed more bedroom space, so each of those girls could have their own bedroom," longtime friend Grace Stumb added. "They had a big back room, and Freddie had pictures, pictures, pictures of every sports event and big-wig sports name around. With that big back porch, where they had hanging baskets of ferns and geraniums and those big wicker chairs, we'd sit out there, have drinks before dinner, and watch the sunset."[8]

Between Russell's penchant for hospitality when visiting sportswriters and coaches were in town, and their active involvement with the neighborhood, not to mention the four girls, 3804 Brighton Road was oftentimes the epicenter for organized chaos.

The four Russell daughters, all of whom are still living, remember those years well. Kay Beasley, the eldest of the four, recalled how it seemed that everyone in the community knew "Miss Kay" and "Mr. Freddie." "People were over all the time, so many coaches and football players and friends," Kay remembered. "We just had a wonderful childhood."[9]

Kay's sister, Lee Brown, summed it up appropriately.

"With four girls, I think everyone had friends in and out all the time," Lee noted. "Our house was like Grand Central Station."

One area that was bound for conflict, however, was the telephone. There was only one telephone line at the house, and with four daughters growing up, that fact by itself was enough to make the phone ring a fair amount. When you add Russell's career as a sportswriter to the mix, there were times when something had to give. Most of the time, the father pulled rank on his daughters.

"Those four girls didn't touch that telephone if their Daddy was expecting a phone call," Grace Stumb recalled with a laugh. "The four of them would have their boyfriends, but they couldn't use it if Freddie needed it for business."[10]

With regard to Russell's job, it wasn't just the telephone that had its set of rules. If there was an important game being played that Russell needed to hear on the radio or watch on the television, the game took priority. The daughters came to realize that watching sports on the television was not an opportunity to spend time with their father.

"That was his work area," Lee noted. "He'd have a radio going, a TV going. You would tiptoe in there and hope you didn't open your mouth."[11]

Even the grandchildren came to learn this rule, as noted by one of Carolyn's two children.

"You just didn't talk during the game, and if the phone rang, it wasn't answered," Carrie Van Derveer recalled. "I would always go early and stay late, because those were the times I knew I could visit with him."[12]

If Russell wasn't on the phone with reporters, coaches, or athletes, it was very common for him and Kay to invite them over for dinner. Whether it was a new Vanderbilt coach, or a coach and his wife visiting from another school, or even just a group of family and friends, the standard procedure was for a big dinner with all involved, followed by stories in the family room from the Russell patriarch.

"It was absolutely commonplace for us to have company for dinner," Lee continued. "There might be a new coach in town, Mother would find out that afternoon, and she'd make a big pot of spaghetti. Everybody would sit around, eat that spaghetti and rye bread, and Daddy would later tell his stories."[13]

At these dinners, even though it was Fred who presided over the closing speeches, Kay was the master of ceremonies who made it all possible.

"Mother was the icebreaker. She would meet the people, make everyone feel at ease, and then Daddy would come in with his little more formal act," Lee noted. "He was shy, believe it or not, but Mother wasn't scared of anything. That was the best thing about her personality."[14]

Roy Kramer, who became a good friend of the Russells later in Fred's life, couldn't talk about the Russell home without first describing Kay. "She was such a gracious Southern lady, such a hostess," Kramer pointed out. "You went to that house, and you just felt that Kay had been waiting all day for you to arrive. She gave you that kind of welcoming."[15]

Kramer was merely one of many before him who had learned that about his friend's wife. The spaghetti dinners were something of a legend, as it turned out. If there were a number of neighborhood kids coming over, Kay would make extra for all who were coming. Two of the more popular gatherings each year were Halloween and Christmas. During the holiday seasons in particular, the Russells used the barn they had in their back yard to tell ghost stories or recreate the nativity scene each year. At Christmastime, families from around the neighborhood were involved as well. Children would dress up in bathrobes to play shepherds, and if a new baby had been born, that baby was the Baby Jesus. The daughters remember the nativity play each year, as it was a tradition that lasted through the decades.

"It was right in the backyard, Mother would read the Bible, and the angels would come," Carolyn remembered. "This was one of Mother's big traditions, reenacting the nativity each year with people from all around the neighborhood."[16]

The Frists were perhaps the closest family friends of the Russells, and memories of the nativity play remain strong years later. Mary (Frist) Barfield was born the same year as Carolyn (1946), and Christmastime was a special memory growing up.

"They would invite neighbors and children of their friends could come participate and dress up for the play," Barfield recalled. "Being a part of that was just an example of how they lived their life the whole year, but it culminated in that event, and that was a special time for all of us. They made it so much that way."[17]

While the holiday events were annual traditions, they of course were not the only parties that friends and family members remember at the Russell home. One particular party that immediately came to mind for one of the sons-in-law was an anniversary celebration. Or perhaps it was Russell's one-liner that Earl Beasley remembered so well.

"They had this anniversary party at their house, and near the end, Fred rose to make a little toast," Beasley said. "He said, 'You know, we have had twenty-eight wonderful years together. And twenty-eight out of forty-one ain't all that bad.' Well, the crowd just went nuts, and his timing was perfect. You never knew what he was going to say next."[18]

Beasley had married Russell's first daughter, Kay, and had a special relationship with his father-in-law.

"I was the first son-in-law to come along, and I was the first male thrown in the group," Beasley reflected. "Here he was living in a house with five women, and he kidded me one day when he said, 'You know the only males in here have been me and my dog.'"[19]

It wasn't only Russell's sense of humor that resonated with his new son-in-law. Beasley had fond memories of the many qualities that made his father-in-law a natural role model. "He had strong convictions and feelings. His mild-mannered exterior and great humor belied a will of steel."[20]

That great sense of humor, however, evokes the strongest memories within the family, especially the grandchildren, who came to see their grandfather as more than just a person they'd see a couple of times per year.

"Every time there was a family gathering, he would wear this red necktie," grandson Will Van Derveer remembered. "It had in white ink all the names of the grandchildren, and that was symbolic of how he constantly paid attention to those around him. He was kind of the quintessential godfather. He always knew what was going on with the grandchildren, and he was a total father figure."[21]

Growing Up with the Russells

While the family events and neighborhood gatherings may have been spirited, the get-togethers were simple. In fact, things at the Russell home were rarely extravagant. As products of the Great Depression, Fred and Kay were thrifty, especially with the task of raising four children.

"Resourceful" was one of the first words Fred would use to describe his wife, according to the daughters. He would often say that Kay could make do with just about anything and rarely complained. Part of this was her own personality, but part of this certainly can be attributed to the lean economic years in which they were raising their family.

"We never were into the materialistic things that some people were, and Mother saw to that," Ellen Sadler recalled of their years growing up.[22]

Her sisters acknowledged that the Depression had affected their parents, without a doubt. "My clothes all came from hand-me-downs," Kay Beasley noted. "There would be a couple of girls older than me who would hand down their clothes, because Mother was a good friend of their family."[23]

"And Mother never cared," Lee Brown continued. "We'd go to church, somebody would ask how she's doing, and she'd say, 'Fine. I'm living in your suit, which is brand-new to me.' She was proud to save money."[24]

The Russells expected their daughters to be tough as well. Not necessarily tough in a physical sense all the time, but mentally and emotionally tough. Their mother set the tone for this, sometimes directly, other times just by leading by example. Ellen remembered a time her mother was sidelined for almost a week and a half due to a ruptured appendix. "That was excruciating pain, and yet she recovered," Ellen recalled. "You needed to be tough. She abhorred hypochondriacs."[25]

As for mental toughness, one example specific to raising four girls was how the Russell parents counseled their daughters in the complicated area of teenage romance. Their parents kept it simple. If one of the girls lost a boyfriend, a common expression from their mother was simply, "Lots of pebbles on the beach."[26]

Lee remembered how romance discussions could also lead into indirect messages of discipline or guidance from her parents. When it came to what she described as "THE crisis of our generation," the advice she and her sisters received was subtle.

"If somebody's daughter had gotten pregnant without being married or had to get married, Mother and Daddy would sit at the table and say things such as, 'Oh. I'm sure it's broken their Mother and Daddy's heart,' or 'That girl was so smart.' That was how they disciplined us," Lee remembered with a laugh. "We had to read between the lines to learn the lesson."[27]

When it came to guidance, much like the "pebbles on the beach" comment, keeping things simple was the no-nonsense approach favored by the Russells, especially with the more debatable subjects. A good example was religion. While quiet in their convictions, Fred and Kay Russell nonetheless were strong Christians. With his own children, Russell preferred the clear-cut answers to religion's tough questions, allowing the more philosophical discussions to occur elsewhere. Lee remembered a conversation she once had with her father on the subject, albeit a short one. "I remember asking Daddy one time, 'Do you think

Jesus could really be God's son?' It was a real deep question," Lee said. "And he just said, real short, 'Couldn't be any other way.' And that was the end of it."[28]

As for things around the house Monday through Saturday, when it came to order, wife Kay and the four daughters took their cues from Russell. The sportswriter's schedule was demanding, but unless Russell was traveling out of town, he was home most nights in time for dinner. But as the daughters remember, there were rules.

"Daddy had two drinks every night, and if he got home, you didn't eat until he had those two drinks," Carolyn remembered. "I wanted to eat at three, but it was always at least seven."[29]

"Everything revolved around Daddy's schedule," Kay added. "Sometimes we would eat so late, there would be curlers in our hair and a date coming in ten minutes."[30]

With Russell out during the day with his duties at the *Banner*, the dinner table became the main gathering place for the family when he returned home. For all the challenges at work, keeping up with the five women in his life sometimes proved to be just as challenging, and the Russell family wouldn't be normal if there weren't a few memorable exchanges.

As members of the family admitted, it was often daughter Lee who found herself at the center of such things, when she reacted to her father's discipline.

"We wouldn't dare have thought of doing some of the things around Daddy that Lee thought of doing and did," daughter Ellen said. "We were just horrified sometimes when she would stand up to him."[31]

"Everybody else was buying into him, and there were times when I was like, 'Oh, you are just full of hot air,'" Lee recalled with a laugh, remembering the times when she would have to out-run her father if her back-talk led to a father-daughter chase through the house.[32]

Youngest daughter Carolyn recalled a specific time they were all at the table, and her sister was testing the limits of their father's patience. Eventually, the response from Russell came: "Not another word out of you!"

Carolyn remembered knowing what was coming next. "I remember thinking: 'She's going to do it. She's going to do it. Here it comes,'" Carolyn said with a smile. "And then there's this long pause, and we knew something bad was coming. And Lee then says, 'Word.' Well, up from the table he goes, and off she goes. Daddy's chasing her, and Lee's running away as fast as she can."[33]

Of course, as was Russell's style at the *Banner* or out with peers, any hard feelings were washed away with his disarming sense of humor. A standing joke at the same dinner table was the happenings among the animals around the house that day.

"Daddy was great at telling stories to us at dinner time. He would tell us that the dogs and cats had a meeting in the barn about something," Kay recalled. "Whichever animals we had at the time, he would use their names and tell us if they were presiding over the meeting and what was decided at these meetings."

If company was coming over for dinner, depending on who it was, that oftentimes allowed Russell to try out a few jokes on the family first.

"He could capture the essence of people, and then turn it around with his sarcasm, his sense of humor," Lee remembered. "For example, with one of the couples with whom they were friends, the husband was real shy and never opened his mouth. Daddy would say things like, 'Gosh, he's gonna talk *all* night, dominate the conversation; we'll never get a word in edge-wise.' Daddy knew that and would just have fun with us."[34]

Beyond invoking his trademark sense of humor to have fun, Russell was also the father in the backyard playing sports with his girls. There was an asphalt badminton court at their home, with basketball goals at each end, and Russell played baseball, softball, and basketball with his four daughters on their property. Described by Kay as a "teaching coach," Russell was involved with the girls as much as his schedule allowed.

Over time, the Russell home at Brighton Road evolved into decades of memories. From the early 1940s, when it was the first home for the last two daughters (Lee and Carolyn), through the early 1990s, it was Fred and Kay's home for fifty-five years. The house today remains in the family, as one of Russell's eleven grandchildren, Russell Harwell, purchased it in 1993.

Losing Kay

When Fred and Kay Russell sold their home of fifty-five years to their grandson in 1993, they moved to Richland Place, a retirement community located less than two miles away. By this time, both were in their eighties, and while Richland Place was not a nursing home, it was established to make everyday living a stress-free experience for retirees, even the ones who wished to remain active.

When it came time for holiday events, the extended Russell family didn't miss a beat. They would have a Thanksgiving or Christmas meal at Richland Place, and the whole family would get together. Carrie Van Derveer remembered how her grandmother, whom they called "Mimi," enjoyed her time there, even though Freddie had not quite come around yet.

"Mimi just adored it. She thought it was like camp," Van Derveer recalled with a laugh. "Freddie hated it, but she loved it, which eventually made him like it, because she loved it so much."[35]

Fred had just turned ninety when Kay, eighty-seven, died, and while he had certainly experienced the deaths of friends and family members over the years, the loss of his wife was devastating.

Roy Kramer, a close friend of Russell's ever since he had become Vanderbilt's athletic director in 1978, remembered how hard it was on his friend. Kramer knew that Russell had lost more than just a wife, but a true companion, someone who had literally been around the world with him, always there to celebrate his successes.

"They were almost one, inseparable. That was such a major blow to Fred," Kramer said of Kay's death, noting that the traveling they did as they got older only brought them closer together. "But even earlier, such as with the football Hall of Fame dinners in New York, Kay would always be part of that. She was always there with Fred in the lobby. She was just a part of his life."[36]

In late summer and early fall 1996, Kay had been moved to a different part of Richland Place. Russell visited her every day, multiple times per day. He knew her time was at hand, and it was important for him to be at his wife's side when she died. In early October, her sickness worsened, and after spending time with Kay during the day on Saturday, 5 October, Russell returned to his room. The next morning, about 6 A.M., just moments before he arrived, Kay died. Not being there made it even more difficult for Russell.

"He was so sad that he had not been with her," Lee recalled. "He had just wanted to be with her at the time of her death, and he regretted that."[37]

Russell's granddaughter saw her grandfather in a way she had never seen. "I knew how much he loved her, but when she died, I saw it. He broke down in a way that was very human, but I wasn't used to seeing that from Freddie," Carrie Van Derveer reflected. "She was always there with him, and he felt so guilty that he wasn't there. She had just died, and he stepped into the room. He hung on to that for awhile, that he wasn't there, he wasn't there, he wasn't there. He kept saying that."[38]

The funeral for his wife proved no easier for Russell.

"I was the one driving him to the funeral in my car, and he kept telling me he was going to have a heart attack," Carolyn recalled of that day.

At the funeral, however, Russell summoned the emotional and physical strength to celebrate his wife. Daughter Kay marveled at her father's ability to stand during the entire visitation. "He was not strong enough to do that, and we kept trying to get him to sit down, but he wouldn't do it," Kay recalled. "Hundreds of people—it had to be excruciating."[39]

In the days and weeks that followed, the death of his wife continued to hit Fred Russell hard. The person who had for years helped him through these times was no longer there for him. Instead, and appropriately so, Russell had his daughters to fill that void. Carolyn remembered how hard those times were on her father.

"When he was first so upset over Mother, he didn't know how to order medicine over the phone, he was crying in the kitchen, absolutely crying," Carolyn recalled. "He would just get so upset. I remember telling him that he just didn't need to worry about things like that, that we would all be there for him, and from that moment on, he was much more open about things."[40]

Over time, Russell improved, of course, but he was never quite the same emotionally. Carolyn's son, Will Van Derveer, couldn't help but notice a difference in his grandfather after his grandmother died.

"He was just a different person. There was the grief of losing her, of course, but most likely he never got over her death," Van Derveer said, adding that toward the end of Russell's own life seven years later, he would sometimes call out to her. "I think that's a sign that he never really got over her."[41]

Will's sister, Carrie, had similar recollections. "Even back in 2001, he was saying to Mom, 'I want to be with your Mother.' He would have these little sad episodes, where he was saying he was ready," Van Derveer said of her grandfather.

Fred Russell lived another six-plus years after Kay's death, passing away in January 2003 at the age of ninety-six. Regardless of the success Fred obtained in his profession, the two of them together were infinitely more successful as parents and grandparents. They raised four children and were grandparents eleven times over. Their oldest daughter, Kay, drawing on her parents' ability to keep things simple, summarized their life appropriately.

"They were just a great pair," Kay Beasley noted. "She was the life of the party, and he was the great, magnetic storyteller."[42]

12

The Scholarship

"I had barely even heard of Vanderbilt. I didn't know anything about it, until a guidance counselor gave me a pamphlet about this scholarship. If there wasn't a scholarship, I wouldn't have learned about Vanderbilt, certainly would not have gone there. But through Vanderbilt, I eventually got to meet Buster, and through Buster, I got a leg up at the *New York Times*, when I was twenty-five. Would that have all happened without the scholarship? Probably not."[1] —Tyler Kepner, *New York Times* sportswriter; 1993 recipient, Fred Russell-Grantland Rice TRA Sportswriting Scholarship

Other than the scholarship itself, one of the more remarkable things about the Fred Russell-Grantland Rice TRA (Thoroughbred Racing Association) Sportswriting Scholarship is hearing past recipients describe their reaction to winning it. The two selections below are from Skip Bayless, 1970 recipient, and Dave Sheinin, 1987 recipient, both of whom made sportswriting their career upon leaving Vanderbilt.

"When I came in from baseball practice one Monday night in 1970, my life changed. I couldn't figure out why my parents were waiting with my late dinner. My mom said, 'Somebody called from Vanderbilt and said you won some scholarship.' The scholarship is something like the Heisman Trophy: it commands attention no matter how professionally talented the recipient."[2] —Skip Bayless

"A math teacher, of all people, at my high school was the one who told me about the scholarship, and I recall being incredulous that such a thing existed. A full scholarship to Vanderbilt for sportswriting? That's unbelievable. When I won the award, I remember driving around to my parents' workplaces and to my grandparents' house to deliver the news in person. I was ecstatic, and I remember my grandfather crying when I told him about it."[3] —Dave Sheiner

Here's a quiz: how many sportswriters (1) have their name attached to a scholarship, (2) share the scholarship's name with Grantland Rice, arguably the godfather of the sportswriting business, and (3) leveraged that scholarship to influence fifty years of future sportswriters?

The answer: one. This scholarship is one-of-a-kind, it still exists today, and the sportswriter for which it is named is Fred Russell.

Despite the numerous awards and accolades that Russell received during his sixty-nine-year run at the *Nashville Banner*, perhaps one of the most tangible aspects of the Russell legacy has nothing to do with any award he received for his own writing. Rather, through this unique sportswriting scholarship to his alma mater, Russell is a common link between his past, the sportswriters of today, and ultimately, the sportswriters of tomorrow.

The scholarship's official title is the Fred Russell-Grantland Rice TRA Sportswriting Scholarship, and it has been in place since 1956. Originally named after Russell's friend and mentor, the "TRA (Thoroughbred Racing Association) Grantland Rice Scholarship" was a four-year award given to an incoming Vanderbilt University freshman. With both Rice (Class of 1901) and Russell (Class of 1927) as Vanderbilt alumni, coupled with the academic prestige of the university itself, the scholarship represented a life-changing opportunity for aspiring writers. When the scholarship received a long-term endowment in 1986, Russell's name was added to the scholarship, and it has attracted some of the nation's top journalistic talent coming out high school for more than fifty years.

Skip Bayless received the scholarship in 1970 and is one of its most well-known recipients. After writing weekly columns for Vanderbilt's school newspaper, the *Hustler*, Bayless went on to become a nationally syndicated columnist with the *Dallas Morning News*, the *Chicago Tribune*, and the *San Jose Mercury News*, before turning primarily to a television career with ESPN.

"I would not be where I am today without that scholarship," Bayless admitted. Reflecting back on his years at Vanderbilt, he immediately thought of Russell. "Like so many freshmen, I was having a hard time getting adjusted to college. But the great joy of my day was to hear the *Nashville Banner* hit the hallway outside my door, because I knew Fred Russell would be there waiting for me."[4]

Bayless, of course, is just one of many past recipients who have parlayed their scholarship at Vanderbilt into professional success. Notable writers before him were Larry Daughtrey (Class of '58), who still writes in Cleveland a half-century after attending Vanderbilt, and Roy Blount (Class of '59), who continues as one of the nation's more successful and popular literary humorists. More recently, over the past twenty years, recipients have included Dave Sheinin (Class of '91), the Baltimore Orioles beat-writer with the *Washington Post*; Tyler Kepner (Class of '97), the New York Yankees beat-writer for the *New York Times*; and Lee Jenkins (Class of '99), who has been with *Sports Illustrated* since 2007.

This elite group of former Vanderbilt students litters the sports desks of America from coast to coast, and even those who didn't win the scholarship, but applied for it and attended Vanderbilt anyway, have made headlines for themselves in the sports business. Most notably in this group is Buster Olney, who fought his way through Vanderbilt's academic rigors to graduate and earn a job at the *Nashville Banner*, working for Russell himself. A favorite of Russell's during their *Banner* days, Olney now works for ESPN as one of its lead baseball analysts.

The history of the scholarship is a fascinating one, in part because of its unique connection to Grantland Rice and Fred Russell, but more for its impact on the generation of writers who followed these two giants of sports journalism. Stories from the recipients themselves on how the scholarship impacted their lives, as well as how they came to know and appreciate Russell in a very special way, provide a personal perspective on how today's generation of scholarship recipients, both young and old, have continued the legacy of Fred Russell.

Origins of the Scholarship

More than a half century ago, in spring 1954, Fred Russell was in New York having lunch at the legendary Toots Shor's restaurant with his good friends Bill Corum and Grantland Rice. Ostensibly, Russell had traveled from Tennessee to meet with a group of Vanderbilt alumni, and while that meeting did occur, this particular trip is memorable for other reasons. Sadly, as mentioned earlier in the book, the trip to New York would be Russell's final visit with Rice. Two months later, Grantland Rice died, just four months shy of his seventy-fourth birthday.

Rice's death laid the foundation for a memorial. In November of that year, back at Toots Shor's, the restaurant's owner made good on a promise to hold a posthumous party for Rice that was unprecedented. Hundreds attended, as sports celebrities, journalists, and other friends and family members paid their respects to one of sportswriting's founding fathers. Among the sportswriting fraternity, and led by Russell and Corum, an idea to honor their friend began to take shape. Wanting to do something more than just a memorial, the men suggested a sportswriting scholarship in Rice's name. They wanted to connect the scholarship to Vanderbilt University, Rice's alma mater, if they could get the funding for it. Corum had a possible solution. As the president of Churchill Downs, Corum suggested that the Thoroughbred Racing Association might be willing to fund such a scholarship. With Rice's love for racing and his passion for writing about the industry, the idea had merit. Corum took the idea to John Morris, president of the TRA, and Morris was sold.

While Corum was taking care of funding the scholarship, Russell took the lead on pulling the scholarship together. As a fellow Vanderbilt man, not to mention the scholarship being named after his mentor, Russell became the easy choice as the person to chair the scholarship selection committee. Russell worked with Vanderbilt chancellor Harvie Branscomb to establish the scholarship, and in 1956, the committee selected the first TRA-Grantland Rice scholar, a young man from Nashville, Tennessee, named Charles "Chuck" Nord.

Fast-forward thirty years. It was 4 May 1986, and on the campus of Vanderbilt University, a reunion was being held. The scholarship was in its thirtieth year, and almost twenty past and current recipients of the TRA-Grantland Rice scholarship gathered for a celebration dinner. It was the first time that such a large group of Rice scholars were united. Vanderbilt chancellor Joe B. Wyatt and vice chancellor John Beasley were there, and Beasley provided the background regarding the genesis of the scholarship and why it was taken so seriously by not only Vanderbilt, but by Russell himself.

"It was designed to be the best sports journalism scholarship in America, as 'best' would be the only kind appropriate to the memory of Grantland Rice," Beasley noted.[5]

Also present that night from TRA was Charles Cella, president at the time, and he had good reason to be excited.

"The message is clear tonight," Cella told the crowded banquet hall. "The thirty-year-old Grantland Rice Memorial Scholarship has been a huge success. Scholars from all over the country have enjoyed this program and have blossomed forth as outstanding sports journalists."

However, despite the efforts of the Thoroughbred Racing Association over the first thirty years of the scholarship, the long-term financial backing for the scholarship was in jeopardy. Cella had an important announcement to address that concern, and it would breathe new life into the scholarship for years to come.

"The Thoroughbred Racing Association announces that no longer will the funding of this scholarship be a spigot, sometimes on, sometimes off," Cella stated. "For tonight, we announce a special endowment gift to Vanderbilt University of $500,000."[6]

The 4 May 1986 celebration was not just about endowing the scholarship. There was one more announcement that night, and it was to honor Fred Russell. While the TRA had taken care of the financial well-being of the scholarship, its caretaker for thirty years had been Russell. He had chaired the selection committee since the scholarship's inception, and true to his character, Russell had remained a mentor to the recipients as they progressed through their years at Vanderbilt.

Local Nashville television anchor Dan Miller narrated a slideshow presentation honoring Russell. As the pictures of Russell's life, his sportswriting adventures, events attended, and contacts within the industry were shown, Miller offered an appropriate tribute:

"Tonight we have honored sportswriting at its best, exemplified in the life and work of one universally acknowledged as the dean of American sportswriters: Grantland Rice.

"We turn now to honor another in that great tradition, a second son of Vanderbilt, whose sentences and paragraphs bring laughter and occasionally tears to countless readers, whose life is a record of straightforwardness and integrity, and whose legacy to the world has been an enrichment of the understanding of sport and its meaning for all people.

"We honor a man whose career embodies the important relationship between athletics and a full life. A man who, like Rice, is a model, perhaps the consummate model for many an aspiring sportswriter, a man without whom there would likely have been no TRA Grantland Rice program and no celebration tonight.

"Fred Russell is a sportswriter in the rare tradition of Grantland Rice, raised in his homeland and educated at his alma mater. He was a close friend, a companion, and a great admirer of Rice. But he climbed the sports world mountain by his own route and with his own personal set of abilities.

"The generous donors who have provided the endowment presented tonight have sought to strengthen this scholarship in two ways: first, by ensuring its continuity through the creation of this handsome and permanent fund; second, by linking the name of 'Fred Russell' with that of Grantland Rice in the title of the scholarship.

"It is the hope of all of us that this tradition of great sportswriting will continue to grow and flourish at Vanderbilt and elsewhere. And it is in that spirit that Vanderbilt is pleased to receive the endowment and to announce for excellence in sports journalism, the Fred Russell-Grantland Rice TRA Sportswriting Scholarship."[7]

Fred's Fingerprints on the Scholarship

Long before his name was officially attached to the scholarship in 1986, Fred Russell was the man behind the scenes with the Thoroughbred Racing Association scholarship. In fact, whether before, during, or after the selection process, Russell's mark on the scholarship was that he was always there. He invested in the process and the recipients, and he cared about them not only during their time spent at Vanderbilt, but in the years after they graduated as well. Once it was in place, it became Russell's annual homage to his mentor and good friend. He took great pride in not just being part of the committee, but spearheading the review process and selecting the recipients. Russell was the scholarship's Wizard of Oz, organizing an annual committee of nine who would gather in Nashville the week after the Kentucky Derby to select that year's recipient. The committee was comprised of three sportswriters, three members of the TRA, and three representatives from Vanderbilt.

An interesting aspect of the scholarship was that it did not require the recipient to be a sportswriter. Vanderbilt did not then (nor does it now) have a journalism department, per se, so even if recipients wanted to major in journalism, they were unable to do so. That recipients did not have to be sportswriters was not an accident or an oversight. Russell put a premium on the Vanderbilt education and always viewed the Vanderbilt degree as the most important thing recipients would take away from their years at the university. The TRA agreed with Russell, and this aspect of scholarship has always remained. Charles Cella of the TRA befriended Russell through the horse racing industry in the 1960s, and by the late 1960s, he was one of the TRA representatives who participated in the selection process.

"Many of them have become great writers, but they don't have to do that for their profession," Cella said, emphasizing that the selection committee always viewed its role as awarding the scholarship to someone who would gain an outstanding education first and foremost. "If you take care of an individual's education, he'll be indebted to you for life."[8]

Each spring, when the committee gathered in Nashville to review writing samples from applicants, there was no denying Russell's involvement in the final selection. And even though there was an official vote every year, Russell himself pored through the applications of the finalists and had the final say if the committee was deadlocked. On many occasions, Russell's instincts as an editor naturally took over.

Lee Jenkins, who wrote for the *Colorado Springs Gazette* and *New York Times* before landing his current job at *Sports Illustrated*, was the 1995 recipient, and he remembered learning of Russell's involvement in the selection process.

"Mr. Russell would look through the clippings and say, 'This is the one.' People would sit around and go through the writings, go through the motions, but when Fred Russell saw the one he wanted, that was it," Jenkins noted, adding that he later learned from Mr. Russell that the veteran sportswriter looked for candidates to show a certain degree of energy in their writing.

"It was his instincts that carried it over," Jenkins added. "He didn't pick things that were bland. He picked a lot of people who wanted to take chances and be writers."[9]

For those who won the scholarship, when the university called them to share the news, it was a day they could hardly forget.

"Except for my wedding day, it was the most thrilling day of my life," David Rapp admitted. Rapp was the recipient in 1969 and had turned to sportswriting in high school when it became clear that playing the sports themselves was not his calling. "The scholarship was like a sign from heaven that I was on the right path."[10]

For others, the news of the award brought out the purest of emotions. Andrew Maraniss, son of Pulitzer Prize-winning and *Washington Post* journalist David Maraniss, remembered the emotions of the day.

"I remember feeling really, really lucky. The day I found out, I was at my high school's All Sports Picnic, and my mom and sister came walking through the park, and my mom was crying," Maraniss recalled. "I could tell by her reaction that they were tears of joy. I felt as if I had used up my one piece of great luck for my whole life."[11]

While most recipients didn't think twice about accepting the scholarship, every once in a while that did happen. Lee Jenkins also had a journalism scholarship to the University of Southern California, but as it turned out, all Vanderbilt needed to do was to bring in the scholarship's namesake to help convince him.

Jenkins was on an official campus visit and was in the admissions office when he heard that Russell himself, at that time in his late eighties, was on campus. Russell took the young Jenkins for a walk around campus, eventually ending up back at Russell's car, where he signed a copy of his autobiography for the prospective student.

"He wrote, 'To Lee: A Perfect Fit for Vanderbilt,'" Jenkins remembered, adding that Russell told him that he wanted Jenkins to take the scholarship and attend Vanderbilt. "Sitting there in his car, I just said, 'Okay, 'I will.' What else were you going to say, to Fred Russell, sitting there in that situation? I surely wasn't going to say, 'You know, I really need a little more time to think about it.'"[12]

Just as the scholarship elicited natural feelings of joy for the victors, those who came close but did not win felt emotions at the other end of the spectrum. In many cases, because the scholarship's financial package was so attractive, if applicants did not win, they were unable to afford Vanderbilt and attended college elsewhere. But there were a number of applicants who finished second or third and attended Vanderbilt anyway, even if there were financial challenges.

Buster Olney fell into the latter category. Growing up poor in Vermont, he learned about the scholarship in high school and applied. His grades were good enough for Vanderbilt, but he finished second runner-up for the Rice scholarship. Now a columnist for ESPN and one its top baseball analysts, Olney recalled the bittersweet aspects of the scholarship. He chose to attend Vanderbilt, but having to work his way through college one semester at a time was not easy.

"Mike Cornwell won it in my year, and when you finish in third place, you don't get anything," Olney recalled. "As I got to know Mike, I learned that Mike didn't really enjoy sports that much. That was an enormous source of frustration for me. It took me six years to get through college because of the money problems we had."[13]

Olney's perseverance paid off, however. His talents did not go unnoticed during his years writing for the *Hustler*, and Olney landed a summer internship with the *Nashville Banner*, where he impressed Russell and others within the sports department. When Olney was twenty-one credits shy of graduating but out of money to pay for school, he went to Russell looking for a full-time job. What he ended up getting was even better.

"Between Mr. Russell and a few others, they went to Irby Simpkins, who was the publisher, and I had a meeting with Irby," Olney remembered. "Irby said that he would pay for the remainder of my school if I went and worked for them for a year. I just can't imagine how lucky I was. The *Banner* completely bailed me out."[14]

Olney stayed at the *Banner* for several years, then had stops in San Diego and Baltimore before landing with the *New York Times* in 1997. He made a significant impression on Russell, and the two stayed close long after Olney left Nashville. Their friendship was well known among scholarship recipients, something Jenkins, a friend of Olney's, was reminded of when he spoke with Russell after he had graduated from Vanderbilt.

"I got a job in Colorado Springs with the *Colorado Springs Gazette*, and he kept telling me how Buster and [1993 recipient] Tyler [Kepner] were writing for the *New York Times*," Jenkins recalled of his conversation with Russell. "He was proud of me that I was still a sportswriter, but he was most proud of Buster, I remember that. He loved Buster, it was very obvious."[15]

Vanderbilt Memories with "Mr. Russell"

For the recipients of the scholarship, some of their most special memories of their times at Vanderbilt can be tied to Russell. In the 1980s, the veteran sportswriter started an annual tradition through which he could meet with the four current recipients.

"My most vivid memories are of the lunches he would host every year at the University Club for the four current scholarship winners," recalled Andrew Maraniss (1988 recipient). "Mr. Russell would tell us stories from the old days—practical jokes he'd pulled, famous athletes he'd known, and we all sat there in awe."[16]

The stories of the Golden Age of Sports and the first half of the twentieth century always captivated the recipients.

"Oh, Lord, that man could tell some stories," Sheinin (1987 recipient) noted, thinking back to the annual lunches. "We would all fill him in on our activities, and then we'd start prodding him to tell us some more stories."[17]

Skip Bayless remembered similar experiences in the early 1970s. Back then, it was a breakfast meeting with Russell, and Bayless remembered the sportswriter's charm and sense of humor. At that time, Russell was still active with his daily column, and the recipients had the opportunity to read Russell's material as often as they liked.

"He was so genuine. I knew right away that he was real, this wasn't an act, this wasn't some phony charm—this was a genuinely good human being who was extremely talented," Bayless recalled of his initial impressions of Russell when he came to Nashville in 1970. "I began to read the *Banner* and he just had such a nice, easy, clean, insightful, pure style—it was one of those effortless styles that I know wasn't effortless. It read effortlessly."[18]

Russell made these types of impressions on many of the recipients, and that was the case for Tena (Robinson) Herlihy, the scholarship's lone female winner. Herlihy had targeted the scholarship her freshman year of high school and had worked for the *Fort Lauderdale Sun Sentinel* since the age of sixteen.

She arrived at Vanderbilt in fall 1983, and despite sensing some skepticism and jealousy from the scholarship's runner-up, as well as the previous year's recipient, Herlihy faced the challenge head-on. She recalled the lasting impression Russell made on her during her Commodore years.

"I felt a little more pressure to prove that I could write well, to show that I deserved it. Mr. Russell definitely took me under his wing, and he was a great mentor to me," Herlihy noted, adding that it was Russell's genuine care for the scholars that made his impact more meaningful. "I remember when I was a student I wasn't always able to go home for holidays, and he and his wife had me over for Thanksgiving dinner one year. That was just who he was—a very special man."[19]

The Scholarship Today: Hard Times

The Fred Russell-Grantland Rice scholarship for sports journalism is still awarded today, but by many accounts, it is a shell of its former state. Perhaps the biggest indicator in its unfortunate decline is that the scholarship was not awarded at all in 2005 or 2006, as the selection committee cited a lack of qualified applicants from which to choose. The reason for this can be traced to money. Despite the $500,000 endowment the scholarship received from the Thoroughbred Racing Association in 1986, the university made a decision in the mid-1990s to limit the scholarship to a $10,000 per year award. Due to rising tuition costs at the close of the twentieth century, the university's thinking was that it needed to cap the award in order to prolong the life of the scholarship. Tuition costs have soared at Vanderbilt in the past two decades, however, and what once was a life-changing financial award now merely makes a dent in the recipient's ability to cover the cost to attend Vanderbilt. Considering the almost $40,000 tuition cost in 2010, the Russell-Rice scholarship today is roughly a quarter of the full-ride financial package that recipients used to receive.

Not surprisingly, in the fifteen years since the decision to cap the award, two things have happened: one, consistently fewer qualified candidates have applied for the scholarship, and two, the number of notable Russell-Rice scholars writing today in prominent publications has gone down significantly.

The turn of the century marked the last time multiple scholars attended Vanderbilt together and have made a name for themselves in the professional ranks. Kepner and Jenkins graduated in 1997 and 1999, respectively, and of the former scholars from the past two decades, they are arguably the most well known. Dan Wolken was the 1997 recipient, graduated in 2001, and worked for the *Commercial Appeal* in Memphis until leaving in 2010 to be part of Rupert Murdoch's *The Daily* iPad newspaper.

Kepner recalled a visit to Vanderbilt several years ago that was upsetting when it came to learning about the current Russell-Rice scholars.

"I stopped by the [*Hustler*] offices, and several people told me they didn't even know who the scholarship winners were, and that was a real shame and a big surprise," Kepner lamented. "Four people on campus somewhere with the scholarship, and people on the paper don't even know who they are.

"The tradition has gone away some, and maybe it's because it's gone from being a full ride to just being $10,000 per year," the 1993 recipient added. "That's a lot money, but at Vanderbilt these days, not that much really."[20]

Beyond Kepner, Jenkins, and Wolken, you have to go all the way back to Dave Sheinin, the 1987 recipient, to find another recipient writing for a major sports publication. Quite simply, the shine has rubbed off the trophy, and Vanderbilt has lost its ability to attract some of the nation's top talent in sportswriting.

It is a noted concern to the Thoroughbred Racing Association, the primary funding body of the scholarship. Charles Cella had been a friend of Russell's through horse racing and sports for more than three decades, and he served on the selection committee beginning in 1968. It was Cella who represented the TRA when announcing the $500,000 endowment check in 1986, and it was painful for him to see the scholarship not awarded in the mid-2000s.

"We have shrunk this thing down to a committee of one, which I don't like, and we're in the throes of trying to rejuvenate it," Cella commented back in 2005. "The applicants last year were just dreadful, and it made me quite upset. I feel responsible right now for this scholarship and to Freddie, and so we decided to waive it that year."[21]

Cella is looking for ways to inject life into the scholarship again, to make it the prestigious award it used to be.

"As old as I am, I still try to come up with new ideas, and I was thinking about dove-tailing the publication of this Russell biography with somehow rejuvenating the scholarship," Cella commented, before adding a more tactical suggestion. "Perhaps we can take one or two of the past members and have them be part of the committee, because it has been very successful in the past."[22]

The latter idea is one that would have the backing of former scholarship recipients. In fact, the idea was floated to the university several years ago by Jenkins, who remembered the days when Cella and Russell were actively involved in the process.

"Something has gone wrong, and it's just not working right now. I remember getting recruited for the scholarship. I remember Cella calling me from his golf cart, talking about the scholarship and asking me to come to Vanderbilt," Jenkins said. "He and Mr. Russell cared about it, and it was this cool thing. They were recruiting." [23]

With Russell gone, and Cella well into his seventies, Jenkins believes that advertising and recruiting for the scholarship is something the former scholars could (and would) do. He feels strongly that the process can be improved, if the former recipients are given the opportunity to get engaged.

"We would get it done. We would recruit the country, and we would get somebody good every year," Jenkins argued, noting that a former recipient's connections within the sportswriting industry would be a significant asset. "Every year, I hear somebody talking about this person or that person, and I meet sportswriters who have sons who want to be sportswriters. Even with $10,000 per year, it can be done."[24]

The reality is this: even though Russell's been gone since 2003, one way that his name and his legacy remain alive today is through the scholarship. Former recipients acknowledge the reputation the Fred Russell name still carries, not to mention his connection to a sportswriting scholarship.

"When I tell people that I covered sports at Vanderbilt, many people ask me, 'Oh, did you get that scholarship?'" Kepner acknowledged. "The fact that I get that question tells me that people are aware of the scholarship and some of the writers who have come before me."[25]

In the years ahead, reviving the Russell-Rice scholarship will be a shared challenge for both Cella and the TRA, and the fraternity of former awardees, such as Jenkins and Kepner. The interest is there, but what remains to be seen is how and when the powers-that-be can come together to make it happen.

Final Thoughts from Past Winners

When contacting dozens of former winners of the Fred Russell-Grantland Rice TRA Sportswriting Scholarship, it was clear that both the scholarship and Fred Russell had made a profound impact on their respective lives. Whether it was simply the opening of the Vanderbilt door to earn an acclaimed education, or if it led to an established career that followed in the footsteps of those for whom the scholarship was named, the scholarship changed lives. Fred Russell changed lives, and his legacy endures through the lives of those whom he not only touched, but in many cases, handpicked to receive this scholarship. The following represent a few final memories and anecdotes from select recipients:

Bill Livingston, 1966 recipient, sportswriter, Cleveland *Plain Dealer*:

"The scholarship was the reason I got the intern job at the *Dallas Morning News*. They took me on as a twenty-two-year-old intern, and then we got baseball when the Senators left and became the Texas Rangers. They put me on full-time, and then the only reason I got hired in Philadelphia was because John Bloom [the 1971 recipient better known for his pseudonym 'Joe Bob Briggs'] had been an intern at Philadelphia, and he had read my stuff at the *Hustler*, so he gave them my name. That's how I got that job in Philadelphia, and it was for more money at that time in my life than I thought existed. It was $440 dollars a week, and my head was spinning."[26]

David Rapp, 1969 recipient, former senior vice president at *Congressional Quarterly*, currently Ideas Editor at Bloomberg Government:

"The scholarship did two things—it validated my early love for journalism; and it made it possible for me to get a first-class education at a top-ranked university. The Vanderbilt entry on my resume carries me to this day. And the Grantland Rice Scholarship remains a signature accomplishment."[27]

Skip Bayless, 1970 recipient, columnist and television personality, ESPN:

"Right after graduation, I was ready to take a job with the *Daily Oklahoman*, but it wasn't going to pay more than about $150 per week. Two nights before graduation, the *Oklahoman*'s sports editor, Frank Boggs, calls me up, and basically tells me that he didn't want to see me get stuck out there. The scholarship essentially saved me. It's what opened the door for other sports editors to at least listen to Boggs when he described my writing. He called Edwin Pope down in Miami, and the next day, I flew to Miami, interviewed, and they hired me on the spot. They knew of Grantland Rice, of course, and the scholarship, and that's what opened the door for me."[28]

Mike Jackson, 1976 recipient, vice president, Rockwell Automation:

"I wasn't aware of it at the time, but the scholarship ended up being the difference between me graduating from college or not. My father passed away suddenly at the beginning of my sophomore year, and if it were not for the scholarship I wouldn't have been able to continue my education."[29]

Andrew Maraniss, 1988 recipient, vice president, McNeely Pigott & Fox:

"Winning the scholarship set the course of my life. I never would have come to Vanderbilt otherwise; never would have moved to Nashville; never would have met the friends I have; never would have gained the experience that led to the jobs in Tampa or back here in Nashville at MP&F. It's a 'seal of approval' that I will carry with me forever."[30]

Mitch Light, 1989 recipient, editor, *Athlon Sports*:

"I tell this to everyone. One of the great things about the scholarship is that I would recommend Vanderbilt to anyone who wants to be a sportswriter rather than a school like Northwestern or Syracuse. Especially as a Grantland Rice winner, at Vanderbilt, you are thrust into a position with the school paper. Three weeks into my freshman year, I'm covering SEC football. At Vanderbilt, if you're a good writer and you show some initiative, you're going to be covering the highest level of college sports for two to three years."[31]

Matt O'Keefe, 1991 recipient, author:
"The *Vanderbilt Hustler*, when looking at the people who have emerged from it, always had a noticeably strong sports section. That extends to the guys who weren't the scholars as well. With all the sportswriters, it really was a fraternity. But the scholarship also led me into some pointlessly arrogant situations. I remember being on my freshman hall, and we'd be arguing about something that not one of us could possibly know the answer to. Well, during my freshman year, when I entered those debates, I'd be like, 'Look, I'm the Grantland Rice scholar, and I'm telling you, this is what would happen. I know what the hell I'm talking about.'" (Laughing.)[32]

Lee Jenkins, 1995 recipient, sportswriter, *Sports Illustrated*:
"One of the last times I saw [Russell], he was working on this project about the '50 Greatest Vanderbilt Football Games Ever.' He's going through all these old documents, and I asked him, 'Well, which one is your favorite one?' And he says, 'Well, I've thought about that for a long time. I've spent weeks on it, and I've come to the conclusion that the best one was 1922, Vanderbilt-Michigan, 0–0.' That's what he thought was the greatest Vanderbilt football game ever, a 0–0 game from 1922." (Laughing.)[33]

Dan Wolken, 1997 recipient, sportswriter, *The Daily* (iPad newspaper):
"When I think about the time I did get to spend with [Russell], I think about sitting in his [Richland Place] apartment and hearing stories, seeing the great pictures he had, the memorabilia. I remember the few times in 1997 when he came into the press box to watch Vanderbilt football games and how reverential everybody was towards him."[34]

Author's note, 1992 recipient:

"It has been almost twenty years since I received a call from Vanderbilt University, informing me that I had been awarded the 1992 Fred Russell-Grantland Rice Scholarship for Sports Journalism. In the fifty-plus years of this scholarship, I have to believe my reaction is one of a kind: believing wholeheartedly that a friend of mine was prank-calling me, I not-so-politely told the person on the other end of the phone that if he really was serious, then he could just call me back in ten minutes. All I can say is this: Charlie, thank you for calling me back."[35]

13

The *Banner* Part 4: Demise

"Let me tell you something about Pop. He gave his heart and soul to the game, only to get it trampled on."[1] —Richard Farnsworth, *The Natural*

February 16, 1998. It is a date that *Nashville Banner* employees wish could have been skipped, and the events of that day wiped away. They wanted a "do over." It was not to be, however, and as longtime *Banner* editor Eddie Jones recalled, it was one of the toughest days he ever endured with his good friend Fred Russell.

"Fred had a hideaway office, so he could come and go as he pleased during those years, and he came in damn near every day. Fred had picked up a sniff that something was coming down. Because of our longevity and our friendship, he would stop by my office when he picked up a rumor, or I'd go upstairs to see him in the same way. One day, a few days before the 'Armageddon,' he came in and said, 'Eddie, there's something going on with the ownership of the paper. I think the paper is being sold.' Well, as it turned out, that would have been great if that had been what it was. But, it wasn't. None of us knew anything until we got the message for a staff meeting. It was 7:00 o'clock on that Monday morning. And it was announced that the paper would close on the following Friday. Later that morning, Fred came to my office, closed the door, sat down, and cried."[2]

* * *

As a fan of baseball more than any other sport, it should come as no surprise that Fred Russell loved the 1984 baseball classic *The Natural*. When you consider the additional context of the film, however—the late 1930s setting, the epic struggle of a forgotten team and its manager, and an over-the-hill star lifting his team to unimaginable heights—you start to appreciate why Russell not only liked this film, but loved it. Along with another baseball movie, *Field of Dreams*, it was one of Russell's favorites. Beyond the obvious sports connection, the movie resonated with the veteran sportswriter on multiple levels, including journalism. Robert Redford plays the late-in-life rookie Roy Hobbs, who gets his one chance at fame, and one of the film's anti-heroes is sportswriter columnist Max Mercy (played by Robert Duvall), who is as ambitious as he is shameless. Ironically, despite his professional connection to the Max Mercy character, Fred Russell had more in common with Redford's character, as Russell was the true natural in the field of journalism. As this chapter's cover quote describes, Roy Hobbs is playing for far more than himself or the fans. He's playing for Pop Fisher (played by Wilford Brimley), the manager of the team, who has endured enough losing seasons to last a lifetime. Fisher had been dealt a tough hand over the years with his teams, but in the final season for both player and manager, it is Hobbs who had one final at-bat to win the pennant. With one magical, final swing, Hobbs delivers a homerun into the night, and Fisher leaves the game on top.

For Fred Russell and the *Nashville Banner*, if only life could have imitated art. If only he were given the chance to leave on his terms. If only things had not come tumbling down one February morning in 1998. If only his paper, the one for which he had written since 1929, the one he had given his heart and soul to for sixty-nine years, could have survived just a bit longer.

If only.

The demise of the *Banner* came swiftly and painfully. While it was a profitable, and probably unavoidable, decision, it resulted in an additional, cruel punishment for the paper's living legend: a depression that left Russell's family initially wondering if the paper's death would take the life of its patriarch as well.

Black Monday

For Russell and the entire *Banner* staff, the Monday morning events of 16 February 1998 were as painful as they were unexpected. For 122 years, the *Nashville Banner* had clawed its way to respectability, and its employees wore the underdog coat well. While the closing decades of the twentieth century had been tough, and circulation was in decline, everyday tenacity, spirit, and pride remained strong. There had been rumors for months, if not years, that the *Banner* was nearing the end of its run or that it might be sold. However, the paper had hung in there each time. As recently as August 1997, publisher and co-owner Irby Simpkins had given a speech stating the *Banner* was healthier than it had ever been and had a long, prosperous future.[3] So when the staff was summoned to a 7 A.M. meeting by Simpkins, very few, if any, of the staffers knew what their boss had in store for them: he had sold the paper to Gannett Company, which owned the *Tennessean*, and Gannett would be shutting down the *Banner*. To add insult to injury, the final publication would be immediate, with operations coming to an end by the close of that week. Desks needed to be emptied by Friday.

For the roughly 100 staffers at the *Banner*, they were suddenly unemployed. For the owners, Irby Simpkins and Brownlee Currey, who sold the paper for $65 million, they would be just fine, each walking away from the *Banner* with more than $25 million apiece after settling the paper's debt.

Family, friends, colleagues, and competitors recalled the impact of this decision on Fred Russell. In the introduction to this chapter, *Banner* editor Eddie Jones shared the painful initial reaction that his longtime friend had, when Russell came to Jones's office after the morning meeting. There was no mystery as to why those tears were shed. Russell was the longest-tenured employee in the paper's history, and he had been the anchor for the *Nashville Banner* in the twentieth century. The *Banner* had become as much a part of Nashville as Russell had become a part of the paper. In an instant, the owners of the paper severed that relationship. A fierce believer that competition results in better reporting and better stories, Russell could not justify a business decision trumping journalistic integrity and civic pride.

"Eddie, I can't believe this is happening to this newspaper," Russell told Jones that morning. "This is just absolutely disastrous."[4]

Across the hall at the *Tennessean*, Russell's equivalent in terms of reputation and longevity was John Seigenthaler. While acknowledging that the financial realities the *Banner* faced were all but insurmountable, Seigenthaler nonetheless frowned upon the way in which Simpkins executed the shut-down as well as how he treated the most revered and prized possession on the staff.

"[Russell's] final encounter with the *Banner* was disgraceful," Seigenthaler said when asked about the infamous Monday. "He resented it, and I resent it still."[5]

Legendary sportswriter Edwin Pope of the *Miami Herald* had known Russell for almost half a century, as the two covered sports across the south, most notably college football, baseball, and golf. In reflecting on Russell's stature and impact on the *Banner*, Pope recalled how much the paper's closing hurt.

"Every sports person knew about the *Nashville Banner* because of Fred. And when that publisher finally sold the *Banner*, he was just livid," Pope said. "I talked to him shortly after that, and it's the only time I've ever seen him in a fine temper. He was just furious that anybody could do such a thing. It was like part of him died."[6]

Family members certainly recalled the emotions and opinions voiced that February day. Russell's oldest daughter, Kay Beasley, shared a feeling that was common among those who knew Russell.

"He never thought that he would outlive the *Banner*," Beasley said.[7]

Kay's sister Carolyn, the youngest of the four daughters, recalled the pain of that Monday. As she had been doing for some time, Carolyn picked her father up that morning to drop him off at the *Banner*. She quickly learned that Russell had been given a heads-up from Currey about the announcement that was coming at 7 A.M.

"When he got in the car, he said Brownlee had called him and told him the paper was closing," Carolyn Russell recalled. "He was crying. He was in shock."[8]

Of the paper's two owners, Currey had the closer friendship with Russell. Russell's relationship with Simpkins had soured years earlier when one of Simpkins's first acts upon buying the paper in the late 1970s was to hire a younger sports editor to run Russell's department. Russell viewed that as a slight, and his relationship with Simpkins over the years was cordial at best. When it came to delivering the news about the paper's end, it was not surprising for the message to come from Currey. Having already called Russell at the start of the day, Currey went to his office later in the day.

"He was shattered, just decimated by the sale," Currey recalled from his talk that day in Russell's office. "He loved walking in that sports room and knowing he was at home. He loved the history of the paper, and I think he took the closing harder than anyone."[9]

Simpkins admitted that the emotions of the day were difficult. He realized the entrepreneurial spirit of his staff made the paper's closing a challenging reality to absorb and would result in initial feelings of anger.

"I suspect they all felt terribly betrayed by Brownlee and me," Simpkins said of the employees left looking for new jobs. "When you close down a business, there's no perfect way to do it. There's no real way to do what we had to do."

Almost a decade after the sale, however, Simpkins stood by his decision as the correct one. He also believed that his former employees eventually understood the rationale behind closing the paper. When asked about Russell specifically, the *Banner*'s former publisher didn't waver. "I think Freddie before he died was ultimately satisfied that we had tried to do the right thing," Simpkins said in 2006.[10]

Such was not the case, however. As noted by one of his daughters, after Monday, 16 February 1998, there was no doubt as to Fred Russell's opinion of Simpkins: "He never wanted his name mentioned again, from that day on."[11]

Arriving at Reality

In the years since the *Banner* folded, it has been well-documented that the paper's fate was inevitable. Emotion, journalistic pride, and history aside, the economic future for the *Nashville Banner* throughout the 1990s was bleak at best. In the immediate aftermath of the sale, editorial opinion in Nashville focused on the decline in circulation as the insurmountable challenge for the *Banner*. By the end of the first week of the announcement, *Nashville Scene* magazine ran a feature story highlighting the history of the *Banner*, its people, and its fate. Bruce Dobie authored the 19 February 1998 cover story and noted that at its healthiest point, the peak for *Banner* circulation exceeded 100,000. However, from the early 1990s to 1998, circulation had dropped from 62,000 to less than 40,000. When Currey and Simpkins sold to Gannett, projections for the *Banner* were less than 25,000 at the turn of the century.[12]

As Currey reflected on the industry trends across the newspaper landscape at the time, the writing was indeed on the wall.

"The newspaper business was not going to be as vibrant with the Internet and other things, and our circulation of our paper was flat to down," the former co-owner of the paper commented, noting that the *Tennessean*'s circulation had taken a hit as well in recent years. "We were going to be in a position at the end of the Joint Operating Agreement that we were not going to have any value whatsoever."[13]

And therein was the truth: the JOA of 1937.

On the surface, a decline in circulation was the reason cited for the *Banner* failing. And that's not an inaccurate statement. But the real reason for the eventual demise of the *Banner* was much deeper than symptomatic circulation figures from the 1980s and 1990s. It was the Joint Operating Agreement that the *Banner* and *Tennessean* signed back in 1937 that sealed the fate for the *Banner*, even though it took sixty years for that fate to be realized.

The *Tennessean*'s Silliman Evans and *Banner* publisher Jimmy Stahlman came to an agreement that was designed to help both papers. Stahlman was looking to trim operations costs to further maximize his strong paper's profits, and Evans was willing to consider options that would allow him to manage his new investment, even if he had to make some initial concessions. The terms were simple: the two papers would share the costs for advertising, printing, and business operations but would maintain different editorial staffs and viewpoints. The two Nashville newspapers would be co-located at 1100 Broadway Street.

Beyond the shared operational costs, there was one additional component to the JOA, and it was this part of the agreement that was the *Banner*'s ultimate undoing. The *Banner* agreed to give up its Sunday edition, and the *Tennessean* dropped its afternoon editions. It was a compromise that served both papers well for a number of years. However, with the advent of television and the evening news, people preferred their morning paper for newspaper information. At the same time, Sunday papers evolved into advertising machines, which worked in favor of the *Tennessean*. These related developments in the second half of the 1900s, coupled with the general decline in newspaper readership across the country, led to the business reality that mid-size markets such as Nashville could probably only support one profitable newspaper. That paper, as it turned out, wasn't the *Nashville Banner*.

Pat Embry was the *Banner*'s executive editor at the time of the sale in 1998, and he acknowledged that, in retrospect, giving up the Sunday edition for the afternoon editions back in the 1930s was an unfortunate concession that cost the paper. The afternoon slot had been the power position before the World Wars and television, Embry noted, and as its history would reveal, "The *Banner* simply chose the wrong horse."[14]

By late 1997, when he considered the long-term viability of the *Banner*, Irby Simpkins looked at various options for growth and profit but ultimately concluded that it was in the best interest of ownership and staff to sell to Gannett. With the financial possibilities of this perfect-storm of data in hand, Simpkins was on the phone with Gannett's CFO Larry Miller the following week. According to Simpkins, negotiations started shortly thereafter but were kept quiet by both parties. With regard to how they arrived at the eventual sale price, it didn't take long.

"We went in with $108 million, and he came back in the mid-30s, and we settled at $65 [million]," Simpkins said, adding that when he shared the news with his co-owner, it took Currey's breath away. "He was very happy, and I told him it was going to be pretty sweet and simple."[15]

Opinion on the decision to sell was generally mixed. Newspaper and journalism purists naturally wanted to see a solution that enabled the *Banner* to continue and allow competition to result in better reporting for both papers. Economists argued that it made sense for Simpkins and Currey to sell when they did, in order to maximize profits from their twenty-year investment.

Within the Nashville media, multiple opinions emerged as well.

"There was no doubt the *Banner*'s circulation was spiraling down, and Irby and Brownlee made a lot of money from the paper, but that was their right. It was their right to sell it," Bruce Dobie said.[16]

Dobie's colleague at the *Nashville Scene*, Henry Walker, was more critical of the two owners. Walker noted that the revenue percentages guaranteed to Simpkins and Currey as part of the JOA allowed each of them to earn more than $1 million each year as far back as the late 1980s. Even if individual profits declined somewhat until the JOA's scheduled expiration in 2015, the two owners could have waited things out until then, or sold to someone other than Gannett. From Walker's perspective, they did neither, choosing profits over people.

"Simpkins and Currey bargained to make a few more dollars while throwing the staff out of work and leaving Nashville a one-newspaper town," Walker wrote. "Despite laments about declining circulation and uncertain profits, the sale and closing of the *Banner* was about greed, not newspaper economics. Currey and Simpkins got richer; Gannett got its monopoly; and the *Banner* staff got pink slips."[17]

At the *Tennessean*, the prevailing emotion from staffers who had once been competitors was one of condolences. Despite the fact that many had battled Fred Russell for years, it was a sad day for them as well.

"People at the *Tennessean* hated to see the *Banner* go. It took some of the fun and the challenge out of the business," sportswriter Jimmy Davy admitted, noting that he felt particularly bad for the man who had been a thorn in his side for years when the two competed for sports stories coming out of Vanderbilt.

"That was a horrible day for Mr. Russell," Davy added. "I went by to see him on the day the paper was sold. I just felt like somebody on the other side should, and I made it a point to go by his office. It was almost like he lost his life. It was a sad, sad day."[18]

Painful Repercussions

As if the closing itself was not enough, the death of the *Nashville Banner* took an unexpected mental toll on Fred Russell. With decades of the proverbial blood, sweat, and tears invested in his career with the paper, Russell fell into a depression in the spring and summer when Simpkins and Currey sold the *Banner* in 1998. It was less than eighteen months after Russell had lost his wife of 63 years, and the two events, so close to one another, were simply too much for him to manage.

"When Mother died, he still had the column," Carolyn Russell noted. "When the *Banner* left, he had nothing."[19]

Hard feelings within the family remain. Russell's first son-in-law, Earl Beasley, married eldest Russell daughter, Kay, and became good friends with his father-in-law.

"It was the cruelest thing I have ever seen happen to a guy. I get really upset at the guys who did that, because of what it did to Freddie," Beasley admitted. "It may have been a good business decision, but it crushed him. Who in the world works somewhere for sixty-nine years and *it* goes out of business?"[20]

Friends saw the impact on Russell as well. C. M. Newton coached the Vanderbilt basketball team for eight years in the 1980s and stayed friends with Russell after taking the athletic director position at Kentucky. Newton remembered that when Russell had been honored with the sports editor emeritus title at the *Banner*, he remained a creature of habit and still went into his office.

"He had no reason to go, no reason to be there other than the fact that was where he wanted to be," Newton pointed out. "And when they closed the *Banner*, it was almost like a death in the family, maybe worse. It deprived him of a place to go, and people to be with, and he had devoted his whole life to it."[21]

All of this took its toll on the ninety-one-year-old Russell. Two of his grandchildren, Will and Carrie Van Derveer, both have vivid memories of their grandfather struggling through depression.

"You couldn't bring up the *Banner*," Carrie Van Derveer said. "You couldn't even say that word."[22]

"His system was so shocked by the *Banner*'s folding, he was in the past," Will Van Derveer added. "We were all very worried about him."[23]

Eventually, though, the right medicine began to help Russell, and he steadily improved. Admittedly, it was a scary time, but Russell survived the ordeal and lived an additional four and a half years. Family members admitted, however, that their father and grandfather was never the same after the *Banner* folded.

A *Banner* Man to the End

Before the depression hit, Russell was respectfully approached by the *Tennessean*. With the blessing of John Seigenthaler, sports editor John Bibb approached his longtime rival from the *Nashville Banner*. The question to the iconic sportswriter: would he be interested in keeping his column going, even if just once a week or once a month?

Hesitantly, Russell agreed. In retrospect, it was as if you couldn't keep a good man down. Like a heavyweight boxer who finds it hard to step away for the final time, Russell went "all in" one last time.

This time, instead of covering the news, the ageless one made it himself. Two weeks after the *Banner* published its final paper on 20

February 1998, *Sports Illustrated* ran a brief article in its 2 March 1998 issue called "Byline for the Ages." Included were references to Russell's remarkable Rolodex of sports figures he had covered during his sixty-eight years of sportswriting, and that beginning in April 1998, his weekly "Sidelines" column would be appearing in the *Tennessean*. The *S.I.* piece closed with the following:

"'One of the luckiest things that can happen to a fellow is to write sports,' Russell once said. Sports is lucky to still have him."[24]

True to his word, Russell's byline appeared in the *Tennessean* beginning in April. Larry Woody, who covered sports for Russell's rival from the 1960s until 2007, recalled how special it was to have Russell join the *Tennessean*.

"We told him how glad we were to have him write for us, because Fred Russell was the best there was," Woody admitted. "From a selfish standpoint, I wanted to keep seeing him write, and from a professional standpoint, how great for the *Tennessean* to land him."[25]

As it turned out, though, the Fred Russell-*Tennessean* experiment wasn't meant to be. Russell recycled five old columns that were of generally timeless topics that he had published before for the *Banner* and submitted them to the *Tennessean*. One column was about Bobby Jones and the Masters, another about the Kentucky Derby in 1941, and so on and so forth. The columns ran once a week beginning 2 April 1998, but it wasn't long before Russell stepped away, once and for all. His last column, in any newspaper, ran 30 April 1998.

Like Larry Woody, Jimmy Davy was another longtime *Tennessean* writer who had slugged it out with Russell over the years. Davy retired from sportswriting that same year and offered a fitting summary to his friend's final columns in a Nashville newspaper.

"You know, he just didn't have his heart in it," Davy acknowledged. "He was a *Banner* man."[26]

14

The Legend and His Legacy

"Freddie had a great sense of humor, and it lasted right there until the end. I went out there to see him at Richland Place, and he was well over ninety at the time. We had a great time, just sitting around talking. He was still very alert, and as we left, when I was at the door saying our goodbyes, Freddie said, 'Edwin, I'll remember this day the rest of my life.' And he must have been ninety-one, maybe ninety-two. Just a great sense of humor, it was so refreshing."[1] —Edwin Pope, *Miami Herald*

"I am not here to say goodbye, but rather to turn the last page and close that little book with its faded blue cover. And as I do, I can very clearly hear Fred simply say in that very distinctive soft voice: I'll Go Quietly." [2] —Roy Kramer, former SEC commissioner, at Russell's standing-room-only funeral

Both in the decades leading up to Russell's death and in the time since, there has been commentary on the altered landscape of sports journalism, its writers, the people they cover, and how they gather and share information. Having witnessed many of these changes firsthand, Russell was often asked to comment on the differences he noticed from the 1930s through the end of the twentieth century. With his national reputation, it wasn't just small-town newspapers searching for answers, nor was it small-time celebrities who commented on Russell. Here are two examples:

"People don't realize how much the sports world has grown. Through World War II, there were only two full-season sports that were well-established nationally: professional baseball and college football. The other important events were once a year, like the Kentucky Derby and the U.S. Open, or once in a while, the big championship prize fights. You'd look forward to those for weeks and cover every conceivable angle in your columns. Sportswriting's changed, too. Back in the '30s and '40s, most of us took our lead from Grantland Rice. His tone was generally positive, and his style was more poetic than hard-news. There's more critical writing now, but I'm not sure it matters much. Athletes are like most people in that they get their news from TV. That's sad, I think."[3] —Fred Russell, 1992

Peyton Manning, NFL quarterback, states: "I think the relationships Mr. Russell had were fascinating. I think the coverage has increased so much with the Internet, things have changed. There are so many outlets nowadays, and those relationships with players and coaches are pretty rare now. The relationships and the trust Mr. Russell had is very, very rare and unique, and I don't think you'll see much more of that anymore today."[4]

* * *

The last decade of Fred Russell's life was not without its share of challenges and sorrow for the veteran sportswriter. In 1993, he and his wife of sixty years moved out of the home they had lived in since 1938. Fred would lose Kay three years later in 1996, and it was the first of two painful tragedies in a relatively short period of time. The second came less than eighteen months later when the *Nashville Banner* shut its doors for good in February 1998.

When you live as long as Russell did, you are bound to outlive not only friends and family, but you may outlive *things* you never expected to lose. Case in point: the *Nashville Banner*. The losses of his wife and the *Banner* were harsh reminders of the price of living almost 100 years. In the immediate months after the *Banner* folded, Russell's depression left his family worried about whether or not their patriarch would make it. It was reasonable to consider that Russell, at the age of ninety-one, might not live more than a few months. Fortunately, Russell did come out of his depression, but in the years that followed, his health and quality of life deteriorated further. Friends and family admitted that he was never the same after the *Banner* folded.

Former *Banner* sports editor Joe Biddle visited Russell often during those final years, oftentimes once a week. He would take his mail to his former boss, they'd watch sports together, and Biddle would listen to Russell rekindle the stories from his life.

"I wish I could have recorded some of that stuff, because he would just tell great, great stories, one right after another," Biddle said years later. "I hated seeing him get in the shape he got at the end, but even when he was so frail, he still had a strong handshake."[5]

By late 2002, Russell's time was near. His body weight dropped considerably, and after the Christmas holidays, it was not a question of if, but when. The answer came the night of 26 January 2003, when Fred Russell died at the age of ninety-six.

In the days that followed, reflections and commentary from around the country poured into Nashville, the net effect of which was a true celebration of Russell's life. Having lived almost a century, he was finally at peace. Reunited with Kay and no longer having the daily reminder of Nashville being a one-newspaper town, the pain of the past ten years had been replaced by a fitting celebration of those who remembered the joy that he brought into their lives, each and every day.

In the years that have followed since Russell's death, the larger questions worth asking address the sportswriter's legacy. Fred Russell's contributions to journalism and sports were significant, and Russell's awards are as impressive as they are deserved. But in the twenty-first century of sports journalism, an era where there is just as much (if not more) emphasis placed on the entertainment value of the reporting as there is on its quality, is there a seat at the table for another Fred Russell? Are the things that made him stand out still even relevant today? In effect, when Fred Russell died, did the fraternity of sportswriters say goodbye to one of its last gentleman writers?

A Week of Memories and Celebration

When news spread in late January 2003 that the sports world had lost one of its most respected commentators, it elicited an array of emotions from those who had known Russell. Young or old, local or national, near or far, people descended upon Middle Tennessee to pay their respects and offer their opinions on how Russell had made a difference in his life of ninety-six years.

The passing of Russell was the lead news story in Nashville that week, and on Monday afternoon, it consumed sports talk radio as well. WTN's "Sportsnight," hosted by radio personality George Plaster and sportswriter Joe Biddle, who had worked for nineteen years at the

Nashville Banner with Russell before the paper shut down in 1998, took calls during the opening hour of the show, and condolences and compliments were the predominant themes of the evening.

Eventually, talked turned to Russell's remarkable ability to forge relationships with people from all walks of life. Biddle offered an appropriate summary of his former boss's relationship skills: "He never met a stranger," Biddle said, "and after you met him, you felt like you knew him all your life."[6]

The following morning, in his 28 January column for the *Tennessean*, Biddle expressed his own feelings of loss. His opening was as concise as it was honest: "I hoped this day would never come."[7]

Biddle had arrived in Nashville in the late 1970s and worked for and with Russell at the *Banner* for two decades. He became one of Russell's closest friends in the latter's final years, and his column that day reflected not only their friendship, but the longevity of Russell's life.

"Like most of those who ever worked in the *Nashville Banner* sports department, I thought Fred Russell would outlive us all. When you work at one newspaper 69 years and have the vitality Russell maintained long after reaching senior-citizen status, you acquire an air of invincibility. His death provides a stark reminder that none of us get out alive. To us, he was Mr. Russell. To his legion of friends, he was Freddie."[8]

As Biddle also pointed out in that column, Russell died exactly twenty years to the day after his longtime friend Paul "Bear" Bryant had died. In the week that followed, the praise Russell received was similar to that which was doled out in 1983 for the famous college football coach. Columnists and writers from across the country acknowledged the loss of one their forefathers. They stopped to remember the past, when the words from Russell delivered to them a dose of warmth, humor, and optimism each day the paper landed on their doorsteps.

The funeral for Russell was held that Wednesday, 29 January, and the pews at West End Methodist Church in Nashville were packed front to back, side to side. Former SEC commissioner Roy Kramer spoke at the service and noted that Russell's passing equated to the passing of a bygone era. Mixed with just the right amount of humor and sentiment, Kramer's words rang true for the thousands who had enjoyed Russell's work over the years.

"Fred's typewriter caught for all time, in an unmatchable way, the thrilling emotion of touchdown runs, birdie putts, photo finishes, and homeruns in the bottom of the ninth. Fred believed in the game and the people who played it. He always came to lift our hearts after the battle rather than second-guess every move. It was this relationship which made almost every well-known player in the majors drift over to the fence for a conversation with Fred during his favorite time of the year, spring training, and every great name in football walk across the lobby of the Waldorf-Astoria at the Hall of Fame dinner to say a special greeting or share a favorite story of yesterday. And I honestly believe the story that even Man of War nodded his famous red head to Fred when he visited him in the rolling pastures outside Lexington."[9]

The funeral itself was a media event in Nashville that week. Members of Russell's family were overwhelmed by the turnout, as former *Banner* employees, friends from the Vanderbilt community, and sportswriters from around the country attended the service. Appropriately so, current and former writers from Russell's rival paper, the *Tennessean*, were on hand as well to pay tribute.

John Seigenthaler recalled the true sense of loss that day for Nashville. "Many times when somebody dies, people say, 'What a loss, what a loss,' and it's almost a cliché," the former editor, publisher, and chairman of the *Tennessean* said, when asked about his attendance at the Russell funeral. "But with him, they really meant it. Performers are honored by standing-room only crowds, and that's how it was that day."[10]

Also on hand were a number of the past recipients of the Fred Russell-Grantland Rice TRA Sportswriting Scholarship, several of whom traveled across the country to pay their final respects.

Dan Wolken attended Vanderbilt in the late 1990s on the Russell-Rice scholarship and had landed a job with the *Colorado Springs Gazette*. He remembered being in the Las Vegas airport on his way back to Denver when he received a call from fellow scholarship recipient Lee Jenkins (Class of '99).

"There was really only one thing I could think about, and that was going back to the ticket counter and finding a way to get to Nashville," Wolken recalled, when Jenkins shared the news of Russell's death. "I was able to rework all my tickets, and by late that night I was there.

Considering all Mr. Russell and the scholarship had done for me, I felt it was my duty to get back and celebrate his life."[11]

Jenkins, now with *Sports Illustrated*, was then covering the UCLA beat for the *Orange County Register*. He, too, made the trip back to Nashville.

"In some ways, he charted the path of my life because he brought me to college [by influencing the decision to attend Vanderbilt over USC], and that opened up doors for what I do now." Jenkins said. "Being around someone with that much history, you couldn't help wanting to be a sportswriter."[12]

Not everyone was able to make the service, and for one man in particular, it was particularly painful to not be there. Charles Cella was a former president of the Thoroughbred Racing Association, the group that had provided financial backing to the Russell-Rice scholarship for decades, giving journalism opportunities to young men such as Wolken. Through the TRA scholarship connection, Cella and Russell had formed a strong friendship since the late 1960s. They shared a love of horse racing, not to mention the same 27 August birthday. When Russell died, it hit Cella hard.

"It was like losing a beloved brother," Cella recalled. "It was the end of a wonderful chapter of sports coverage at its best."[13]

For those who knew Russell well, his death was a reminder of living a life of strong values and conviction. This was recognized by his colleagues within the sports world, but especially with family and friends. One such example included U.S. Senator Bill Frist, a former Majority leader of the United States Senate.

Bill Frist grew up attending Frist-Russell family events in Belle Meade. Frist's father, Dr. Thomas Frist, was the founder of Nashville's Hospital Corporation of America in 1968, and the two families had been close since the 1950s.

"When Mr. Russell died, it made me very conscious of the loss of a generation," Frist said in 2006 from his Senate office in Washington, D.C. "It made me realize that the passing of the baton was almost complete and reminded me of the values that we must pass on to our children."[14]

Finally, there was the sad, undeniable connection to the *Nashville Banner*. It had been a relatively short five years since the 122-year-old paper had folded, and Russell had been the owner of one of the paper's most notable bylines for sixty-nine of those years. When he died, many former colleagues could not help but think back to the final, dark days of February 1998. For Eddie Jones, Russell's longtime friend, the wounds had not yet healed.

"When I was at the service, my thoughts kept going to Fred and the newspaper," Jones recalled. "I felt gratified that there were so many friends, so much power and influence, and so many people there to give him a magnificent tribute and tremendous sendoff, but losing Fred for me rekindled the whole loss of the paper."[15]

From Memories to Recognition

When considering Russell's legacy, it is impossible to do so without acknowledging the astounding array of awards the journalist received, not to mention the leadership positions he held and the many honors that were bestowed upon him. The following represents a select list of some of the many honors Fred Russell received through the years:

Year	Award/Honor
1936	National Headliners Club Award
1955	Named vice president, *Nashville Banner*
1955	Grantland Rice Memorial Award (inaugural recipient)
1964–91	Chairman, National Football Foundation Hall of Fame Honors Court
1965	President, Football Writer's Association of America
1966	Jake Ward Award
1974	Elected to Tennessee Sports Hall of Fame
1976	Distinguished Journalism Award (U. S. Olympic Committee)
1980	National Football Foundation's Distinguished American Award
1981	Amos Alonzo Stagg Award
1981	Bert McGrane Award
1983	Turf Writer's Walter Haight Award
1983	Kappa Sigma National Man of the Year
1984	Red Smith Award
1988	National Sportscasters and Sportswriters Hall of Fame
2005	Tennessee Sportswriters Hall of Fame (charter member)

The National Headliners award that Russell received in 1936 for his coverage of a kidnapping case involving a former law student classmate of Russell's was just the beginning. His dual skills as sportswriter and editor put the *Nashville Banner* on the map in the middle decades of the twentieth century, and he catapulted to national recognition when the *Saturday Evening Post* tapped Russell to be its annual college football prognosticator. His "Pigskin Preview" ran from 1949 to 1962, and when Russell leveraged his relationships within college football into a position on the Hall of Fame Honors Court with the National Football Foundation, he was *the* voice of integrity and respectability within college football from the 1960s through the 1980s.

One of Russell's former staffers in the late 1960s at the *Banner* was Delbert Reed, who remembered Russell's national popularity during this era. Reed recalled how Russell was an in-demand speaker on the so-called "banquet" tour. Universities would have end-of-season football award dinners, and they would attract keynote speakers, sometimes coaches, other times college football personalities, who were recognized across the country.

"Russell did these all the time, and this was not common for sportswriters back then. Nobody else did that," Reed noted. "When he served a term as the president of the Football Writers Association of America [1965], he was the biggest name in the South. He was always going places to make speeches, he was involved with the Heisman committee, and he was famous throughout the country."[16]

As for the awards Russell received, they were as noteworthy as they were numerous.

In 1966, shortly after his term as Football Writers Association of America (FWAA) president, Russell received the Jake Ward Award, which is presented annually to an individual who has made an outstanding contribution in the media to the field of intercollegiate athletics. Recent winners have included Billy Packer (2008), Christine Brennan (2003), Dick Vitale (2001), and Dan Jenkins (1999). Russell also received the United States Olympic Committee's Distinguished Journalism Award (1976), the National Football Foundation's Distinguished American Award (1980), and the Bert McGrane Award (1981) for service to the FWAA, to name a few. Russell has also been named to numerous halls of fames within his profession, and even obtained "Man of the Year" recognition from his Kappa Sigma fraternity in 1983.

Of all the recognition that Fred Russell received over the years, though, there are three that warrant additional attention, because of their importance to Russell.

The first is the Red Smith Award that Russell received in 1984. Presented by the Associated Press Sports Editors, the award is given annually by the APSE to a person who has made "major contributions to sports journalism." Smith was awarded the inaugural award in 1981, but then passed away in early 1982 at the age of seventy-six. Jim Murray (*L.A. Times*) and Shirley Povich (*Washington Post*) followed in 1982 and 1983 before Russell. It was a special award for Russell, in part because of the respect he had for the three men who held it before him, but also because of his close friendship with Smith, which had lasted over thirty years.

In June 1984, the APSE held its annual meeting in Philadelphia, and Russell was at his humorous best during his acceptance speech. He took a few moments to honor his friend, recollecting one particular story from the days he and Red had traveled through the South covering different events.

"One spring day during an automobile drive from Florida spring training to the Masters in Augusta, Red and I were trying to write the next day's columns on portable typewriters perched on our laps," Russell told the packed banquet hall. "Red said to the lady driving, 'Please don't get arrested. So far, no officer could be convinced that this stuff is going to appear in a newspaper.'"[17]

The second award that had special significance to Russell came a few years prior to the Smith award. In 1980, the American Football Coaches Association (AFCA) presented Russell with its Amos Alonzo Stagg Award, which honors those "whose services have been outstanding in the advancement of the best interests of football." The Stagg award is one of the premier AFCA awards, and what is unique about Russell receiving this honor is that it typically goes to football coaches, not sportswriters. A look through its list of winners offers a glimpse into the biggest names of football in the past fifty years. Bill Walsh (2008), Joe Paterno (2002), Vince Dooley (2001), and Paul "Bear" Bryant (1983) are just a few of the signature recipients of the Stagg award.

Dooley coached at Georgia and received the Stagg award in 2001, and he acknowledged Russell's achievement as well.

"It is a tremendous tribute to Freddie. The ones who aren't coaches that receive it, they have to be extremely well thought of and respected by the coaches association," Dooley said. "Freddie is a classic example of that, of someone who was not a coach, but yet held in the highest esteem by all the coaches."[18]

It wasn't just the support from the former coaches whom he had covered that made this award special for Russell. Russell is one of only two sportswriters ever to receive the award in its seventy-year history. The other sportswriter? It was 1946, and the recipient was none other than Russell's fellow Vanderbilt alum, mentor, and close friend—Grantland Rice.

The connection to Rice with the Stagg award underscores the third award that had special significance for Russell. In 1955, just one year after Rice had died in July 1954, Russell was the inaugural recipient of the Grantland Rice Memorial Award, an honor given to a sportswriter who in his writing most nearly approaches the Rice tradition. What separated Russell from the other candidates was his utter devotion to the spirit of sportsmanship, a critical component of Rice's style as well. Several months prior to receiving the Rice award, Russell's 10 June 1955 column was titled, "Maybe It's Time to Update the True Meaning of Sportsmanship." In it, he lamented the direction the sports world was headed, specifically as it related to poor losing, and the public's willingness to condone, if not encourage, such behavior. Russell feared for the sanctity and appreciation for selfless play.

"Competitive sport is the friend of motion and grace; it tightens the body and tempers the mind," Russell wrote. "But its priceless teachings—of respect for the rights of others, of discipline, of devotion to an ideal, of unselfishness—may be endangered."[19]

The Rice award was a noteworthy achievement for the Nashville writer, made more impressive by the competition of that era, specifically the writers from the big cities who could reach a larger audience. Over the next few years, notable recipients of the award included Red Smith (New York) in 1956 and Frank Graham (New York) in 1958.

Russell received his Rice award in 1955, and more than forty years later, Russell was honored in a similar fashion. Much like Russell had organized the annual *Banner*'s "Banquet of Champions" in the 1930s, the Nashville Sports Council started a "Dinner of Champions" awards night in the late 1990s. In 1998, at its inaugural banquet, a Lifetime Achievement Award was announced, and it was named the Fred Russell Lifetime Achievement Award. As a tribute to Russell's remarkable run of almost seven decades at the *Banner*, the veteran sportswriter was the first recipient.

Local Nashville sports radio personality George Plaster has been involved with the "Dinner of Champions" since its beginning, and he had the privilege of introducing Russell in 1998.

"It was one of the few public speaking things that I was really nervous about, because I wanted to make sure that when I introduced him, people in the audience who were not Nashville-born would absolutely know why he was getting it," Plaster said in 2005.

"When he got up there to accept that award, it was one of the most electric moments I've ever seen with that Dinner of Champions," Plaster added, recalling that he used his introduction speech to point out how far Nashville had come over the years. "All these things we have. The Predators, the Titans, the new sports. None of this would have ever happened without this guy, because back when we weren't known for anything else, we were known for Mr. Russell."[20]

Russell's Living Legacy

It has now been well over ten years since that first "Dinner of Champions", and a similar amount of time has passed since Russell's *Nashville Banner* printed its last issue. While it is undeniable that he had a profound impact on Nashville, Vanderbilt, and the South, the larger question that remains is this: what is the legacy of Fred Russell?

In answering that question, it's important to acknowledge just how much has changed from the time Russell began writing in the 1930s to the time he put away his typewriter in the late 1990s. A fair criticism of sportswriters from fifty years ago has been that they were, at times, far too biased for the cities in which they wrote and the teams that played there. For Russell, it was a penchant for Vanderbilt and Nashville, for Furman Bisher, it was Georgia Tech and Atlanta. Likewise, for Red Smith, Jim Murray, and Blackie Sherrod, there was favoritism toward teams from New York, Los Angeles, and Dallas, respectively. In and of itself, this information isn't ground-breaking. Writers today are well aware of how things were different for their predecessors. The rationale for highlighting this core difference, though, is to illustrate a secondary or subsequent distinction between the two eras. Particularly with collegiate athletics, once Russell had established a relationship, there was no telling where it might lead.

A worthy example comes from his interactions in the South when he was covering college football after World War II. When All-American Charley Trippi was running roughshod over defenses in the Southeastern Conference, Russell wrote a feature story in 1946 on the Georgia running back. The story appeared in the *Saturday Evening Post*, and Russell received a number of telegrams from the university thanking him for the story. Nothing wrong with that, as it's not uncommon for writers to be acknowledged for such pieces of work, especially if the article is on the lighter side or is mostly human interest in nature. It is the last telegram from Georgia that is the rather remarkable one. In a final gesture of thanks to Russell, the athletic department, on behalf of coach Wally Butts and the University of Georgia, offered Russell an all-expense paid trip to its upcoming Sugar Bowl game against North Carolina...as a guest of the school!

Today, this would be unheard of, as it's almost laughable to consider any sports organization, collegiate or professional, making such an offer to a member of the media. It would be the equivalent of the New York Yankees winning the pennant and offering to pay for a writer's trip to the World Series. By today's standards, such a thought wreaks of conflict of interest. But two generations ago, that was not the case. Bottom line: times were different. Russell knew the rules of the game and played them exceptionally well. He cultivated one of the most impressive lists of contacts within American sports, and he did so one relationship at a time.

It wasn't just the nature of relationships that changed over the years. There were wholesale changes in journalism, and not just limited to the sports page. The post-Watergate era of journalism in general introduced an investigative culture rarely seen during the prime years of Russell's career. At the sports end of the journalism spectrum, a new level of scrutiny from reporters infiltrated the business as well. No longer did coaches and players get a "free pass" on morally questionable off-the-field activities. The unwritten codes that existed between reporters and their subjects no longer applied. In the old days, coaches knew they were off the record until the reporter's notebook came out; that has been replaced with the generally accepted belief that one is always on the record, unless he or she has stated otherwise. This "notebook" example is a subtle distinction between the current environment and the time in which Russell carved his niche, but it is a by-product of a reporting culture and journalistic landscape that changed dramatically in the second half of his long career.

Blackie Sherrod wrote for the *Dallas Morning News* for years, and remembered conversations he and Russell would have regarding the shift. "Our press box generation is of the WWII era, and we had a hard time accepting sports as anything other than fun and games," Sherrod noted. "A popular theory of our day was, 'The World Series is not Judgment at Nuremberg.' Everything is changed now."[21]

Just as Watergate changed the *type* of information that was researched and reported, television had a similar impact on the way in which that information was delivered to the public. The television medium butted against the newspaper model, where warm, friendly relationships between players and writers were developed and nurtured over the years. With the television boon from the 1960s on, it became considerably easier for sports figures to catapult—seemingly overnight—from regional popularity to celebrity status at the national level. It wasn't just television that impacted the invaluable relationship between writer and subject. For all its conveniences and benefits, basic logistics and overall technological capabilities have worked against a reporter's ability to build grassroots relationships. In Russell's day, he traveled everywhere, because if he wanted the story, he had to be there in person. Travel itself was different, and oftentimes meant going by train with the coaches, players, and other writers themselves. Russell parlayed that kind of access into having friends across the country in every locker room and press box. Contrast that with today's reporting environment, where access is monitored and limited, even for the daily beat writers who do nothing but cover one team. Athletes are coached not just on being athletes but on interacting with the media; in the end, the relationships between writer and sports figure have become, at best, professional.

The enormous amount of money involved in sports today has made a difference as well. A veteran and notable reporter from Russell's era who is still active today is Frank Deford, currently a senior writer for *Sports Illustrated* and an HBO sports correspondent. In addition to the advent of television and the coverage of off-the-field events, Deford cited money as one of the three most significant changes that has impacted the relationships between writers and players.

"Beforehand, they'd had to depend on writers to give them some 'ink,' to help their profile," Deford said of players from a half-century ago, before contrasting them to the players of today. "When you're making millions of dollars a year, why bother with writers unless you absolutely have to."[22]

Similar evolutions have occurred with the reporter's relationship with the coach as well.

"Nowadays, coaches don't trust the media. The reason is: they get burnt so much. Internet, talk shows, *USA Today*, and ESPN—those are the culprits for the college coach," former coach and current ESPN analyst Lee Corso said. "Remember also, Fred had one advantage. Fred could come and be with you. You could talk to him."[23]

The net effect of these developments has been an erosion of trust between sports figure and reporter, and the benefit of the doubt once afforded to players and coaches has all but disappeared. Where there used to be an assumption of trust, there is now a wall that divides writers from their subjects.

The wall is not impenetrable, however. It just requires more skill to get around, over, or through. One solution that warrants consideration is to examine Russell's approach and learn from it. In doing so, the approach to successful reporting may come full circle in the years ahead. What was once considered outdated could be rejuvenated. To be fair, journalism will never return to the portrayal of players and coaches as mythical heroes, nor should it go back to such a period of sensationalism and borderline fictional reporting. Certain elements of the Russell era absolutely need to remain in that century, but the hallmarks of what made Russell last in this business for so many years warrant acknowledgement and celebration.

Consider Russell's own words in his 1957 autobiography.

"Nobody can teach another person how to write," Russell wrote. "But if I reduced to simplest terms the things I think sportswriters strive for most, they would be: Accuracy, speed, and sparkle. Beyond those, he's blessed if he has originality and a sense of the dramatic." [24]

These are skills that transcend time and technology, and Russell was a testimony to that. He was successful for four more decades after he wrote his own life story. More importantly, in the ten-plus years since his last column, it is Russell's living legacy that continues. He put his heart and soul into developing the staff at the *Banner*, and through the Russell-Rice sportswriting scholarship at Vanderbilt University, Russell put his fingerprints on the next generation of successful writers, many of whom are in their prime today.

Pick up a copy of the *New York Times* and find the latest article by Tyler Kepner. Flip through a current issue of *Sports Illustrated* and see what Lee Jenkins has to say about baseball. Or go online and check out Buster Olney's latest blog at ESPN.com, Dave Sheinin at the *Washington Post*, Skip Bayless with ESPN2, Bill Livingston at the Cleveland *Plain Dealer*...the list goes on and on.

The fundamentals he espoused then are just as relevant today: fairness, accuracy, efficiency, and competitive fire. Throw in a sense of humor, that "sense of the dramatic" (as Russell referred to it), and a love for what you are covering, and that's as good a foundation for a successful career in journalism as you'll find.

The proof in this formula is in that list of writers with ties to Russell who are active today in the field of journalism. These are some of the top writers of today's generation, excelling at the highest levels of their profession, and a common denominator for each of them is Fred Russell. Much like Grantland Rice has been labeled the "Dean of American Sportswriters," Russell is at the epicenter of our current generation's top writers. For forty years, he handpicked aspiring journalists like Livingston, Bayless, Sheinin, Kepner, and Jenkins to receive scholarships to attend Vanderbilt; for others like Olney and Joe Biddle, they worked for Russell at the *Nashville Banner*. All of them benefitted from their interactions with the mentor or legend, and the sportswriting world today is better because of the lessons they learned, and the ripple effect Russell had, within the sportswriting community.

When asked how Russell himself would have fared in today's sportswriting environment, Olney didn't hesitate.

"He would have *loved* it. He would have loved the velocity of the journalism, with the Internet. It would have fed right into how competitive he was," the former Vanderbilt graduate and *Banner* staffer said. "Working at an afternoon paper, his challenge was to find a way to beat a morning newspaper. Well, by God, on the Internet, he could have done that every day.

"He would have stood out even more because his work had so much integrity," Olney continued. "I think we've seen less integrity in work since the advent of the Internet, where people are just firing stuff out there. Mr. Russell would have put thought into it. He would have thrived in this atmosphere."[25]

Before his stint at ESPN, Olney worked his way to the *New York Times* and covered the Yankees. While there, he met veteran columnist Dave Anderson, who had crossed paths with Russell numerous times over the years at national events. Since the turn of the century, Anderson has seen a number of writers with ties to Russell pass through the *Times*, a fact not lost on the veteran columnist.

"The *Times* is indebted to Fred Russell, because of writers like Tyler Kepner, Lee Jenkins, and Buster Olney," Anderson noted in 2005.[26]

At that time, Jenkins and Olney were still at the paper. Kepner joined the staff in 2000 and has covered the Yankees beat since 2002. Kepner attended Vanderbilt from 1993 to 1997, and his passion for sports and his discipline to be as thorough as he is fair are just two of the traits that stand out. With Kepner's love for baseball, it's easy to see why Russell selected him as the 1993 scholarship recipient, another reminder of Russell's eye for talent.

"If you have some humility about yourself, and don't try to come off like you know more than they do, and show players that you are interested, they respect that," Kepner said of reporting in today's environment. "As long as I ask smart questions and know what I am talking about, ninety-nine times out of 100, I'll get the answers I need."[27]

Russell's path to success is not lost on these writers.

"I think about Fred sometimes when certain situations come up. I think Tyler does this, too, and we try to incorporate elements of the way Mr. Russell did the job," Jenkins said. "How to foster relationships with these athletes, for example. I think today's media could stand to learn more than a few lessons from the way Mr. Russell conducted his business."[28]

"The fact that he was so precise, so competitive and had so much integrity with the words he wrote. I learned from that," Olney added. "He devoted an awful lot of time to getting to know people in sports, and that became a big part of my thinking."[29]

That type of discipline and approach is evident more and more today, and for some old-school members of the media who remember times when they were different, this is a positive step. Ernie Harwell, legendary baseball announcer for the Detroit Tigers, has seen generations of writers come and go and knows what is needed to see more of today's generation emulate his old friend Fred Russell.

"People are better writers today, they are more educated, and all in all, the writers today do work harder," Harwell said, noting that the dividends of journalism schools are starting to pay off. "They write better and it's of a higher quality. I think that's part of the reason Russell and Rice stood out so much, they just out-worked almost all their contemporaries."[30]

Old-school coaches have an opinion on this as well, such as the renowned Lou Holtz, who now works for CBS Sports. Holtz commented on how eras change for coaches as well, even though some have shown remarkable resilience.

"I'll tell you this: it's easier to replace a great coach than it is to replace a great sportswriter, I promise you," said Holtz, who coached from 1969 to 2004. "Someone will always come along and replace the Bobby Bowdens and Joe Paternos, but to replace Fred Russell, I don't know who's going to take his place, or if it can be. The most difficult people to replace are the ones like Fred Russell."[31]

Closing Thoughts

In summer 2005, Wake Forest asked golfing icon Arnold Palmer to deliver its commencement address. In the speech that he gave to the graduating class of his alma mater, Palmer made headlines with his hard-cutting comments.

"Many adults of my generation despair of your generation. All too often in my primary field of endeavor—sports—the headlines go to the players who defy authority and misbehave on and off the field, players who showboat and show up others," Palmer stated matter-of-factly. "Instead, those who should be recognized more often are the fine athletes who are also fine citizens and role models for the youngsters following in their footsteps."[32]

Within this quote lies the essence of Fred Russell, or at least a significant piece of it. Just as much as he loved the spirit of sports and competition, Russell was a firm believer in the integrity of sports, the virtues of fair play, and celebrating the athletes who competed, whether they won or lost. While often compared to his predecessor Grantland Rice, one area in which he clearly departed from Rice was that of myth-making. Russell was not out to make fictional heroes out of everyday athletes. Rather, he merely extolled their passion for competition, and if that passion led to heroic actions, he would be there to tell that story.

At Vanderbilt, Russell befriended basketball coach C. M. Newton, who coached the Commodores in the 1980s. Newton appreciated Russell's firm stance on ethics within sports and once noted that Russell "would rather see a team or an athlete compete within the rules and lose, than compete outside the rules and win."[33]

Within the world of college basketball, one of Russell's friends was Bobby Knight. To equate the two, Russell was to the *Banner* what Knight was to Indiana University basketball. Over the years, Russell made a strong impression on Knight, not an easy thing to do as a member of the media, and the two discussed the changes in media coverage.

"Fred was just a guy interested in what was going on that was positive," Knight pointed out. "He was certainly chagrined at the direction writing had taken during his lifetime, but I think he did everything he conceivably could to keep it the way he wanted it, and the way he envisioned writing being."[34]

And while that style is what drew some criticism over the years, it is also what elevated Russell to the stature that he had. He chose to focus on the positive, and for a vast majority of the reading public, it resonated year after year. Turn to the last two pages of his autobiography, in which he's included his own "Top Ten" list, entitled "A Sportswriter's Well-Thumbed Rulebook." Rule number one states simply, "Tie goes to the runner. Favor the positive side over the negative."[35]

Adherence to this rule served Russell well his entire career. It's why he loved the Roy Hobbs character in *The Natural*, as that was an against-all-odds story of good triumphing over evil. In a real-life example, going back to Russell's earliest years at the *Banner*, the inspiring story of heavyweight fighter James "Jim" Braddock and his improbable upset of Max Baer in 1935 is what Russell loved about sport. That's just one example of hundreds he witnessed during his career, at all levels of play, and what Russell loved more than the event itself was writing about the triumph. Through the years, whether covering Vanderbilt football, spring training in Florida, or the Masters in Augusta, he sought out the uplifting stories that were of interest to him. As one Russell-Rice scholar from the 1970s noted, "Russell had it right—at its core, these are just games. Let's enjoy them for what they are."[36]

Equally important in telling the story was the way in which Russell delivered his messages. He wrote with a clarity and precision that was admired by his peers, two of whom recalled how challenging that can be.

"He did what we all wanted to do: he wrote a column as if he was talking to you," noted Jesse Outlar, former columnist and editor at the *Atlanta Constitution*.[37]

"The other thing he did, and Lord knows I tried to copy this, don't try to write too hard," added Tom McEwen of the *Tampa Tribune*. "Write simply if you can, and write for the guys at the country club, at the bar, and at the junior high school."

Roy Kramer spent thirteen years as Vanderbilt's athletic director and witnessed (and appreciated) Russell's style firsthand, through good times and bad times. If times were bad, Russell didn't pour salt in the wound. He tried to stitch it up as best he could, and when he did, that clarity and precision made a difference.

"If we lost a game, he would do his job and report that somebody fumbled the ball at the two-yard line, but he loved sport so much, that he always found a way to put some sort of positive twist on the day," Kramer said. "When you get through talking to Fred, or reading Fred, you felt better in some way. There was something there at the end of the tunnel, there was light there."[38]

As for being tough when players or coaches deserved it, Russell didn't back down from these situations either. But his philosophy was founded in treating people fairly from the beginning. He garnered respect through a lifetime of leveling with people when he had information and giving them the benefit of the doubt.

"This is what Russell said: go out there and write the good stories about the good teams, and the good players, and the good coaches," former *Banner* staffer Delbert Reed recalled from his years working for Russell. "There's no need to go out there and hunt for dirt on anybody. You go write what's there and write about it well, and treat everybody with respect.

"He always told us, there's going to be plenty of bad stuff you'll have to write, that you're going to have to suck it up and write it," Reed continued. "But if you've treated them fairly all the time, they will give you the story when they get fired, or when they quit, or when things get tough. They will know that you've been fair."[39]

And therein was Fred Russell.

He was the Tom Landry of sportswriters, dignity and class to the core, undeniable talent, a passion for sport, and a competitive drive that pushed him to excel beyond even his own wildest imagination. Beginning in 1930 and coming to a close in 1998, Russell worked his way to the highest echelons of his trade on his own steam, one relationship at a time, one game at a time, and one column at a time. He was serious about what he did, but he never took himself too seriously, as evidenced by his celebrated status as practical joker extraordinaire. Along the way, as Russell's reputation grew, he was unaffected by the national stature that he attained or the people whose company he kept. In doing so, it was this "everyman" quality that won the hearts of those he touched. His "Sidelines" column ran for Middle Tennesseans for decades, but what ultimately pushed Fred Russell into the national spotlight was his desire to do more and give back. He wanted to have the best Monday through Friday sports department in the country, so he challenged his *Nashville Banner* sports staff to excel and compete every day against their rivals at the *Tennessean*. He wanted other potential journalists to have the same educational opportunities that he and Grantland Rice had at Vanderbilt, so he established, developed, and nurtured a once-in-a-lifetime sportswriting scholarship that cultivated a legion of outstanding writers in the twenty-first century worthy of the Russell-Rice scholarship that is on their resumes.

Two final but fair questions to ask: if he were writing today, would Russell's modest and grassroots approach be successful? Would it result in the biggest headlines, the largest paychecks, or the most notoriety? The answer to the first question, absolutely. The answer to the second question, probably not. But then again, he never sought such things. Fred Russell just wanted to cover sports and be a writer. He did that, and he did it exceptionally well.

At Russell's funeral in January 2003, on the back of the funeral program was a reprint of Grantland Rice's 1953 "To Fred Russell" poem. Because he was not healthy enough to attend the banquet honoring Russell's twenty-five years with the *Banner*, Rice had paid tribute to his old friend and fellow alum with prose. The following is the first verse of that poem, and a fitting conclusion to a man who lived a life of dreams:

> Freddie, the south wind's calling
> From far and far away
> I see the twilight falling
> On hills of yesterday.
> I find an old, old yearning
> And when I turn to you,
> I meet old pals returning
> To find a dream come true.[40]

Eulogies from the Fred Russell Memorial Service, Wednesday, 29 January 2003

Roy Kramer, former SEC commissioner and close friend of Russell's:

"It may well be the most humbling experience of my entire life to stand in this sanctuary and for one brief shining moment share with you in honoring your friend and mine, Fred Russell.

"And what a man he is...For you see in my world Fred will always be here, smiling under that old wrinkled hat he always wore in the press box, nodding to each of us with that special twinkle in his eye, always full of anticipation for sharing the latest joke he had heard from one of his sportswriting buddies. You always laughed at Fred's jokes, whether they were any good or not, just because Fred enjoyed telling them so much. If we could only see on the other side of the mountain, I strongly suspect that Fred has already written his first column over there, with tongue in check, of why Jesus should have been penalized for having twelve disciples on the field instead of eleven. Certainly the love he carried so deep in his heart for his family and especially for that most gracious lady of his life, the one and only Kay.

"This man was able to catch in the beautiful words of the English language so many wonderful moments that have been forever enshrined in our memories of almost every possible sporting event from the betting window at Churchill Downs, to the smell of azaleas at the Masters, to the taste of a hot dog at old Sulphur Dell park on a warm summer afternoon, to the golden days of autumn in the great stadiums of this land.

"More than fifty years ago, I enrolled in a freshman English composition class at a little college in east Tennessee. My instructor remains one of the most influential individuals in my life today. She had a special interest in those of us who thought we were athletes. She knew so well that the last thing I was interested in at that time was the use of the English language. But she did understand my love of the game. So after one rather boring class session, she called me to her desk and handed me a small book with a blue paper cover. The title of that little book was *I'll Go Quietly*.

"As I began to read those poetic lines in the columns written so many years ago in his beloved *Nashville Banner*, I was first introduced to Fred Russell, the tales, the jokes, the artful descriptions of hundreds of sporting events and most of all, an appreciation of the people he knew so intimately who had played the game.

"Thus it is that I am deeply indebted to share in this special moment in time as we remember Fred Russell and the blessings he bestowed on each of us as he painted so many masterpieces of the world of sport through his writings.

"Fred's typewriter caught for all time, in an unmatchable way, the thrilling emotion of touchdown runs, birdie putts, photo finishes, and homeruns in the bottom of the ninth. Herein is the fame and fortune that Fred Russell brought to this community from all over the world. All of the giants of his profession from Grantland Rice to Red Smith looked up to him. He was an inspiration for decades to almost every young and aspiring sportswriter.

"He brought a dignity and a class to the game that unfortunately is often lost today. There was a relationship between Fred and the heroes of sport that afforded him access and friendship we do not often see in the media in these times.

"Fred believed in the game and the people who played it. He always came to lift our hearts after the battle rather than second-guess every move. It was this relationship which made almost every well-known player in the majors drift over to the fence for a conversation with Fred during his favorite time of the year, spring training, and every great name in football walk across the lobby of the Waldorf-Astoria at the Hall of Fame dinner to say a special greeting or share a favorite story of yesterday. And I honestly believe the story that even Man of War nodded his famous red head to Fred when he visited him the rolling pastures outside Lexington.

"I could go on forever, for you see Fred's world is my world and the people he knew and who knew him are forever my idols. This is the world I love so much, and in so many ways the fertile fields of that world have been sowed, cultivated, and harvested for each of us by this great gentleman.

"Thank you, Fred, for your friendship but most of all, thank you for a lifetime of memories that shall never be forgotten by those of us assembled in this sanctuary today.

"I am *not* here to say goodbye...but rather to turn the last page and close that little book with its faded blue cover.... And as I do, I can very clearly hear Fred simply say in that very distinctive soft voice.... 'I'll go quietly.'"

Andrew Derr, 1992 recipient, Fred Russell-Grantland Rice TRA Sportswriting Scholarship:

"It is a great honor to stand here today and say a few words about Mr. Russell. It is truly humbling.

"Regrettably, I only knew Mr. Russell during the final chapters of his remarkable life. I came to Nashville in the fall of 1992, as one of the very fortunate Fred Russell-Grantland Rice scholarship recipients at Vanderbilt University.

"My first chance to meet Mr. Russell occurred just a little over ten years ago. Each semester, Mr. Russell would join the scholarship recipients for a lunch at the University Club. It wasn't more than fifteen minutes into this luncheon—maybe less than that—after hearing about the people he had met and the events he had covered, that I thought to myself, "This man is really, really cool." As a wide-eyed freshman sports reporter...I knew I was in the presence of a legend.

"Through my years of knowing him, I developed a great affection for Mr. Russell, and it began at that first meeting. And I think it was because he reminded me so much of my own grandfather. My grandfather played college baseball in the 1920s for the University of Maryland and loved to share with me his stories and his affection for sports. Mr. Russell played ball here at Vanderbilt in the 1920s, and when it came to storytelling, there was no one better. He painted pictures with his words—it was as if you were right there beside him.

"What astounded me was his memory—it was always razor-sharp. Mr. Russell would not only remember Don Newcombe giving up that ninth inning homerun to lose Game 1 of the '49 World Series to the New York Yankees, he would remember that it was a 2–0 count, that

Newcombe threw a fastball, and that Tommy Hennrich probably winked at Newcombe as he rounded first base.

"In a word, he was remarkable.

"Most importantly, he cared. Mr. Russell truly and genuinely cared about us. Talk to any one of the former *Hustler* sportwriters, and you will hear about the encouragement that Mr. Russell provided us...not only about journalism, but about living a good life, about being a good person. His advice to us as sports journalists was simple yet profound: write from your heart and be proud of your hard work; be serious about what you do, but don't take yourself too seriously.

"At the time, we thought we were simply receiving advice on being good writers. Little did we know that we were the beneficiaries of wisdom that sometimes only a grandfather can impart.

"I will close with this last story. Last fall, I had the wonderful opportunity to try and document the impact Mr. Russell had on the scores of aspiring sports reporters that wrote for the *Vanderbilt Hustler*. I caught up with writers such as Skip Bayless, Dave Sheinin, Buster Olney, Tyler Kepner, and Lee Jenkins. Each had a story about Mr. Russell, and I loved this comment from Skip Bayless, as he recalled his early times at Vanderbilt:

"'Like so many freshmen, I was having a hard time getting adjusted to college. But the great joy of my day was to hear the *Nashville Banner* hit the hallway outside my door, because I knew Fred Russell would be there waiting for me.'

"Mr. Russell, we will miss you. But we will certainly never forget you. God bless you and thank you."

Select Bibliography

Barra, Allen. *The Last Coach: A Life of Paul "Bear" Bryant* (New York: W. W. Norton, 2005).

Bisher, Furman. *Face to Face* (Champaign IL: Sports Publishing, 2005).

Carnegie, Dale. *How to Win Friends & Influence People* (New York: Simon & Schuster, 1936).

Fountain, Charles. *Sportswriter* (New York/Oxford: Oxford University Press, 1993).

Harper, William. *How You Played the Game: The Life of Grantland Rice* (Columbia MO: University of Missouri Press, 1999).

Holtzman, Jerome. *No Cheering in the Press Box* (New York: Holt, Rinehart and Winston, 1973).

Kirby, James. *Fumble* (New York: Harcourt Brace Jovanovich, 1986).

Rice, Grantland. *Only the Brave and Other Poems* (New York: A. S. Barnes & Company, 1941)

Rice, Grantland. *The Tumult and the Shouting: My Life in Sport* (New York: A. S. Barnes & Company, 1954)

Russell, Fred. *Bury Me in an Old Press Box: Good Times and Life of a Sportswriter* (New York: A. S. Barnes & Co., 1957).

Russell, Fred. *Funny Thing about Sports* (Nashville TN: McQuiddy Press, 1948).

Russell, Fred. *I'll Go Quietly* (Nashville TN: McQuiddy Press, 1944).

Russell, Fred. *I'll Try Anything Twice* (Nashville TN: McQuiddy Press, 1945).

Smith, Red. *To Absent Friends from Red Smith* (New York: New American Library, 1982).

Notes

Chapter 1

[1] C. M. Newton to author, 1 August 2005, personal interview.

[2] Fred Russell, speech to Quinq Club, Vanderbilt University, Nashville, TN, 28 May 1994.

[3] Tom Siler, daily column, *Knoxville* (TN) *News Sentinel*, 9 September 1953.

[4] Fred Russell, *Bury Me in an Old Press Box: Good Times and Life of a Sportswriter* (New York: A. S. Barnes and Co., 1957) 2.

[5] Fred Russell, "Old Nashville Town" television show, hosted by Libby Fryer, October 1986.

[6] Kay Russell Beasley to author, 17 January 2006, personal interview.

[7] Ibid.

[8] Russell, Quinq Club, 28 May 1994.

[9] Carolyn Russell to author, 12 September 2006, personal interview.

[10] Russell, *Bury Me*, 10–11.

[11] C. M. Newton to author, 1 August 2005, personal interview.

[12] Jimmy Davy to author, 13 September 2005, personal interview.

[13] John Seigenthaler to author, 28 October 2005, personal interview.

[14] Mark McGee to author, 21 April 2006, personal interview.

[15] George Plaster to author, 22 July 2005, personal interview.

[16] John Seigenthaler to author, 28 October 2005, personal interview.

[17] Jimmy Webb to author, 26 June 2005, personal interview.

[18] Roy Kramer to author, 27 July 2005, personal interview.

[19] John Beasley to author, 8 February 2006, personal interview.

[20] Ibid.

[21] George Plaster to author, 22 July 2005, personal interview.

[22] Russell, Quinq Club, 28 May 1994.

[23] Dick Philpot to author, 26 June 2005, personal interview.

[24] Ibid.

[25] Skip Bayless to author, 12 February 2006, personal interview.

[26] Ibid.

Chapter 2

[1] Dan Miller, speech at Fred Russell-Grantland Rice Scholarship for Sports Journalism banquet, Vanderbilt Loews Plaza, Nashville, TN, 4 May 1986.

[2] Eddie Jones to author, 18 November 2005, personal interview.

[3] Fred Russell, "Old Nashville Town" television show, hosted by Libby Fryer, October 1986.

[4] Russell, "Old Nashville Town," October 1986.

[5] Fred Russell, *Bury Me in an Old Press Box: Good Times and Life of a Sportswriter* (New York: A. S. Barnes and Co., 1957) 14.

[6] Russell, "Old Nashville Town," October 1986.

[7] Fred Russell to William Harper, 27 June 1986, personal interview.

[8] Russell, *Bury Me*, 32.

[9] Edwin Pope to author, 28 October 2005, personal interview.

[10] John McLain to author, 8 September 2005, personal interview; Jeff Klinkenberg, "Thanks Babe," *St. Petersburg* (FL) *Times*, 21 March 2004, 1.

[11] Fred Russell to Dick Horton, Golf House of Tennessee, 15 May 1996, personal interview (audiotape courtesy of Russell family archives, Nashville, TN).

[12] Ibid.

[13] Russell, *Bury Me*, 30.

[14] Freddie Russell, "Kidnapper Tells of Gay $45,000 Spree in Which He Crisscrossed Continent Three Times Spending Stoll Ransom," *Nashville* (TN) *Banner*, 17 May 1936, 1.

[15] Russell, *Bury Me*, 30.

[16] Russell, *Bury Me*, 30–31.

[17] Russell, "Kidnapper," 1.

[18] Ibid.

[19] Ibid.

[20] Russell, "Old Nashville Town," 1986.

[21] Ibid.

[22] Vince Dooley to author, 28 September 2005, personal interview.

[23] C. M. Newton to author, 1 August 2005, personal interview.

[24] David E. Sumner, "Nashville Banner" (25 December 2009). Tennessee Encyclopedia of History and Culture; http://tennesseeencyclopedia.net/entry.php?rec=965.

[25] John Seigenthaler to author, 28 October 2005, personal interview.

[26] Ibid.

[27] Ibid.

[28] Edwin Pope to author, 28 October 2005, personal interview.

[29] Eddie Jones to author, 18 November 2005, personal interview.

[30] Carolyn Russell to author, 26 June 2005, personal interview.

[31] John Seigenthaler to author, 28 October 2005, personal interview.

[32] Ibid.

[33] Eddie Jones to author, 18 November 2005, personal interview.

[34] Carolyn Russell to author, 26 June 2005, personal interview.

[35] Joe Biddle to author, 30 June 2005, personal interview.

[36] Jimmy Webb to author, 26 June 2005, personal interview.

[37] Jimmy Webb to author, 26 June 2005, personal interview.

[38] Nancy Siler to author, 7 September 2005, personal interview.

Chapter 3

[1] *Field of Dreams,* directed by Phil Alden Robinson, Universal City, CA: Universal Studios, 1989. Terence Mann (James Earl Jones) speaking to Ray Kinsella (Kevin Costner).

[2] Buzz Davis to author, 21 November 2005, personal interview.

[3] Fred Russell, *Bury Me in an Old Press Box: Good Times and Life of a Sportswriter* (New York: A. S. Barnes and Co., 1957) 150–51.

[4] Ibid., 4–5.

[5] Ibid., 100.

[6] Ibid., 99.

[7] Fred Russell, "Old Nashville Town" television show, hosted by Libby Fryer, October 1986.

[8] Mark McGee to author, 21 April 2006, personal interview.

[9] Tom McEwen to author, 15 September 2005, personal interview.

[10] Edwin Pope to author, 28 October 2005, personal interview.

[11] Tommy Lasorda to author, 28 November 2005, personal interview.

[12] Ernie Harwell to author, 21 July 2005, personal interview.

[13] Ibid.

[14] Lee Russell Brown to author, 20 November 2005, personal interview.

[15] Mark McGee to author, 21 April 2006, personal interview.

[16] George Steinbrenner to author, 27 July 2005, personal interview.

[17] Tom Robinson to author, 26 June 2006, personal interview.

[18] Roy Kramer to author, 27 July 2005, personal interview.

[19] Russell, "Old Nashville Town," 1986.

[20] Kay Russell Beasley to author, 17 January 2006, personal interview.

[21] Bill Roberts to author, 2 September 2005, personal interview.

[22] Larry Schmittou to author, 21 October 2005, personal interview.

[23] Russell, *Bury Me,* 102–103.

[24] Fred Russell to William Harper, 27 June 1986, personal interview.

[25] Larry Schmittou to author, 21 October 2005, personal interview.

[26] Ibid.

[27] Russell, *Bury Me,* 140.

[28] Fred Russell, "Fred Russell Remembers" in "The Masters," advertising supplement, *Wall Street Journal,* 6 April 1995.

[29] Ibid.

[30] Arnold Palmer to author, 22 November 2005, personal interview.

[31] Jake Wallace to author, 14 March 2006, personal interview.

[32] Fred Russell to Dick Horton, Golf House of Tennessee, 15 May 1996, personal interview (audiotape courtesy of Russell family archives, Nashville, TN).

[33] Ibid.

[34] Russell, "Old Nashville Town," 1986.

[35] Ibid.

[36] Fred Russell to Dick Horton, Golf House of Tennessee, 15 May 1996, personal interview (audiotape courtesy of Russell family archives, Nashville, TN).

[37] Fred Russell, "Fred Russell Remembers" in "The Masters," advertising supplement, *Wall Street Journal*, 6 April 1995.

[38] John Boyette, "Reporters' hut has been upgraded," *Augusta* (GA) *Chronicle*, 8 April 2004. http://www.augusta.com/masters2004/stories/040804/cou_557953.shtml.

[39] Edwin Pope, as quoted by John Boyette in "Reporters' hut has been upgraded," *Augusta* (GA) *Chronicle*, 8 April 2004. http://www.augusta.com/masters2004/stories/040804/cou_557953.shtml.

[40] Tom McEwen to author, 15 September 2005, personal interview.

[41] Buzz Davis to author, 21 November 2005, personal interview.

[42] Fred Russell to Dick Horton, Golf House of Tennessee, 15 May 1996, personal interview (audiotape courtesy of Russell family archives, Nashville, TN).

[43] Ibid.

[44] Ibid.

[45] Dick Horton, speech at Tennessee Golf Association Sports Hall of Fame banquet, Opryland Hotel, Nashville, TN, 16 November 1990.

[46] Russell, *Bury Me*, 142.

[47] Russell, *Bury Me*, 147.

[48] Ibid., 150–51.

[49] Ibid., 147.

[50] Tom McEwen to author, 15 September 2005, personal interview.

[51] Charles Cella to author, 4 August 2005, personal interview.

[52] Russell, *Bury Me*, 149–50.

[53] Tom Robinson to author, 26 June 2006, personal interview.

[54] Ibid.

Chapter 4

[1] William Harper, speech at Vanderbilt University Library, Nashville, TN, 14 November 1999. Harper is a Grantland Rice biographer and was comparing Russell and Rice.

[2] Russell, *Bury Me*, 195.

[3] Fred Russell, *Bury Me in an Old Press Box: Good Times and Life of a Sportswriter* (New York: A. S. Barnes and Co., 1957) 196.

[4] Fred Russell, "Sidelines," *Nashville* (TN) *Banner*, 14 July 1954, sports section, 20.

[5] Grantland Rice, "Alumnus Football" in *Only the Brave and Other Poems* (New York: A. S. Barnes and Company, 1941) 144.

[6] Fred Russell, "Old Nashville Town" television show, hosted by Libby Fryer, October 1986.

[7] Fred Russell, keynote address, 1986 Fred Russell-Grantland Rice Scholarship for Sports Journalism banquet, Vanderbilt Loews Plaza, Nashville, TN, 4 May 1986.

[8] Fred Russell, as told to Jerome Holtzman, *No Cheering in the Press Box*, rev. ed. (New York: Holt, Rinehart and Winston, 1995) 303.

[9] Fred Russell, keynote address, 1986 Fred Russell-Grantland Rice Scholarship for Sports Journalism banquet, Vanderbilt Loews Plaza, Nashville, TN, 4 May 1986.

[10] Roy Kramer to author, 27 July 2005, personal interview.

[11] Grantland Rice, *The Tumult and the Shouting* (New York: A. S. Barnes and Company, 1954) 8.

[12] Charles Fountain, *Sportswriter* (New York/Oxford: Oxford University Press, 1993) 68.

[13] NSSA Public Relations material (http://nssafame.com/our-history/).

[14] Fred Russell to William Harper, 27 June 1986, personal interview.

[15] Lou Holtz to author, 18 November 2005, personal interview.

[16] "U.S. sports figures praise Fred Russell," *Nashville* (TN) *Banner*, 28 August 1981, sports section, 1.

[17] John Seigenthaler to author, 28 October 2005, personal interview.

[18] Fred Russell article on Grantland Rice for 1984 PGA Championship at Shoal Creek Golf and Country Club. From the Russell family archives, Nashville, TN.

[19] Bill Weiss and Marshall Wright, "[Number] 47. 1940 Nashville Vols" from Weiss's and Wright's compilation of the 100 best Minor League baseball teams of the twentieth century. http://web.minorleaguebaseball.com/milb/history/top100.jsp?idx =47.

[20] Holtzman, *No Cheering*, 303.

[21] Tom McEwen to author, 15 September 2005, personal interview.

[22] Russell, "Old Nashville Town," 1986.

[23] Fred Russell to William Harper, 27 June 1986, personal interview.

[24] Ibid.

[25] Guest list, Grantland Rice commemorative dinner party, 31 October 1954, Russell family archives, Nashville, TN.

[26] Blackie Sherrod to author, 24 October 2005, personal interview via email correspondence.

[27] Fred Russell, keynote address, 1986 Fred Russell-Grantland Rice Scholarship for Sports Journalism banquet, Vanderbilt Loews Plaza, Nashville, TN, 4 May 1986.

[28] Holtzman, *No Cheering*, 304.

[29] Skip Bayless to author, 12 February 2006, personal interview.

Chapter 5

[1] Lou Holtz to author, 18 November 2005, personal interview.

[2] Lee Corso to author, 17 November 2005, personal interview.

[3] Tom McEwen to author, 15 September 2005, personal interview.

[4] Western Union telegram from Jimmy Jones of the University of Georgia to Fred Russell. Russell Family archives, Nashville, TN.

[5] Ibid., 15 December 1946.

[6] Dale Carnegie, *How to Win Friends & Influence People* (New York: Simon & Schuster, 1936).

[7] Jimmy Jones to Robert Fuoss of the *Saturday Evening Post*, telegram. Russell Family archives, Nashville, TN.

[8] John Seigenthaler to author, 28 October 2005, personal interview.

[9] Gus Manning to author, 31 January 2006, personal interview.

[10] Curtis Publishing Company receipt, July 1949, Russell family archives, Nashville, TN.

[11] Johnny Majors to author, 28 November 2005, personal interview.

[12] Carolyn Russell to author, 20 November 2005, personal interview.

[13] Fred Russell, speech to Quinq Club, Vanderbilt University, Nashville, TN, 28 May 1994.

[14] Fred Russell, "Writer Who Knew Him Best Tells About Dan McGugin," *Nashville* (TN) *Banner*, 25 January 1936.

[15] Haywood Harris to author, 11 November 2005, personal interview.

[16] Gus Manning to author, 31 January 2006, personal interview.

[17] Fred Russell, "Sidelines," *Nashville* (TN) *Banner*, 29 November 1948, 16.

[18] Ibid., 4 December 1950.

[19] Gus Manning to author, 31 January 2006, personal interview.

[20] Vince Dooley to author, 28 September 2005, personal interview.

[21] Jesse Outlar to author, 16 March 2006, personal interview.

[22] Vince Dooley to author, 28 September 2005, personal interview.

[23] Tom McEwen to author, 15 September 2005, personal interview.

[24] Tom McEwen to author, 15 September 2005, personal interview.

[25] Norm Carlson to author, 10 February 2006, personal interview.

[26] Ibid.

[27] Ibid.

[28] Dick Philpot to author, 26 June 2005, personal interview.

[29] Robert Casciola to author, 13 September 2005, personal interview.

[30] Lou Holtz to author, 18 November 2005, personal interview.

[31] Gene Corrigan to author, 30 September 2005, personal interview.

[32] Robert Casciola to author, 13 September 2005, personal interview.

[33] William "Bill" Wallace, 25 August 2005, personal interview via email correspondence.

[34] Robert Casciola to author, 13 September 2005, personal interview.

[35] Dave Campbell to author, 24 September 2005, personal interview.

[36] Gene Corrigan to author, 30 September 2005, personal interview.

[37] Lee Corso to author, 17 November 2005, personal interview.

[38] Art Demmas to author, 2 September 2005, personal interview.

[39] Dick Philpot to author, 26 June 2005, personal interview.

[40] Ibid.

[41] Brownlee Currey to author, 15 March 2006, personal interview.

[42] Dick Philpot to author, 26 June 2005, personal interview.

[43] National Football Foundation Hall of Fame award program, "Fred Russell Retires after 31 Years," December 1991, Waldorf-Astoria Hotel, New York City.

Chapter 6

[1] Johnny Majors to author, 28 November 2005, personal interview.

[2] Joe Biddle to author, 30 June 2005, personal interview.

[3] Furman Bisher to author, 14 September 2005, personal interview.

[4] Bill Corum, "Sports," *New York Journal American*, 9 May 1953.

[5] Fred Russell, "Sidelines," *Nashville* (TN) *Banner*, 9 May 1953, 9.

[6] Grantland Rice to Fred Russell (September 1953), Russell family archives, Nashville, TN.

[7] Dizzy Dean to Fred Russell, summer 1953, Russell family archives, Nashville, TN.

[8] Ed Danforth to Fred Russell, 8 September 1953, telegram, Russell family archives, Nashville, TN.

[9] Joe Biddle to author, 30 June 2005, personal interview.

[10] George Steinbrenner to author, 27 July 2005, personal interview.

[11] Roy Kramer to author, 27 July 2005, personal interview.

[12] Harold Huggins, "Russell's legacy lives on through his protégés," *Nashville* (TN) *City Paper*, 29 January 2003, sports section, 1.

[13] Delbert Reed to author, 14 March 2006, personal interview.

[14] Ibid.

[15] Harold Huggins to author, 1 June 2006, personal interview.

[16] Blackie Sherrod to author, 24 October 2005, personal interview via email correspondence.

[17] Delbert Reed to author, 14 March 2006, personal interview.

[18] Dave Campbell to author, 24 September 2005, personal interview.

[19] John McLain to author, 18 July 2005, personal interview.

[20] Dave Anderson to author, 18 July 2005, personal interview.

[21] Ed Temple to author, 2 September 2005, personal interview.

[22] Ibid.

[23] Ibid.

[24] Ibid.

[25] Ed Temple to author, 2 September 2005, personal interview.

[26] Ibid.

[27] Ibid.

[28] Ibid.

[29] Eddie Jones to author, 18 November 2005, personal interview.

[30] Ibid.

Chapter 7

[1] Frank Graham, Jr., "The Story of a College Football Fix: A Shocking Report of how Wally Butts and 'Bear' Bryant Rigged a Game Last Fall, "*Saturday Evening Post,* 236/11 (23 March 1963): 80. Editorial text box on the cover page of its story.

[2] Fred Russell to Dick Horton, Golf House of Tennessee, 15 May 1996, personal interview (audiotape courtesy of Russell family archives, Nashville, TN).

[3] Edwin Pope to author, 28 October 2005, personal interview.

[4] Fred Russell, "Sidelines," *Nashville* (TN) *Banner*, 5 August 1963.

[5] Ibid., 6 August 1963.

[6] "College Football Fix," *Saturday Evening Post,* 23 March 1963, 82.

[7] Fred Russell, "Sidelines," *Nashville* (TN) *Banner*, 12 August 1963.

[8] Ibid., 6 August 1963.

[9] Ibid., 7 August 1963.

[10] Ibid., 8 August 1963.

[11] Ibid.

[12] Fred Russell, "Sidelines," *Nashville* (TN) *Banner*, 10 August 1963.

[13] Ibid., 19 August 1963.

[14] Ibid.

[15] Fred Russell, "A Juror's Account of Verdict: Butts Became a Symbol to Jury," *Nashville* (TN) *Banner*, 20 August 1963.

[16] Fred Russell, "Sidelines," *Nashville* (TN) *Banner*, 21 August 1963.

[17] Paul Bryant, as quoted in *Sports Illustrated*, "Black Days After a Black Charge," 25/10 (5 September 1966): 32.

[18] Ibid.

[19] Judge Lewis Morgan to Fred Russell, 27 August 1963, Russell family archives, Nashville, TN.

[20] James Kirby, *Fumble* (New York: Harcourt Brace Jovanovich, 1986) 173.

[21] Delbert Reed to author, 14 March 2006, personal interview.

[22] Frank Graham, Jr., to author, 18 May 2006, personal interview.

[23] Ibid.

[24] Ibid.

[25] Kirby, *Fumble*, 57–58.

[26] Edwin Pope to author, 28 October 2005, personal interview.

[27] Charley Trippi to author, 4 April 2006, personal interview.

[28] Frank Graham, Jr., to author, 18 May 2006, personal interview.

[29] Furman Bisher, *Face to Face* (Champagne IL: Sports Publishing, 2005) 40–41.

[30] Furman Bisher to author, 29 April 2006, personal interview.

Chapter 8

[1] Bobby Knight to author, 29 July 2005, personal interview.

[2] Buster Olney to author, 15 November 2005, personal interview.

[3] C. M. Newton to author, 1 August 2005, personal interview.

[4] Fred Russell, *Bury Me in an Old Press Box: Good Times and Life of a Sportswriter* (New York: A. S. Barnes and Co., 1957) 16.

[5] Russell, *Bury Me*, 18.

[6] Ibid., 21.

[7] Fred Russell, "Old Nashville Town" television show, hosted by Libby Fryer, October 1986.

[8] Russell, *Bury Me*, 21.

[9] Robert "Bobby" Jones to President Eisenhower, 13 January 1958, Russell family archives, Nashville, TN.

[10] Lou Holtz to author, 18 November 2005, personal interview.

[11] Lee Corso to author, 17 November 2005, personal interview.

[12] Ibid.

[13] Frank Broyles to author, 10 November 2005, personal interview.

[14] Jake Wallace to author, 14 March 2006, personal interview.

[15] Peyton Manning to author, 26 July 2005, personal interview.

[16] Fred Russell interview with Darryl Sanders in the early 1990s for potential college football television show.

[17] Fred Russell, "Sidelines," *Nashville* (TN) *Banner*, 24 September 1981, sports section, 1.

[18] Fred Russell interview with Darryl Sanders in the early 1990s for potential college football television show.

[19] Ibid.

[20] Allen Barra, *The Last Coach: A Life of Paul "Bear" Bryant* (New York: W. W. Norton & Co., 2005) 85.

[21] Paul Bryant, "U.S. sports figures praise Fred Russell," *Nashville* (TN) *Banner*, 28 August 1981.

[22] Delbert Reed to author, 14 March 2006, personal interview.

[23] Ibid.

[24] Fred Russell interview with Darryl Sanders in the early 1990s for potential college football television show.

[25] Tom Robinson to author, 26 June 2006, personal interview.

[26] Johnny Majors to author, 28 November 2005, personal interview.

[27] Robert Casciola to author, 13 September 2005, personal interview.

[28] Blackie Sherrod to author, 24 October 2005, personal interview via email correspondence.

[29] Larry Woody to author, 12 September 2005, personal interview.

[30] Fred Russell, "Sidelines," *Nashville* (TN) *Banner*, 27 January 1983, section A, 1.

[31] Fred Russell interview with Darryl Sanders in the early 1990s for potential college football television show.

[32] Ibid.

[33] Buster Olney to author, 15 November 2005, personal interview.

[34] Joe Biddle to author, 30 June 2005, personal interview.

[35] Ibid.

[36] Ibid.

[37] George Plaster to author, 22 July 2005, personal interview.

[38] Tommy Lasorda to author, 28 November 2005, personal interview.

[39] Mark McGee to author, 21 April 2006, personal interview.

[40] George Plaster to author, 22 July 2005, personal interview.

[41] Eddie Fogler to author, 17 May 2006, personal interview.

[42] C. M. Newton to author, 1 August 2005, personal interview.

[43] Ibid.

Chapter 9

[1] Jimmy Davy to author, 13 September 2005, personal interview.

[2] John Seigenthaler to author, 28 October 2005, personal interview.

[3] Joe Biddle to author, 30 June 2005, personal interview.

[4] John Rich to author, 3 February 2006, personal interview.

[5] Fred Pancoast to author, 5 December 2005, personal interview.

[6] Jimmy Davy to author, 13 September 2005, personal interview.

[7] Fred Pancoast to author, 5 December 2005, personal interview.

[8] Ibid.

[9] John Rich to author, 3 February 2006, personal interview.

[10] Interview with Clay Stapleton, *Des Moines* (IA) *Register*, 20 August 2002.

[11] Larry Woody to author, 12 September 2005, personal interview.

[12] Jimmy Davy to author, 13 September 2005, personal interview.

[13] John Seigenthaler to author, 28 October 2005, personal interview.

[14] Ibid.

[15] Joe Biddle to author, 30 June 2005, personal interview.

[16] John Seigenthaler to author, 28 October 2005, personal interview.

[17] Pat Embry to author, 5 May 2006, personal interview.

[18] Buster Olney to author, 15 November 2005, personal interview.

[19] Harold Huggins to author, 1 June 2006, personal interview.

[20] Jimmy Davy to author, 13 September 2005, personal interview.

[21] Ibid.

[22] Ibid.

[23] John Seigenthaler to author, 28 October 2005, personal interview.

[24] Joe Biddle to author, 30 June 2005, personal interview.

[25] Larry Woody to author, 12 September 2005, personal interview.

[26] Delbert Reed to author, 14 March 2006, personal interview.

[27] Ibid.

[28] Tom Robinson to author, 26 June 2006, personal interview.

[29] Buster Olney to author, 15 November 2005, personal interview.

[30] Ibid.

[31] Mark McGee to author, 21 April 2006, personal interview.

[32] Joe Biddle to author, 30 June 2005, personal interview.

[33] Ibid.

[34] Ibid.

[35] Mark McGee to author, 21 April 2006, personal interview.

[36] Joe Biddle to author, 30 June 2005, personal interview.

[37] Mark McGee to author, 21 April 2006, personal interview.

[38] Ibid.

[39] Ibid.

[40] Ibid.

[41] Ibid.

[42] Greg Pogue to author, 19 May 2006, personal interview.

[43] Ibid.

[44] Ibid.

[45] Joe Biddle to author, 30 June 2005, personal interview.

[46] Bill Roberts to author, 2 September 2005, personal interview.

[47] Larry Woody to author, 12 September 2005, personal interview.

Chapter 10

[1] Earl Beasley to author, 17 January 2006, personal interview.

[2] Carolyn Russell to author, 26 June 2005, personal interview.

[3] Fred Russell to William Harper, 27 June 1986, personal interview.

[4] Roy Kramer, speech at Vanderbilt University Library: Russell-Rice Gallery Talk, Nashville, TN, 14 November 1999.

[5] Bob Broeg to author, 14 September 2005, personal interview.

[6] John Beasley to author, 8 February 2006, personal interview.

[7] Carolyn Russell to author, 8 April 2006, personal interview.

[8] Fred Russell to Dick Horton, Golf House of Tennessee, 15 May 1996, personal interview (audiotape courtesy of Russell family archives, Nashville, TN).

[9] Fred Russell, *I'll Go Quietly* (Nashville TN: McQuiddy Press, 1944) 46–49.

[10] Fred Russell to Dick Horton, Golf House of Tennessee, 15 May 1996, personal interview (audiotape courtesy of Russell family archives, Nashville, TN).

[11] Russell, *I'll Go Quietly*, 48.

[12] Ibid., 49.

[13] Fred Russell to Dick Horton, Golf House of Tennessee, 15 May 1996, personal interview (audiotape courtesy of Russell family archives, Nashville, TN).

[14] Fred Russell, *I'll Go Quietly*, 49.

[15] Ibid.

[16] Carolyn Russell to author, 26 June 2005, personal interview.

[17] Jerry Patterson, "Getting Even Is the Best Revenge: The Art of Practical Joking," *Nashville* (TN) *Scene*, 11 April 1996, 17–18.

[18] Fred Russell, "Golf's 14 Cardinal Principles," Russell family archives, Nashville, TN.

[19] Jack Hairston to author, 3 February 2006, personal interview.

[20] Fred Russell, speech to Quinq Club, Vanderbilt University, Nashville, TN, 28 May 1994.

[21] Steve Sloan to author, 28 September 2005, personal interview.

[22] Tom McEwen, induction speech for Fred Russell into the NSSA Hall of Fame, Salisbury, NC, 3 May 1988.

[23] Jimmy Davy to author, 13 September 2005, personal interview.

[24] Gene Corrigan to author, 30 September 2005, personal interview.

[25] Orville Henry, "Fred Russell's Fun and Games," *Arkansas Gazette*, 18 January 1968, 2B.

[26] Fred Russell, "Old Nashville Town" television show, hosted by Libby Fryer, October 1986.

[27] Bill Roberts to author, 2 September 2005, personal interview.

[28] Tom Robinson to author, 26 June 2006, personal interview.

[29] Jimmy Webb to author, 26 June 2005, personal interview.

[30] Eddie Jones to author, 18 November 2005, personal interview.

[31] Gag letter authored by Fred Russell, pretending to be Maxwell Benson, 28 May 1942. Russell family archives, Nashville, TN.

[32] Gag letter authored by Fred Russell, pretending to be Chancellor-elect Harvie Branscomb, 23 August 1946. Russell family archives, Nashville, TN.

[33] Buzz Davis to author, 21 November 2005, personal interview.

[34] Multiple sources. Russell family archives, Nashville, TN.

[35] Fred Russell, "Sidelines," *Nashville* (TN) *Banner*, 1 November 1974, 33.

[36] Paul Dietzel to author, 9 November 2005, personal interview.

[37] Ibid.

[38] Robert Casciola to author, 13 September 2005, personal interview.

Chapter 11

[1] Kay Russell Beasley to author, 17 January 2006, personal interview.

[2] Grace Stumb to author, 27 January 2006, personal interview.

[3] Fred Russell, *Bury Me in an Old Press Box: Good Times and Life of a Sportswriter* (New York: A. S. Barnes and Co., 1957) 33.

[4] Ibid., 34.

[5] Carolyn Russell to author, 20 November 2005, personal interview.

[6] Russell, *Bury Me*, 34.

[7] Art Demmas to author, 2 September 2005, personal interview.

[8] Grace Stumb to author, 27 January 2006, personal interview.

[9] Kay Russell Beasley to author, 17 January 2006, personal interview.

[10] Grace Stumb to author, 27 January 2006, personal interview.

[11] Lee Russell Brown to author, 20 November 2005, personal interview.

[12] Carrie Van Derveer to author, 22 May 2006, personal interview.

[13] Lee Russell Brown to author, 20 November 2005, personal interview.

[14] Ibid.

[15] Roy Kramer to author, 10 February 2006, personal interview.

[16] Carolyn Russell to author, 20 November 2005, personal interview.

[17] Mary Barfield to author, 6 February 2006, personal interview.

[18] Earl Beasley to author, 17 January 2006, personal interview.

[19] Ibid.

[20] Earl Beasley to author, 17 February 2011, personal interview.

[21] Will Van Derveer to author, 22 May 2006, personal interview.

[22] Ellen Russell Sadler to author, 20 November 2005, personal interview.

[23] Kay Russell Beasley to author, 17 January 2006, personal interview.

[24] Lee Russell Brown to author, 20 November 2005, personal interview.

[25] Ellen Russell Sadler to author, 20 November 2005, personal interview.

[26] Ibid.

[27] Lee Russell Brown to author, 20 November 2005, personal interview.

[28] Ibid.

[29] Carolyn Russell to author, 20 November 2005, personal interview.

[30] Kay Russell Beasley to author, 17 January 2006, personal interview.

[31] Ellen Russell Sadler to author, 20 November 2005, personal interview.

[32] Lee Russell Brown to author, 20 November 2005, personal interview.

[33] Carolyn Russell, Ellen Sadler, and Lee Russell Brown, 20 November 2005, personal interviews; Kay Russell Beasley, 17 January 2006, personal interview.

[34] Lee Russell Brown to author, 20 November 2005, personal interview.

[35] Carrie Van Derveer to author, 22 May 2006, personal interview.

[36] Roy Kramer to author, 10 February 2006, personal interview.

[37] Lee Russell Brown to author, 20 November 2005, personal interview.

[38] Carrie Van Derveer to author, 22 May 2006, personal interview.

[39] Kay Russell Beasley to author, 17 January 2006, personal interview.

[40] Carolyn Russell to author, 20 November 2005, personal interview.

[41] Will Van Derveer to author, 22 May 2006, personal interview.

[42] Kay Russell Beasley to author, 17 January 2006, personal interview.

Chapter 12

[1] Tyler Kepner to author, 29 September 2005, personal interview.

[2] Skip Bayless to Charles J. Cella, chairman of the TRA Grantland Rice com-mittee, April 1986. Russell family archives, Nashville, TN. Syndicated sports columnist and television personality; 1970 scholarship recipient.

[3] Dave Sheinin to author, 28 November 2005, personal interview.

[4] Skip Bayless to author, personal interview; originally quoted in "Vanderbilt Sportswriters: From Coast to Coast," which appeared in Vanderbilt University's *Flagship* sports magazine; January 2002.

[5] John Beasley, representing Vanderbilt University at Russell-Rice scholarship banquet, Vanderbilt Loews Plaza, Nashville, TN, 4 May 1986.

[6] Charles Cella, representing the Thoroughbred Racing Association at Russell-Rice scholarship banquet, Vanderbilt Loews Plaza, Nashville, TN, 4 May 1986.

[7] Dan Miller, narrator at Russell-Rice scholarship banquet, Vanderbilt Loews Plaza, Nashville, TN, 4 May1986.

[8] Charles Cella to author, 4 August 2005, personal interview.

[9] Lee Jenkins to author, 28 November 2005, personal interview.

[10] David Rapp, email response to scholarship survey, 18 November 2005.

[11] Andrew Maraniss, email response to scholarship survey, 7 April 2005.

[12] Lee Jenkins to author, 28 November 2005, personal interview.

[13] Buster Olney to author, 15 November 2005, personal interview.

[14] Ibid.

[15] Lee Jenkins to author, 28 November 2005, personal interview.

[16] Andrew Maraniss, email response to scholarship survey, 7 April 2005.

[17] Dave Sheinin to author, 28 November 2005, personal interview.

[18] Skip Bayless to author, 12 February 2006, personal interview.

[19] Tena (Robinson) Herlihy, email response to scholarship survey, 6 December 2005.

[20] Tyler Kepner to author, 29 September 2005, personal interview.

[21] Charles Cella to author, 4 August 2005, personal interview.

[22] Ibid.

[23] Lee Jenkins to author, 28 November 2005, personal interview.

[24] Ibid.

[25] Tyler Kepner to author, personal interview; originally quoted in "Vanderbilt Sportswriters: From Coast to Coast," which appeared in Vanderbilt University's *Flagship* sports magazine; January 2002.

[26] Bill Livingston to author, 28 November 2005, personal interview.

[27] David Rapp, email response to scholarship survey, 18 November 2005.

[28] Skip Bayless to author, 12 February 2006, personal interview.

[29] Mike Jackson, email response to scholarship survey, 14 November 2005.

[30] Andrew Maraniss, email response to scholarship survey, 7 April 2006.

[31] Mitch Light to author, 30 November 2005, personal interview.

[32] Matt O'Keefe to author, 7 December 2005, personal interview.

[33] Lee Jenkins to author, 28 November 2005, personal interview.

[34] Dan Wolken, email response to scholarship survey, 23 November 2005.

[35] Andrew Derr, originally quoted in "Vanderbilt Sportswriters: From Coast to Coast," appearing in Vanderbilt University's *Flagship* sports magazine; January 2002.

Chapter13

[1] *The Natural*, directed by Barry Levinson, Culver City, CA: Tri-Star Pictures, 1984. Pop Fisher, played by Wilford Brimley, is a veteran baseball manager trying to win the pennant but who has had nothing but heartache during his years managing the New York Knights. Richard Farnsworth plays one of the assistant coaches, and in this

exchange, he informs Robert Redford's Roy Hobbs of the hard-luck career Fisher has endured.

[2] Eddie Jones to author, 18 November 2005, personal interview.

[3] Henry Walker, "Death Blow: The Deal That Brought the *Banner* Down," *Nashville* (TN) *Scene*, 17/2 (19 February 1998).

[4] Eddie Jones to author, 18 November 2005, personal interview.

[5] John Seigenthaler to author, 28 October 2005, personal interview.

[6] Edwin Pope to author, 28 October 2005, personal interview.

[7] Kay Russell Beasley to author, 17 January 2006, personal interview.

[8] Carolyn Russell to author, 20 November 2005, personal interview.

[9] Brownlee Currey to author, 15 March 2006, personal interview.

[10] Irby Simpkins to author, 5 April 2006, personal interview.

[11] Carolyn Russell to author, 20 November 2005, personal interview.

[12] Bruce Dobie, "Stop the Presses," *Nashville* (TN) *Scene*, 17/2 (19 February 1998).

[13] Brownlee Currey to author, 15 March 2006, personal interview.

[14] Pat Embry to author, 4 May 2006, personal interview via email correspondence.

[15] Irby Simpkins to author, 5 April 2006, personal interview.

[16] Bruce Dobie to author, 10 May 2006, personal interview via email correspondence.

[17] Walker, "Death Blow."

[18] Jimmy Davy to author, 13 September 2005, personal interview.

[19] Carolyn Russell to author, 20 November 2005, personal interview.

[20] Earl Beasley to author, 17 January 2006, personal interview.

[21] C. M. Newton to author, 1 August 2005, personal interview.

[22] Carrie Van Derveer to author, 22 May 2006, personal interview.

[23] Will Van Derveer to author, 22 May 2006, personal interview.

[24] *Sports Illustrated*, 2 March 1998, 22, 24.

[25] Larry Woody to author, 12 September 2005, personal interview.

[26] Jimmy Davy to author, 13 September 2005, personal interview.

Chapter 14

[1] Edwin Pope to author, 28 October 2005, personal interview.

[2] Roy Kramer, eulogy at Russell memorial service, West End Methodist Church, Nashville, TN, 29 January 2003.

[3] Fred Russell, as quoted by Frederick C. Klein, "On Sports: An Old-Time Scribe," *Wall Street Journal*, 27 November 1992, Leisure and Arts section, 1.

[4] Peyton Manning to author, 26 July 2005, personal interview.

[5] Joe Biddle to author, 30 June 2005, personal interview.

[6] Joe Biddle, WTN "Sportsnight" radio show transcript, 27 January 2003. Russell family archives, Nashville, TN.

[7] Joe Biddle, "Missing an Old Friend on the Sidelines," the (Nashville) *Tennessean*, 28 January 2003.

[8] Ibid.

[9] Roy Kramer, eulogy at Russell memorial service, West End Methodist Church, Nashville, TN, 29 January 2003.

[10] John Seigenthaler to author, 28 October 2005, personal interview.

[11] Dan Wolken to author, 23 November 2005, personal interview.

[12] Lee Jenkins, as quoted by Joe Biddle, "Mr. Russell: End of an Era," the (Nashville) *Tennessean*, 28 January 2003, sports section, 1.

[13] Charles Cella to author, 4 August 2005, personal interview.

[14] Bill Frist to author, 26 May 2006, personal interview.

[15] Eddie Jones to author, 18 November 2005, personal interview.

[16] Delbert Reed to author, 14 March 2006, personal interview.

[17] Fred Russell, typewritten speech notes. Russell family archives, Nashville, TN.

[18] Vince Dooley to author, 28 September 2005, personal interview.

[19] Fred Russell, "Sidelines," *Nashville* (TN) *Banner*, 10 June 1955, 26.

[20] George Plaster to author, 22 July 2005, personal interview.

[21] Blackie Sherrod to author, 24 October 2005, personal interview via email correspondence.

[22] Frank Deford to author, 13 March 2006, personal interview via email correspondence.

[23] Lee Corso to author, 17 November 2005, personal interview.

[24] Fred Russell, *Bury Me in an Old Press Box: Good Times and Life of a Sportswriter* (New York: A. S. Barnes and Co., 1957) 39.

[25] Buster Olney to author, 15 November 2005, personal interview.

[26] Dave Anderson to author, 18 July 2005, personal interview.

[27] Tyler Kepner to author, 29 September 2005, personal interview.

[28] Lee Jenkins to author, 28 November 2005, personal interview.

[29] Buster Olney to author, 15 November 2005, personal interview.

[30] Ernie Harwell to author, 21 July 2005, personal interview.

[31] Lou Holtz to author, 18 November 2005, personal interview.

[32] Arnold Palmer, commencement address at Wake Forest University, 16 May 2005.

[33] C. M. Newton to author, 1 August 2005, personal interview.

[34] Bobby Knight to author, 29 July 2005, personal interview.

[35] Russell, *Bury Me*, 226.

[36] Mike Jackson to author, 14 November 2005, personal interview.

[37] Jesse Outlar to author, 16 March 2006, personal interview.

[38] Roy Kramer to author, 27 July 2005, personal interview.

[39] Delbert Reed to author, 14 March 2006, personal interview.

[40] Grantland Rice, "To Fred Russell," September 1953. Russell family archives, Nashville, TN.

Index